English Language Arts
Activity Book

3

K12 Summit
CURRICULUM

Book Staff and Contributors

Kristen Kinney-Haines   *Director, English Language Arts*
Amy Rauen   *Director, Instructional Design*
Allyson Jacob, Susan Raley   *Text Editors*
Tricia Battipede   *Senior Creative Manager*
Julie Jankowski   *Senior Visual Designer*
Caitlin Gildrien   *Visual Designer*
Sheila Smith   *Cover Designer*
Robyn Campbell, Alane Gernon-Paulsen, Allyson Jacob, Tisha Ruibal   *Writers*
Amy Eward   *Content Specialist; Senior Manager, Writing and Editing*
Dan Smith   *Senior Project Manager*

Doug McCollum   *Senior Vice President, Product Development*
Kristin Morrison   *Vice President, Design, Creative, and UX*
Kelly Engel   *Senior Director, Curriculum*
Christopher Frescholtz   *Senior Director, Program Management*
Erica Castle   *Director, Creative Services*
Lisa Dimaio Iekel   *Senior Production Manager*

Illustrations Credits

All illustrations © K12 unless otherwise noted.
Characters: Tommy DiGiovanni, Matt Fedor, Ben Gamache, Shannon Palmer
Cover: Rabbit. © Andrew Cribb/Alamy Stock Photo; Origami butterfly. © brulove/Shutterstock;
Spiral. © Silmen/iStock.

About K12 Inc.
K12 Inc. (NYSE: LRN) drives innovation and advances the quality of education by delivering state-of-the-art digital learning platforms and technology to students and school districts around the world. K12 is a company of educators offering its online and blended curriculum to charter schools, public school districts, private schools, and directly to families. More information can be found at K12.com.

ISBN: 978-1-60153-603-7

Printed by Walsworth, Saint Joseph, MI, USA, July 2020

Table of Contents

Author Study

Fables

Folktales and Legends

Snowy Days

What Do You Think?

Lessons Learned

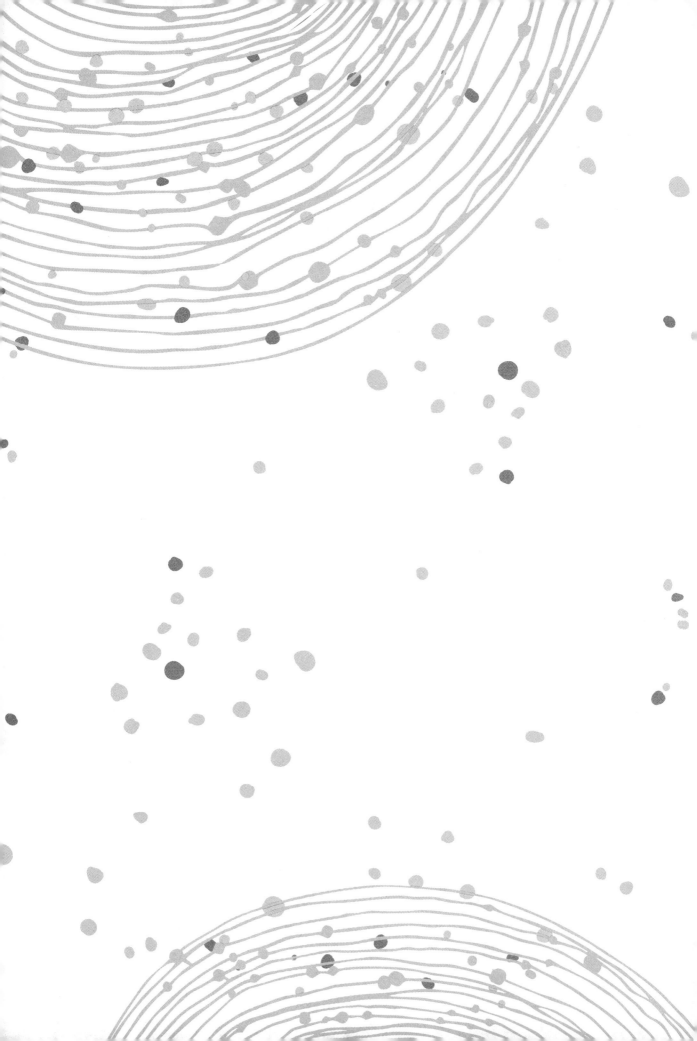

Allen Say (A)

Spelling List 1 Pretest

1. Open the Spelling Pretest activity online. Listen to the first spelling word. Type the word. Check your answer.

2. Write the correct spelling of the word in the Word column of the Spelling Pretest table.

Word	✓	✗
1 blindfold		

3. Put a check mark in the ✓ column if you spelled the word correctly online.

   Put an X in the ✗ column if you spelled the word incorrectly online.

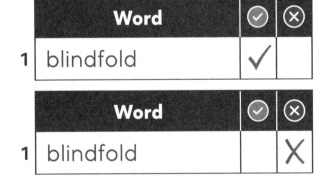

Word	✓	✗
1 blindfold	✓	

Word	✓	✗
1 blindfold		✗

4. Repeat Steps 1–3 for the remaining words in the Spelling Pretest.

Allen Say (A)

Spelling List 1 Pretest

Write each spelling word in the Word column, making sure to spell it correctly.

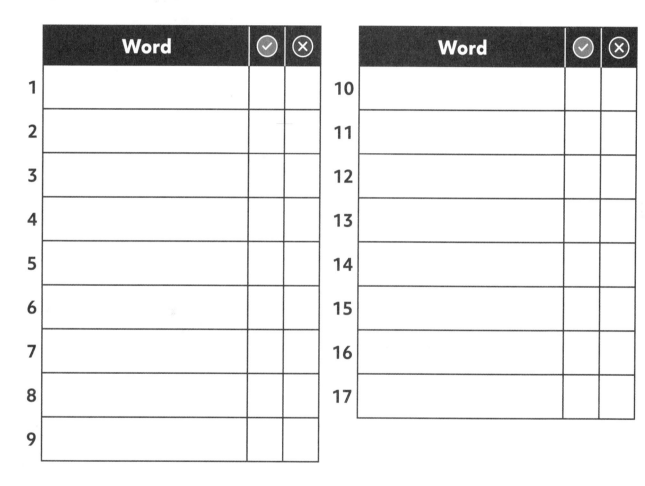

	Word	✓	✗
1			
2			
3			
4			
5			
6			
7			
8			
9			

	Word	✓	✗
10			
11			
12			
13			
14			
15			
16			
17			

Allen Say (A)

Sequence of Events in *Grandfather's Journey*

Number the events in the correct order. Use the text in *Grandfather's Journey* to help you. The first one has been done for you.

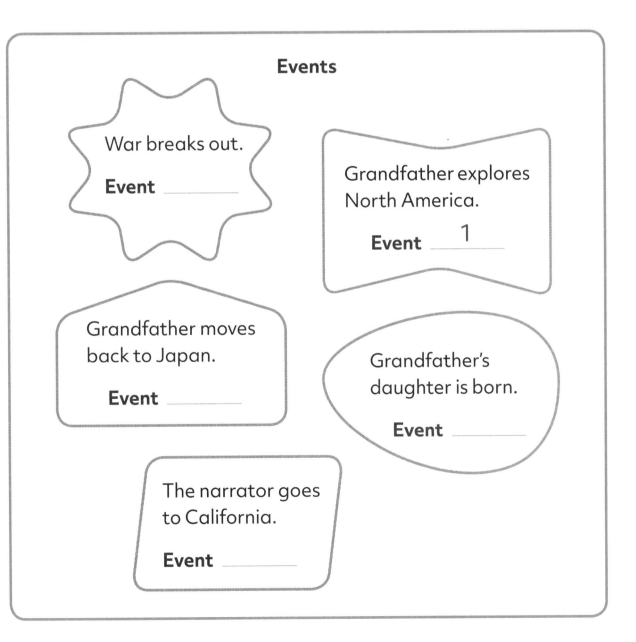

Events

War breaks out.

Event _____

Grandfather explores North America.

Event _____1_____

Grandfather moves back to Japan.

Event _____

Grandfather's daughter is born.

Event _____

The narrator goes to California.

Event _____

Use the information from the box to write the sequence of events in *Grandfather's Journey*. The first one has been done for you.

First, Grandfather explores North America.

Second, _____

_____

Next, _____

_____

Then, _____

_____

Finally, _____

_____

Allen Say (B)

Spelling List 1 Activity Bank

Circle any words in the box that you did not spell correctly on your pretest. Choose one activity to do with your circled words. Do as much of the activity as you can in the time given.

Did you spell all the words on the pretest correctly? Do the one activity with as many spelling words as you can.

children	expect	himself	problem	sudden
difficult	fantastic	invent	publish	ticket
establish	finish	pocket	rabbit	until
exact	happen			

Spelling Activity Choices

Alphabetizing

1. In the left column, write your spelling words in alphabetical order.

2. Correct any spelling errors.

Vowel-Free Words

1. In the left column, write only the consonants in each of your spelling words. Put a dot where each vowel should be.

2. Spell each word aloud, stating which vowels should be in the places with dots.

3. In the right column, rewrite the entire spelling word.

4. Correct any spelling errors.

Rhymes

1. In the left column, write your spelling words.

2. In the right column, write a word that rhymes with each spelling word.

3. Correct any spelling errors.

Uppercase and Lowercase

1. In the left column, write each of your spelling words in all uppercase letters.

2. In the right column, write each of your spelling words in all lowercase letters.

3. Correct any spelling errors.

Complete the activity that you chose.

My chosen activity: _____

1. _____ _____

2. _____ _____

3. _____ _____

4. _____ _____

5. _____ _____

6. _____ _____

7. _____ _____

8. _____ _____

9. _____ _____

10. _____ _____

11. _____ _____

12. _____ _____

13. _____ _____

14. _____ _____

15. _____ _____

16. _____ _____

17. _____ _____

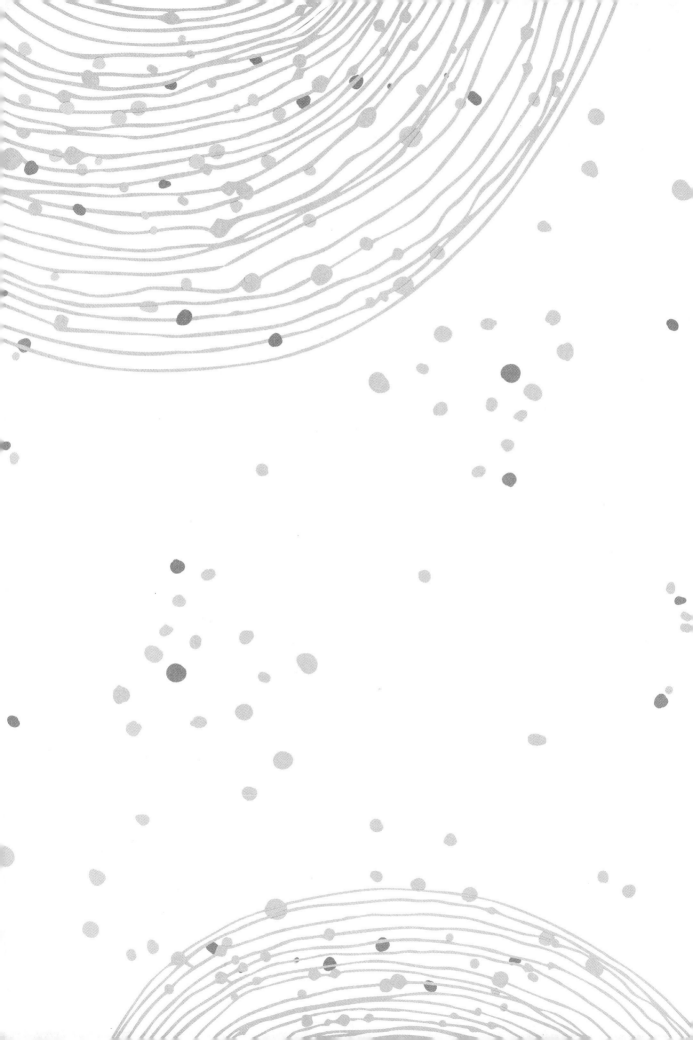

Characters, Illustrations, and Mood

Read the excerpt from *Tea with Milk* by Allen Say.

On the following weekend, the matchmaker introduced Masako and her mother to a young banker and his mother. In a fancy restaurant they drank tea and ate lunch and drank more tea. Then the young couple was left alone for the afternoon....

In the evening, Masako came home fuming.

"Isn't he a charming young man?" her mother asked.

"Charming like a catfish!" Masako answered.

"His family owns the bank where he works," her mother said.

"I won't marry a moneylender!" Masako replied.

Masako could not sleep that night. Mother is determined to find a husband for me, she told herself. I could never marry someone like that. Never! What can I do?

Answer the questions in complete sentences.

1. What mood does the text convey?

   _____

   _____

2. What details in the text support that mood?

   _____

   _____

   _____

3. Look at the illustration of two people on a bench on page 13 of *Tea with Milk*. What details in the illustration support your choice of mood?

   _____

   _____

   _____

   _____

Write About Supporting Details

Read the excerpt from *Tea with Milk* by Allen Say.

The next morning, Masako returned to the department store office. No one had read her application yet, the clerk said. Masako asked to see the manager. She was very insistent. After a while, the supervisor interviewed her.

"Can you really drive a car?" he asked, looking at her application. "I've never seen a woman drive."

"Many women drive in America," she said.

"I see." He nodded and picked up his telephone.

Soon a girl appeared and took Masako to a changing room and gave her a uniform. An hour later, Masako was driving an elevator cage up and down, bowing to customers, and announcing the floors.

She rented a room in a rooming house for university students. Her parents were not happy, especially her mother. It was shameful for ladies to work, she said. Masako did not tell her she was an elevator girl.

One theme in *Tea with Milk* is that it takes determination to be successful. List at least two details from the excerpt that support this theme.

_____

_____

_____

_____

_____

_____

_____

_____

_____

_____

_____

_____

_____

Allen Say (D)

Write a Paragraph to Contrast Two Texts

Fill in the blanks to write a paragraph that contrasts Grandfather from *Grandfather's Journey* with Masako from *Tea with Milk*. Begin with a topic sentence that states the main idea of your paragraph.

Grandfather and Masako are _____ .

First, _____

_____

_____ .

Another difference is _____

_____

_____ .

Finally, _____

_____

_____ .

In conclusion, _____

_____ .

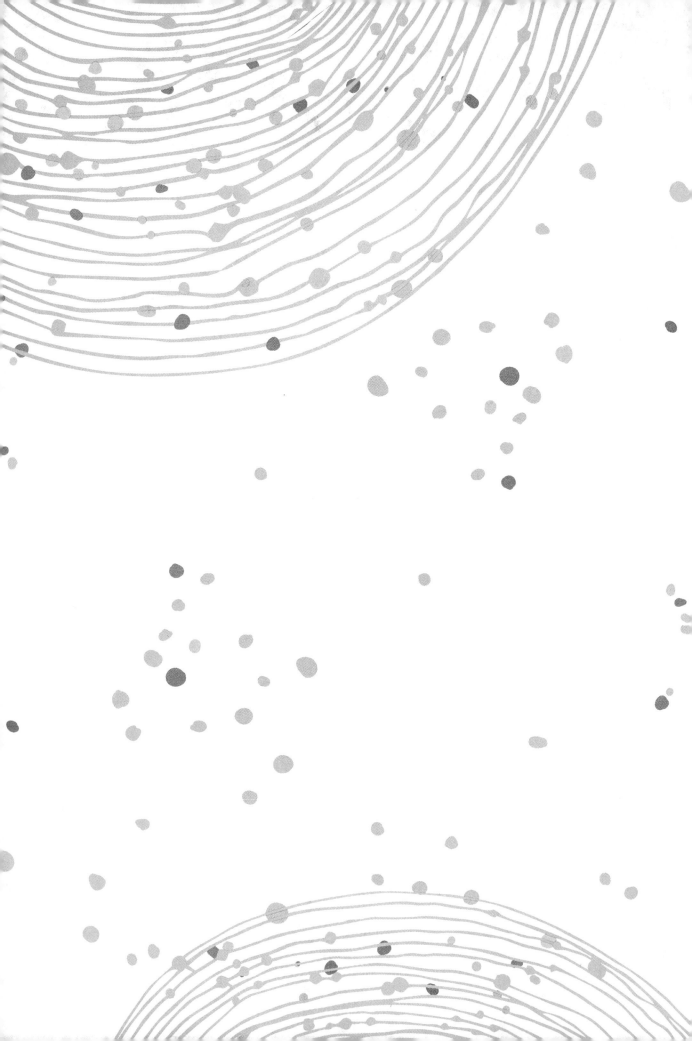

Allen Say (E)

Spelling List 2 Pretest

1. Open the Spelling Pretest activity online. Listen to the first spelling word. Type the word. Check your answer.

2. Write the correct spelling of the word in the Word column of the Spelling Pretest table.

Word	✓	✗
1 blindfold		

3. Put a check mark in the ✓ column if you spelled the word correctly online.

   Put an X in the ✗ column if you spelled the word incorrectly online.

Word	✓	✗
1 blindfold	✓	

Word	✓	✗
1 blindfold		✗

4. Repeat Steps 1–3 for the remaining words in the Spelling Pretest.

Allen Say (E)

Spelling List 2 Pretest

Write each spelling word in the Word column, making sure to spell it correctly.

	Word	✓	✗
1			
2			
3			
4			
5			
6			
7			
8			
9			

	Word	✓	✗
10			
11			
12			
13			
14			
15			
16			
17			

Describe an Illustration

Read the writing prompt.

Prompt: **Write a paragraph that describes an illustration.**

Follow the instructions to brainstorm for your paragraph.

1. Choose an illustration from *Grandfather's Journey*, *Tea with Milk*, or *The Sign Painter*.

   Book I chose: _____

   Page number of illustration: _____

2. What sights, sounds, feeling, tastes, and smells does the illustration make you think of? List words and phrases that describe the illustration. Sample words that describe the illustration on page 13 of *The Sign Painter* are shown.

   > **Sample words:** hot, dry, dusty, empty, silent

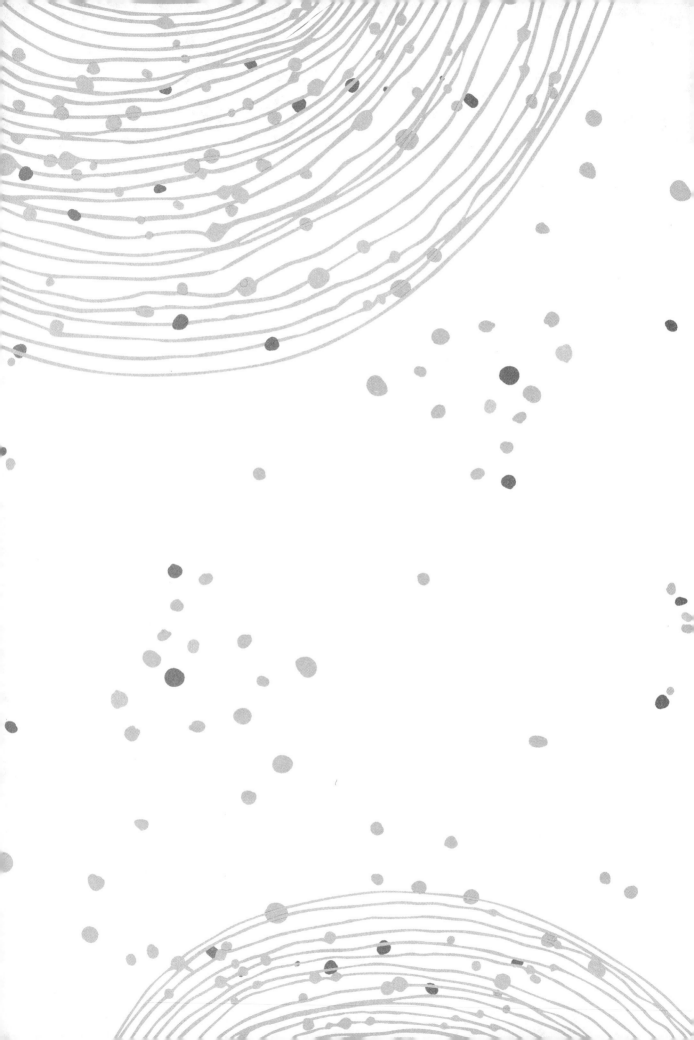

Spelling List 2 Activity Bank

Circle any words in the box that you did not spell correctly on the pretest. Choose one activity to do with your circled words. Do as much of the activity as you can in the time given.

Did you spell all the words on the pretest correctly? Do the one activity with as many spelling words as you can.

facts	numbers	products	foxes	quizzes
hundreds	objects	systems	gashes	riches
insects	plants	dresses	inches	sandwiches
napkins	presidents			

Spelling Activity Choices

Silly Sentences

1. Write a silly sentence for each of your spelling words.

2. Underline the spelling word in each sentence.
   Example: The dog was <u>driving</u> a car.

3. Correct any spelling errors.

Spelling Story

1. Write a very short story using each of your spelling words.

2. Underline the spelling words in the story.

3. Correct any spelling errors.

Riddle Me This

1. Write a riddle for each of your spelling words.
   Example: "I have a trunk, but it's not on my car."

2. Write the answer, which is your word, for each riddle.
   Example: Answer: elephant

3. Correct any spelling errors.

RunOnWord

1. Gather some crayons, colored pencils, or markers. Use a different color to write each of your spelling words. Write the words end to end as one long word.
   Example: dogcatbirdfishturtle

2. Rewrite the words correctly and with proper spacing.

3. Correct any spelling errors.

Complete the activity that you chose.

My chosen activity: _____

_____

_____

_____

_____

_____

_____

_____

_____

_____

_____

_____

_____

_____

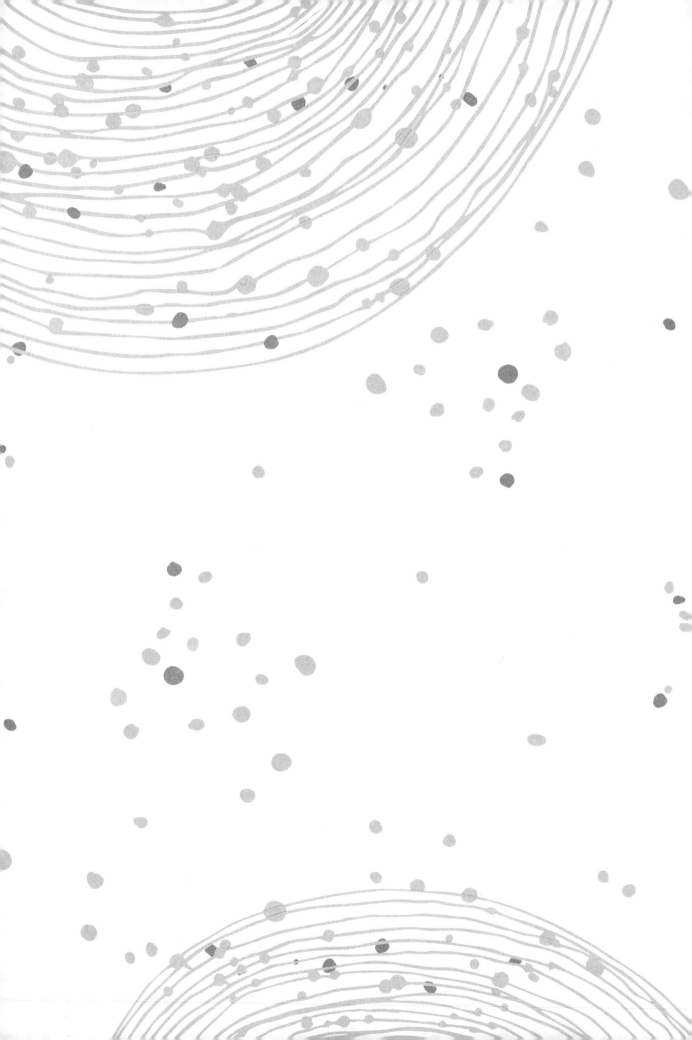

Allen Say (F)

Plan a Descriptive Paragraph

Read the writing prompt.

Prompt: **Write a paragraph that describes an illustration.**

Follow the instructions to plan your paragraph. Use complete sentences.

1. State the **purpose** of your paragraph.

_____

_____

_____

_____

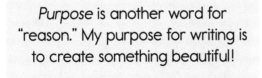

Purpose is another word for "reason." My purpose for writing is to create something beautiful!

2. Complete the graphic organizer to plan your descriptive paragraph. Use the sensory words that you brainstormed to help you. Sample answers are shown.

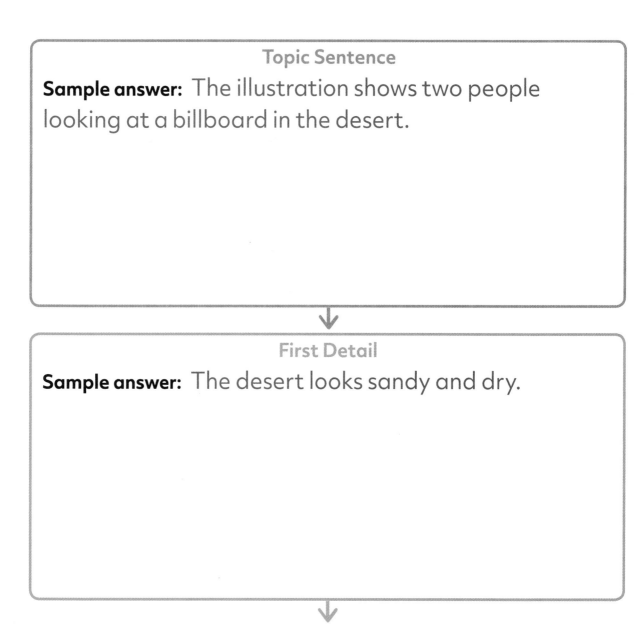

Topic Sentence

Sample answer: The illustration shows two people looking at a billboard in the desert.

↓

First Detail

Sample answer: The desert looks sandy and dry.

↓

Second Detail

Sample answer: It is very sunny and bright. The metal car is shiny in the sun.

Third Detail

Sample answer: It feels hot because there is no shade.

Conclusion

Sample answer: In the illustration, there are two people in the middle of the desert.

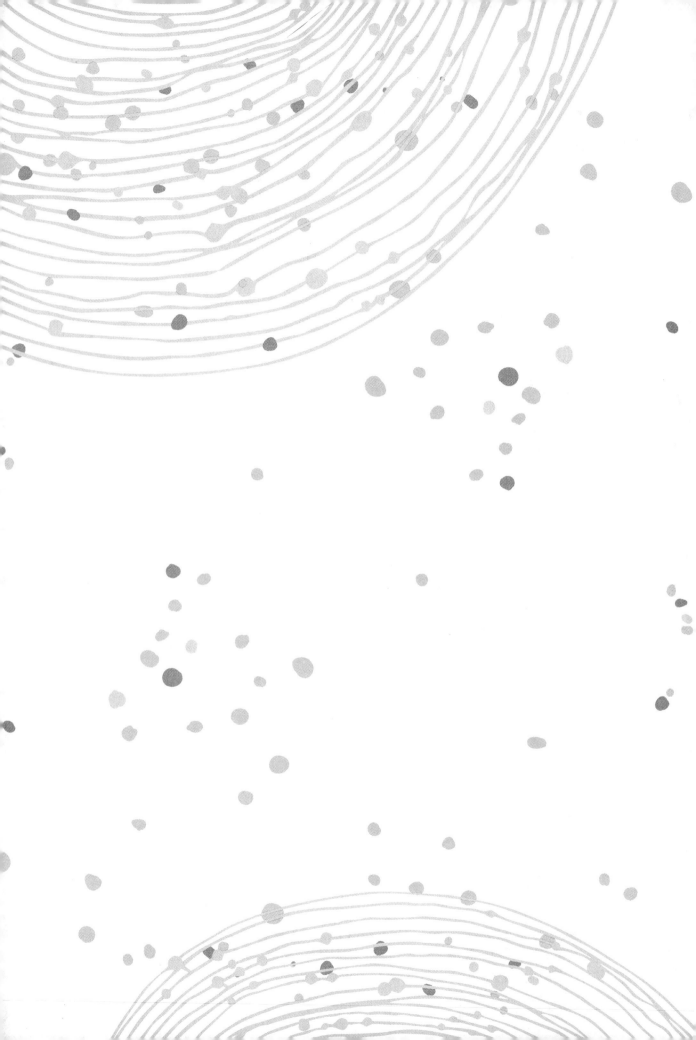

Allen Say (G)

Write a Descriptive Paragraph

Read the writing prompt.

Prompt: **Write a paragraph that describes an illustration.**

Respond to the writing prompt. Use your prewriting work to help you. Indent your paragraph. Write a topic sentence, supporting details, and a concluding sentence.

Allen Say Wrap-Up

Revise and Proofread a Descriptive Paragraph

Read your descriptive paragraph. Use the checklist to revise and proofread your paragraph.

Ideas

☐ Did I include a topic sentence that states the main idea of the paragraph?

☐ Did I include sensory details?

☐ Did I include a concluding sentence?

Grammar

☐ Are all sentences complete and correct?

☐ Does every sentence begin with a capital letter?

☐ Does every sentence end with the correct punctuation?

☐ Did I indent the first sentence in the paragraph?

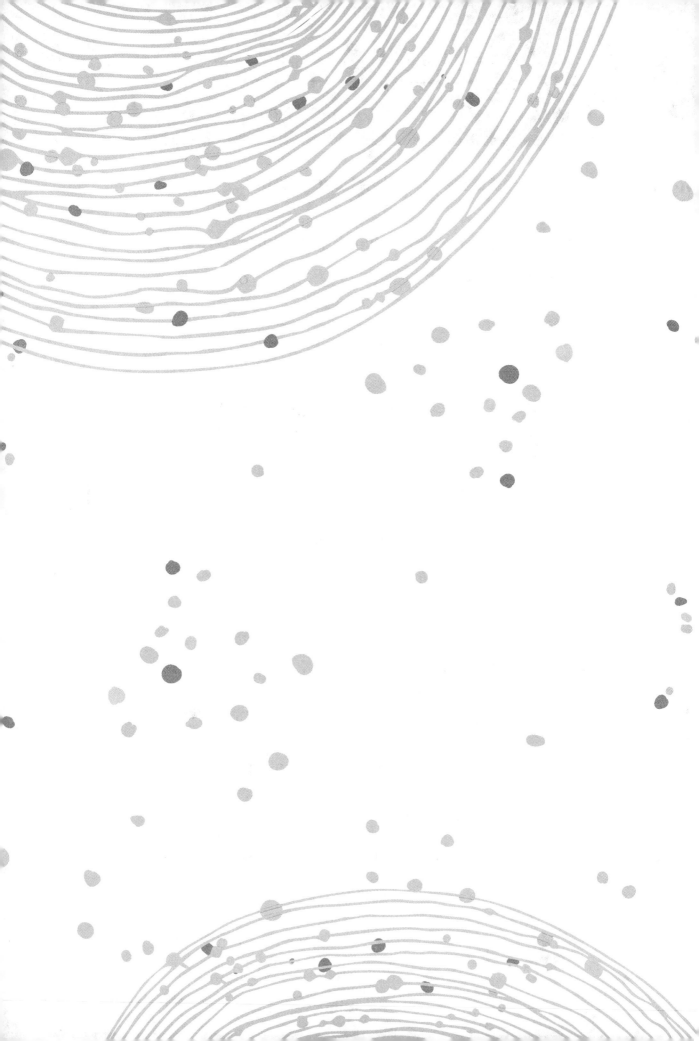

Word Relationships and Context Clues

Apply: Word Relationships and Context Clues

Use a dictionary or thesaurus to find and list synonyms and antonyms for the vocabulary word.

1. **comprehend**

   synonyms: _____

   antonyms: _____

2. **develop**

   synonyms: _____

   antonyms: _____

3. **organize**

   synonyms: _____

   antonyms: _____

WORD RELATIONSHIPS AND CONTEXT CLUES   **31**

Rewrite the sentence or add a second sentence to include a context clue for the vocabulary word's meaning. Use the synonyms and antonyms you listed in Questions 1–3 to help create the context clue. The first one has been done for you.

4. I could **comprehend** the math lesson.

   Sample response: I could comprehend the math lesson. The teacher showed me how to do the math problem in a way that I understood.

5. Juan was worried the strong winds would **develop** into a bad storm.

   _____

   _____

   _____

6. Kelly's mom told her to **organize** her toys before dinner.

   _____

   _____

   _____

Word Relationships and Context Clues

Go Write! Who Are You?

Respond to the prompt. Or, write about a topic of your choice!

Prompt: Who are you? Describe yourself by writing about what
you like, what you don't like, and what things are most
important to you.

My Journal

Narrative Writing Skills (A)

Spelling List 3 Pretest

1. Open the Spelling Pretest activity online. Listen to the first spelling word. Type the word. Check your answer.

2. Write the correct spelling of the word in the Word column of the Spelling Pretest table.

Word	✓	✗
1 blindfold		

3. Put a check mark in the ✓ column if you spelled the word correctly online.

Word	✓	✗
1 blindfold	✓	

Put an X in the ✗ column if you spelled the word incorrectly online.

Word	✓	✗
1 blindfold		✗

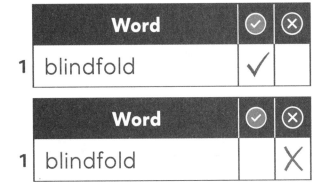

4. Repeat Steps 1–3 for the remaining words in the Spelling Pretest.

Narrative Writing Skills (A)

Spelling List 3 Pretest

Write each spelling word in the Word column, making sure to spell it correctly.

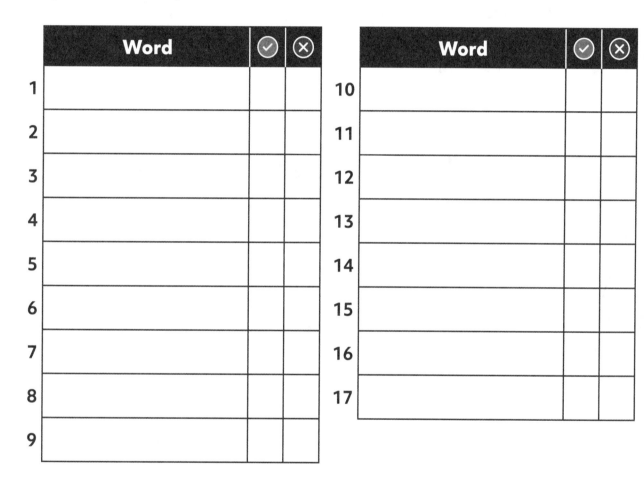

	Word	✓	✗
1			
2			
3			
4			
5			
6			
7			
8			
9			

	Word	✓	✗
10			
11			
12			
13			
14			
15			
16			
17			

Narrative Writing Skills (A)

Model Personal Story

Use this model to help you as you complete your own personal story.

The Big Drop

ook ⎡ Click, click, click. On the ride to the
top, the roller coaster clicked. Thump,
thump, thump. My heart beat really
fast. Next to me was my friend, Marc. In
front of us were a few feet of track. Below   beginning
us were all the people at Astroland. I   of story
gripped Marc's hand, and the wind blew
my hair. We were at the top of the hill.

Whoosh! Down we went. The ground
came closer. The people seemed to be
getting bigger. I screamed, and I think
I heard Marc scream, too. There was   middle
of story
lots of shaking and rumbling. Then we
zoomed up. That's when I started to

have fun. I smiled and shouted with joy. We laughed the whole time.

middle of story

Screech! The roller coaster came to a stop. Marc and I were the first ones out. We ran so fast that it felt like we were flying. We ran to our families. Mom took our picture, and Marc's uncle Jerry gave us high fives. My dad said he was proud of us for riding a roller coaster all by ourselves for the first time. I was proud of myself, too, because I had faced one of my biggest fears. But I only had one thing to say—I wanted to know when I could ride it again!

importance of event

end of story

Narrative Writing Skills (A)

Plan Your Personal Story

Read the writing prompt.

Prompt: **Write a true story about a meaningful experience in your life.**

- Describe the experience from start to finish.

- Use chronological order.

- Include important details about what happened, who else was there, and how you felt at the time.

- Be sure a reader can tell why this experience is important to you.

I might write about moving to a new neighborhood.

Follow the instructions to begin planning your personal story.

1. List as many possible topics for your story as you can think of.
    Topics should be small, meaningful moments.

    _____   _____

    _____   _____

    _____   _____

    _____   _____

    _____   _____

    _____   _____

2. Read your list of topics. Cross off ideas until you have one
    left. That idea is your topic. Circle it.

3. Answer the questions to plan the details of your
    personal story.

    a. **Who** are the important people?

    _____

    _____

    _____

b. What are the important events?

_____

_____

_____

c. When do the events take place?

_____

_____

_____

d. Where do the events take place?

_____

_____

_____

4. Complete the chart to organize your story. List as many details as you can in each box.

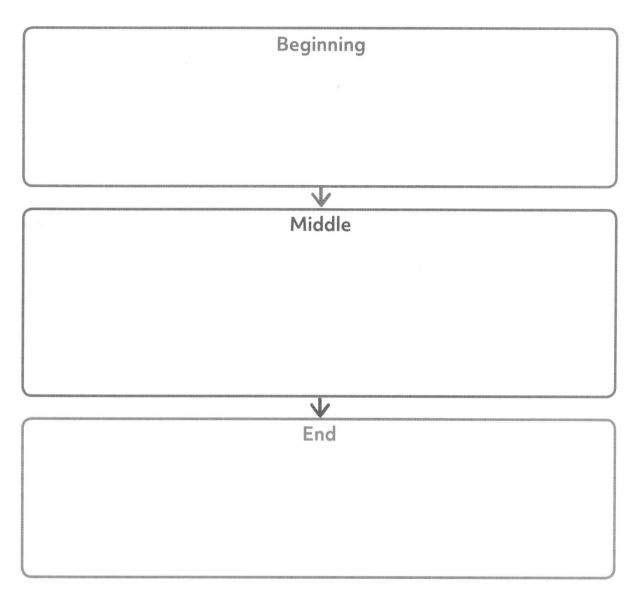

Beginning

↓

Middle

↓

End

5. **Why** are the events in your story important to you?

_____

_____

_____

Narrative Writing Skills (B)

Spelling List 3 Activity Bank

Circle any words in the box that you did not spell correctly on your pretest. Choose one activity to do with your circled words. Do as much of the activity as you can in the time given.

Did you spell all the words on the pretest correctly? Do the one activity with as many spelling words as you can.

chunk	think	lungs	singing	strong
drink	yanking	mustang	something	thing
honk	cling	nothing	string	wings
shrink	hangs			

Spelling Activity Choices

Hidden Words

1. Draw a picture. "Hide" as many of your spelling words as you can inside the picture.

2. See if others can find the words you hid in the picture.

Triangle Spelling

Write each of your spelling words in a triangle.

```
    d
   do
  dog
```

Ghost Words

1. Use a white crayon to write each of your spelling words.

2. Write over the words in white crayon with a colored marker.

Complete the activity that you chose.

My chosen activity: _____

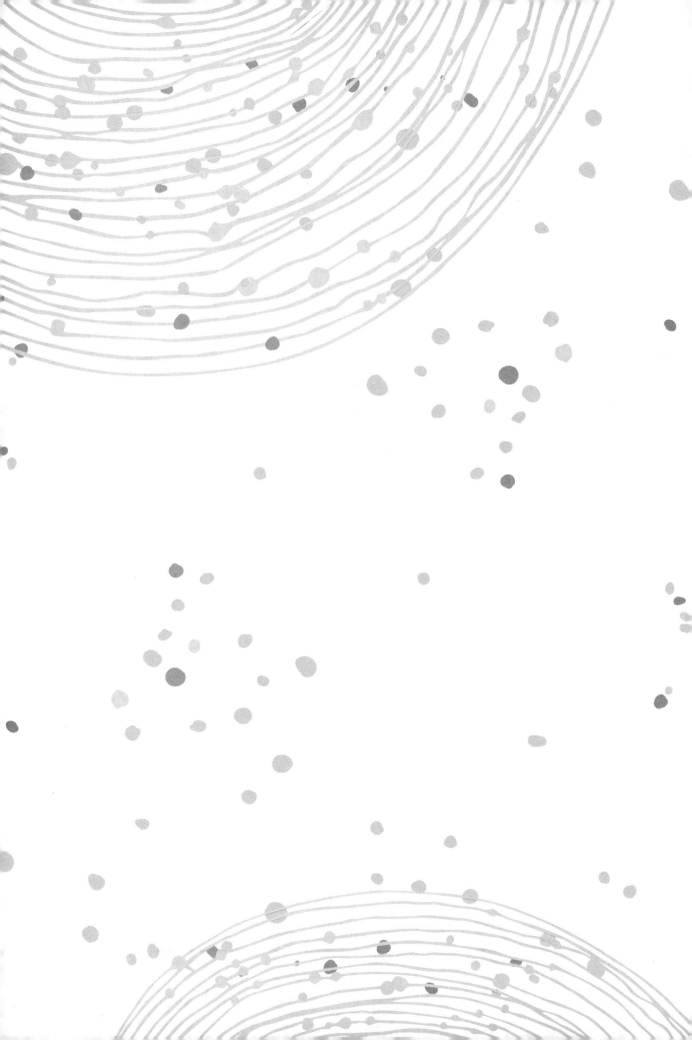

Narrative Writing Skills (B)

Show What Happened

Read the writing prompt.

Prompt: **Tell a true story about a meaningful experience in your life.**

- Describe the experience from start to finish.

- Use chronological order.

- Include important details about what happened, who else was there, and how you felt at the time.

- Be sure a reader can tell why this experience is important to you.

Follow the instructions to plan how you will describe the events in your story.

1. Draw an important part of your meaningful experience.

2. Describe your drawing. Use words that will help readers imagine what was happening.

   Example from "The Big Drop": Whoosh! Down we went. The ground came closer. The people seemed to be getting bigger.

   _____

   _____

   _____

   _____

Follow the instructions to plan how you will describe your feelings in your story.

3. Complete the chart to show how you felt during your meaningful experience. A sample answer is shown.

Tell How You Felt	Show How You Felt
Sample answer: I felt nervous.	**Sample answer:** My hands started to shake.

Follow the instructions to plan the hook for your story.

4. Think about your meaningful experience.

   a. What does the reader need to know right away about the setting?

   _____

   _____

   b. What does the reader need to know right away about the situation?

   _____

   _____

5. Use your answers to Question 4 to draft the first few sentences of your personal story. Write sentences that *show* instead of tell.

   Example from "The Big Drop": Click, click, click. On the ride to the top, the roller coaster clicked.

   _____

   _____

   _____

   _____

Narrative Writing Skills (C)

Write Your Personal Story

Read the writing prompt.

Prompt: **Tell a true story about a meaningful experience in your life.**

- Describe the experience from start to finish.

- Use chronological order.

- Include important details about what happened, who else was there, and how you felt at the time.

- Be sure a reader can tell why this experience is important to you.

Respond to the writing prompt. Use your prewriting work to help you.

_____

_____

_____

_____

_____

If you wish, draw a picture of an important part of your story.

Narrative Writing Skills Wrap-Up

Reflect on Your Personal Story

Read your personal story. Then, answer the questions in complete sentences.

1. A strong narrative begins with a strong introduction.

   a. What do you think you did well in your introduction?

   _____

   _____

   b. What do you think you could improve?

   _____

   _____

2. Good writers use sensory details to describe events and show how characters feel.

   a. List two examples of sentences that *show* instead of *tell*.

   _____

   _____

   _____

   _____

   b. Rewrite one sentence that you could improve with descriptive writing.

   _____

   _____

   _____

3. Good writers use transitions to show order.

   a. List one sentence that includes a transition.

   _____

   _____

b. Rewrite one sentence that you could clarify by adding a transition.

_____

_____

4. A strong narrative ends with a strong conclusion.

a. Does your conclusion explain why the event in your story is important to you? Explain.

_____

_____

_____

b. If not, what could you add to let readers know why the event is important?

_____

_____

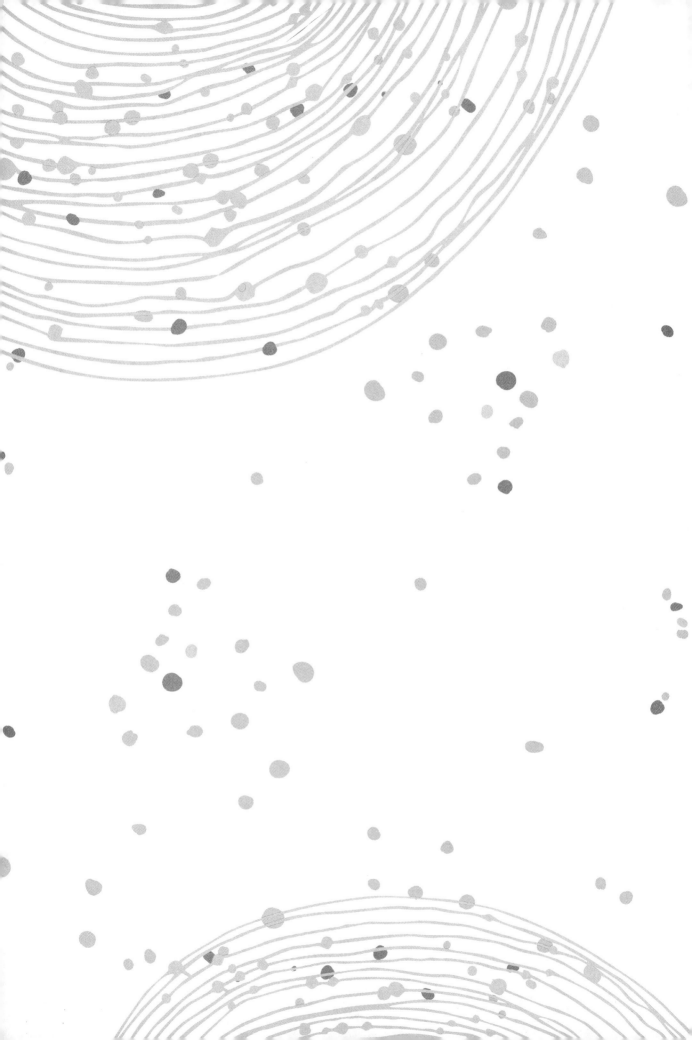

"The Wind and the Sun"

Spelling List 4 Pretest

1. Open the Spelling Pretest activity online. Listen to the first spelling word. Type the word. Check your answer.

2. Write the correct spelling of the word in the Word column of the Spelling Pretest table.

Word	✓	✗
1 blindfold		

3. Put a check mark in the ✓ column if you spelled the word correctly online.

Word	✓	✗
1 blindfold	✓	

Put an X in the ✗ column if you spelled the word incorrectly online.

Word	✓	✗
1 blindfold		✗

4. Repeat Steps 1–3 for the remaining words in the Spelling Pretest.

"The Wind and the Sun"

Spelling List 4 Pretest

Write each spelling word in the Word column, making sure to spell it correctly.

	Word	✓	✗
1			
2			
3			
4			
5			
6			
7			
8			
9			
10			
11			
12			
13			

	Word	✓	✗
14			
15			
16			
17			
18			
19			
20			
21			
22			
23			
24			
25			

"The Wind and the Sun"

Write About Sequence and Moral

Fill in the boxes with plot events from the story in sequence. Then, state the moral of the story.

At the beginning of the story,

In the middle of the story,

At the end of the story,

The moral of the story is _____

_____ .

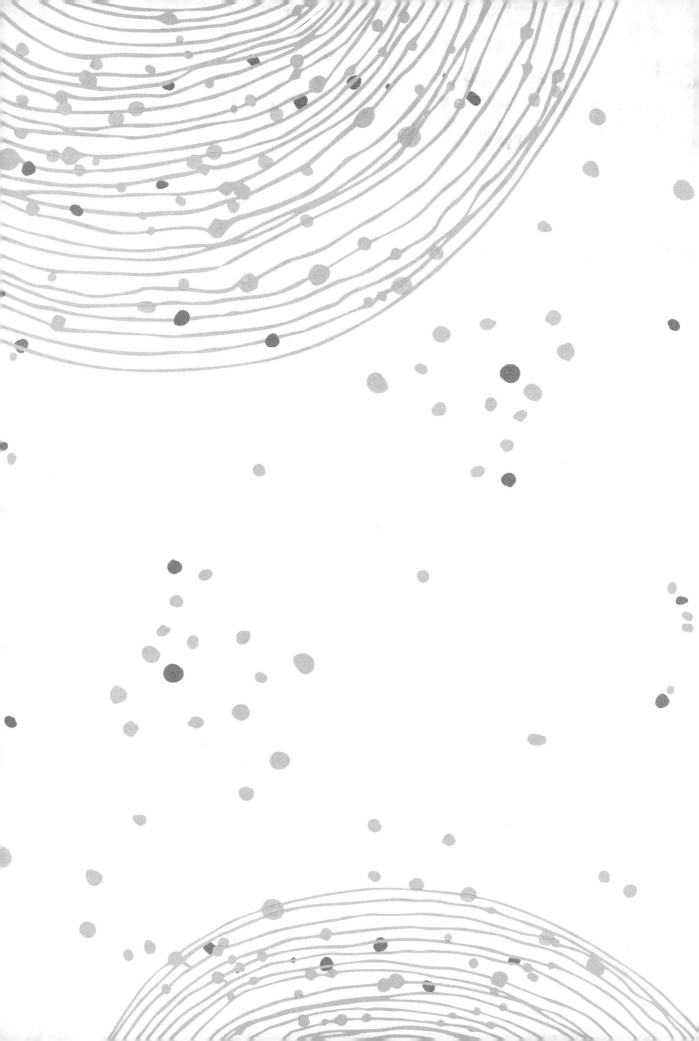

GET READY

"The Wind and the Sun" Wrap-Up

Spelling List 4 Activity Bank

Circle any words in the box that you did not spell correctly on your pretest. Choose one activity to do with your circled words. Do as much of the activity as you can in the time given.

Did you spell all the words on the pretest correctly? Do the one activity with as many spelling words as you can.

able	cupcake	flare	label	sleigh
always	decade	freight	ladle	snail
away	dictate	glare	maintain	Sunday
basic	eight	gravy	neighbor	training
claim	explain	holiday	payment	weight

Spelling Activity Choices

Create a Crossword

1. Write one of your spelling words going down in the center of the grid.

2. Write another spelling word going across that shares a letter with the first word. See how many words you can connect.

Example:

			p				
		k	i	s	s	e	s
	d		n				
r	o	c	k	s			
	g						
	s						

Word Search Puzzle

1. Draw a box on the grid. The box should be large enough to hold your spelling words.

2. Fill in the grid with your spelling words. Write them across, up and down, and diagonally. You can write them forward and backward.

3. Fill in the rest of the box with random letters.

4. Ask someone to find and circle your words in the puzzle.

Complete the activity that you chose.

My chosen activity: _____

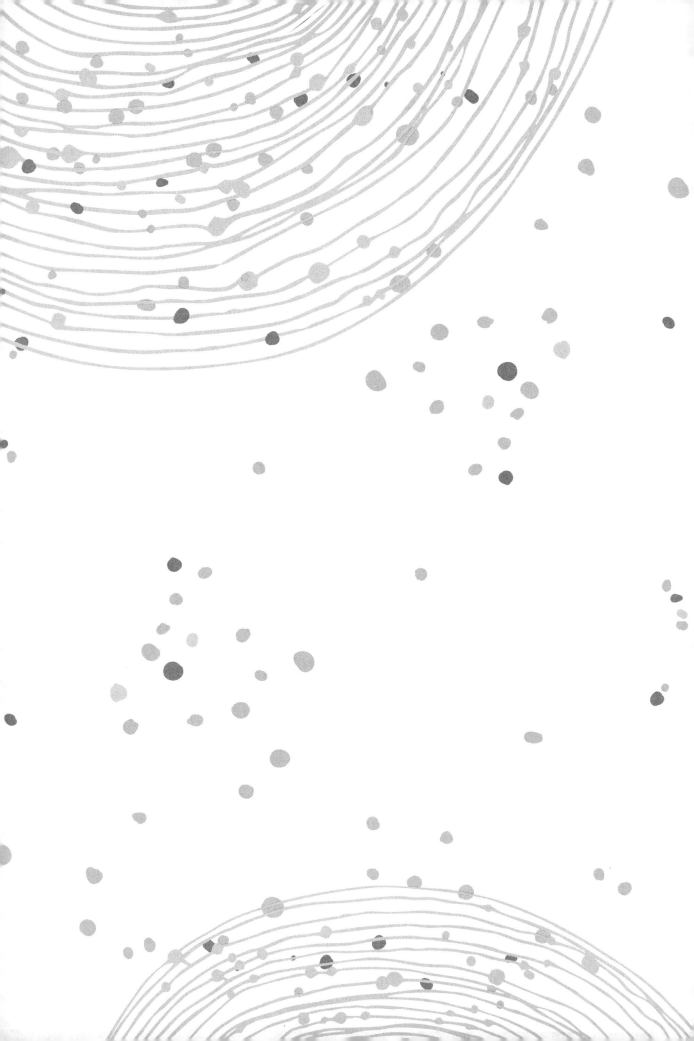

"The Wind and the Sun" Wrap-Up

Write About a New Fable

Read "The Crow and the Pitcher," adapted from a fable by Aesop.

A Crow, half-dead with thirst, found a pitcher with a little water in it. But the pitcher was tall with a narrow neck. No matter how hard he tried, the Crow could not reach the water. Then he had an idea. He found some pebbles and began dropping them into the water one by one. He saw the water rising higher and higher. After dropping in a few more pebbles, the water was at last high enough for the Crow to drink.

In a pinch, use your brains.

Answer the questions in complete sentences.

1. What happens at the beginning of the fable?

_____

_____

_____

2. What happens in the middle of the fable?

_____

_____

_____

3. What happens at the end of the fable?

_____

_____

_____

4. How would you describe the Crow?

_____

_____

5. How do the Crow's actions support the moral, "In a pinch, use your brains"?

_____

_____

"The Cruel Lion and the Clever Rabbit"

Write About Characters and Evidence

Sort the words in the Word Bank according to the character each word describes.

1.   Word Bank

cruel	caring	clever
brave	scared	mighty
proud	strong	hungry

Bhaksuraka, the lion	Rabbit

Answer the questions in complete sentences.

2. What is one word that you used to describe Bhaksuraka, the lion? What evidence from the story supports this description?

_____

_____

_____

_____

_____

_____

_____

My brother is "generous." Why? He let me borrow his lucky button-down shirt!

"The Cruel Lion and the Clever Rabbit" Wrap-Up

Write More About Characters and Evidence

Answer the questions in complete sentences. Refer to the Write About Characters and Evidence activity page for words that describe Rabbit.

1. What is one word that you used to describe Rabbit? What evidence from the story supports this description?

_____

_____

_____

_____

_____

_____

_____

2. What is another word that you used to describe Rabbit? What evidence from the story supports this description?

_____

_____

_____

_____

_____

_____

_____

_____

Do you think this rabbit will notice my slippers?

"Why the Larks Flew Away"

Compare Two Stories

Read the beginning of "Cinderella."

Once upon a time, there was a lovely young woman named Cinderella. She lived in a small kingdom with her wicked stepmother and two stepsisters. They treated her like a servant. Even though they made her do all the work, she was always kind. One day, they were all invited to a ball in honor of the prince. But Cinderella's stepmother would not let her go. Instead, she was forced to help her stepsisters prepare for the ball. When they left for the palace, Cinderella stayed behind.

As the door closed, Cinderella began to cry. Suddenly, a fairy godmother appeared. She said, "Do not weep. I will help you go to the ball." This made her cry harder, saying, "I have nothing to wear but rags." At that, the fairy godmother waved her magic wand. Cinderella's rags turned into a beautiful gown. Then the fairy godmother touched Cinderella's feet with her wand. In a blink, tiny glass slippers appeared on her feet.

Complete the chart to compare "Cinderella" with "Why the Larks Flew Away." You do not need to use complete sentences.

Story Element	"Cinderella"	"Why the Larks Flew Away"
Characters		
Setting		
Problem		

Story Element	"Cinderella"	"Why the Larks Flew Away"
Solution		
Is the story a fable or fairy tale? How do you know?		

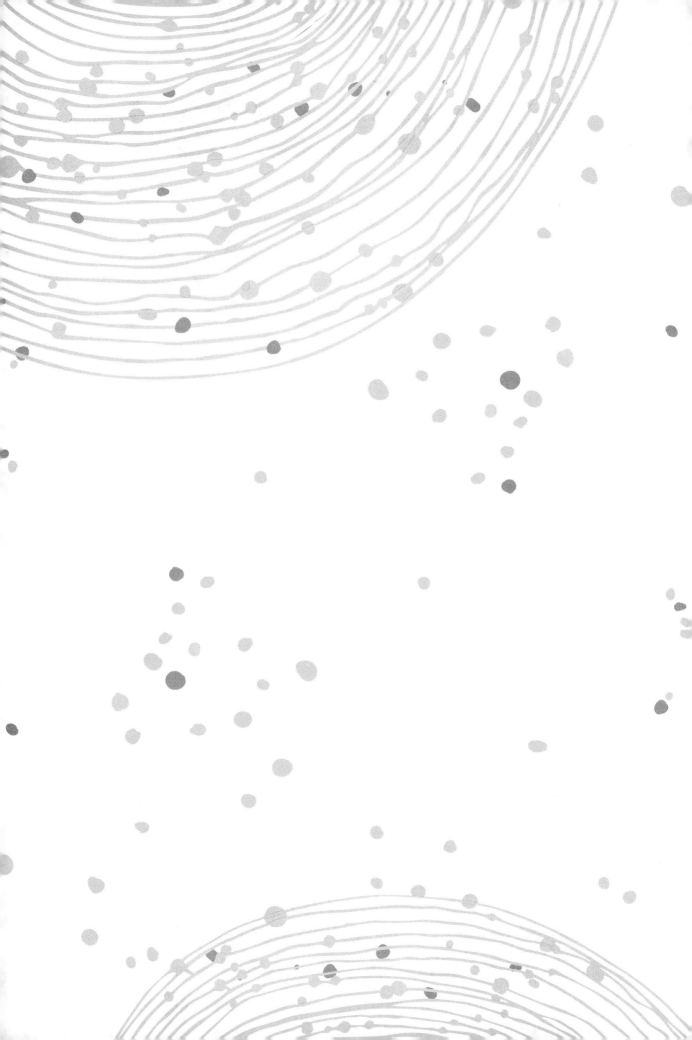

"Why the Larks Flew Away" Wrap-Up

Write About Two Stories

Answer the questions in complete sentences to compare "Cinderella" and "Why the Larks Flew Away." Use the chart on the Compare Two Stories activity page to help you.

1. Characters: Who are the characters in each story?

_____

_____

_____

_____

2. Setting: What is the setting of each story? Is the setting the same or different in the stories?

_____

_____

_____

_____

3. Problem: What is the problem in each story?

_____

_____

_____

_____

_____

_____

_____

4. Solution: How does the problem get solved in each story?

_____

_____

_____

_____

_____

_____

5. Are the two stories the same kind of story or are they different? How can you tell?

_____

_____

_____

_____

_____

_____

_____

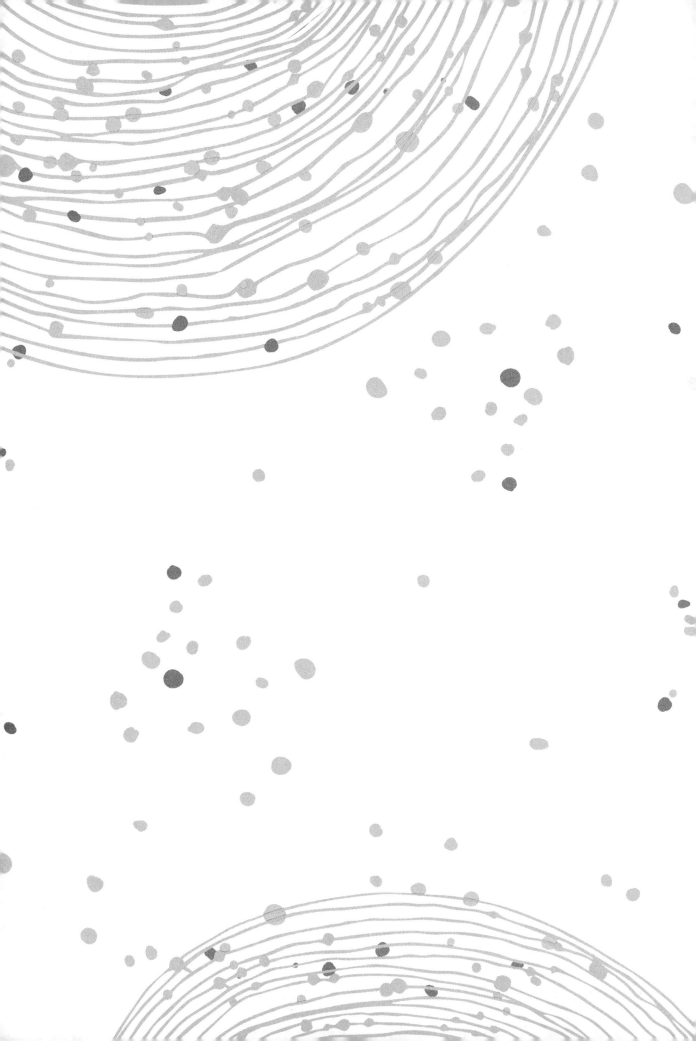

Narrative Writing: Prewriting (A)

Spelling List 5 Pretest

1. **Open the Spelling Pretest activity online. Listen to the first spelling word. Type the word. Check your answer.**

2. **Write the correct spelling of the word in the Word column of the Spelling Pretest table.**

	Word	✓	✗
1	blindfold		

3. **Put a check mark in the ✓ column if you spelled the word correctly online.**

	Word	✓	✗
1	blindfold	✓	

   Put an X in the ✗ column if you spelled the word incorrectly online.

	Word	✓	✗
1	blindfold		✗

4. **Repeat Steps 1–3 for the remaining words in the Spelling Pretest.**

Narrative Writing: Prewriting (A)

Spelling List 5 Pretest

Write each spelling word in the Word column, making sure to spell it correctly.

	Word	✓	✗
1			
2			
3			
4			
5			
6			
7			
8			
9			

	Word	✓	✗
10			
11			
12			
13			
14			
15			
16			
17			

Narrative Writing: Prewriting (A)

Model Short Story

Use this model to help you as you complete your own short story. Note: Only the most important plot events and one example of dialogue are labeled.

The Incredible Special Shoes

Mary lived in a forest with her twin sister Molly. The forest was full of tall trees and high mountains. It was a very pretty place. 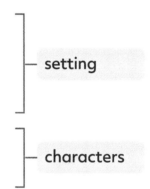 — setting

Mary and Molly were normal girls — characters with red hair and freckles. Yet their shoes were not normal. Their shoes were special. Their shoes could make them jump very high and run very fast. Once, their shoes helped the girls catch up to an airplane and jump on it as it was taking off!

One morning, Mary and Molly were swimming in a pond. Their shoes were on the grass nearby. Just then, a mean

character boy named Gordy stole Mary's shoes.

Gordy was jealous of Mary. He wanted

to be able to jump high and run fast

like Mary.

"Hey!" Mary called from the water.

"What are you doing?"

"I'm taking your shoes, Mary,"

problem laughed Gordy as he picked up Mary's

shoes from the grass. "And there is no

way you can stop me."

Then Gordy put on the shoes and

jumped high into a tree. He smiled and

clapped his hands. He thought about all

the things he would do, now that he had

Mary's special shoes.

What Gordy did not know was that

Molly had a pair of special shoes, too.

Molly's shoes were on the grass, near

where Mary's shoes had been. So as

Gordy laughed, Mary put on Molly's

shoes. Then she jumped high up into the

tree. She landed next to Gordy.

"How did you do that?" Gordy asked with surprise.

"Just give me my shoes back, Gordy," Mary told him.

— dialogue

Gordy decided to jump to an even higher branch in the tree. Mary followed him. Gordy jumped again, and so did Mary. Soon Mary was chasing Gordy all through the forest.

— plot event

They jumped high over the trees. They dashed through streams and rivers. They even jumped over a mountain. After an hour, Gordy and Mary were both tired. They stopped to rest on a low branch of a tree. Their legs hung down below them.

"Let's have a contest," said Mary. "If you win, you can keep my shoes. If I win, you have to give them back."

— plot event

"That sounds interesting. What is the contest?" Gordy asked.

"We'll have a race," Mary replied. "The first one to run around the entire pond wins."

Gordy thought for a minute. He scratched his head. He and Mary were both wearing special shoes, but he thought he was faster than she was.

plot event — He agreed to race Mary. Yet because Gordy was mean, he tried to cheat, too. He wanted to get a head start in the race.

"Go!" he shouted, as he jumped from the branch and started to run.

solution — Oops! Gordy fell down quickly. While he was thinking, Molly had sneaked up under him and tied the laces on the special shoes together. Now Gordy could not run at all. Mary jogged around the pond and easily won the race.

"Thanks, sister," Mary said to Molly. Then she turned to Gordy. "Now give my shoes back, you mean boy!"

Narrative Writing: Prewriting (A)

Brainstorm for Your Short Story

Read the assignment. You will complete the assignment in steps over multiple lessons.

Prompt: **Write a short story.**

Requirements: Your short story should have the following:

- A **title**

- **Beginning** paragraphs that describe the **characters** and **setting**, and present a **problem**

- **Middle** paragraphs that develop the **plot**, include **dialogue**, and make readers want to know what happens next

- **Ending** paragraphs that wrap up the story and show how the characters solve the problem

- **Transitions** that show order

- **Description** of characters and events

- Correct **grammar**, **punctuation**, **capitalization**, and **spelling**

Audience: Your teacher, peers, and Learning Coach

Purpose: Tell a short story that entertains and makes sense to readers.

Length: 300–400 words long, approximately 4–6 handwritten drafting pages or 1–$1\frac{1}{2}$ pages typed and double spaced

Begin brainstorming ideas. Answer the questions in complete sentences.

1. Do you want to write a funny story about people who are like your friends or family?

   _____

   _____

2. Do you want to write a scary story about places or people that are unusual and frightening?

   _____

   _____

3. Do you want to write a sad story about characters who face a difficult and upsetting problem?

   _____

   _____

4. Do you want to write an exciting story about characters who have a thrilling adventure?

   _____

   _____

Use your imagination to think about story ideas. Write four short story ideas in the boxes. Include some key plot events and the problem that your characters will face.

Idea 1: _____

_____

_____

_____

Idea 2: _____

_____

_____

_____

Idea 3: _____

_____

_____

_____

Idea 4: _____

_____

_____

_____

Answer the questions to choose one of your ideas for your short story.

5. Which story's characters seem least interesting to you? Cross off that story idea.

6. Are any stories too complicated to tell in a few pages? Cross off those story ideas.

7. Do any of the stories seem too much like another story you have read or a TV show or movie you have seen? If so, cross them off.

8. Which story's characters are most interesting to you? What story would be most fun to write? What story already has you imagining some settings, characters, and important events? Circle that idea.

Wow! I just got the best idea!

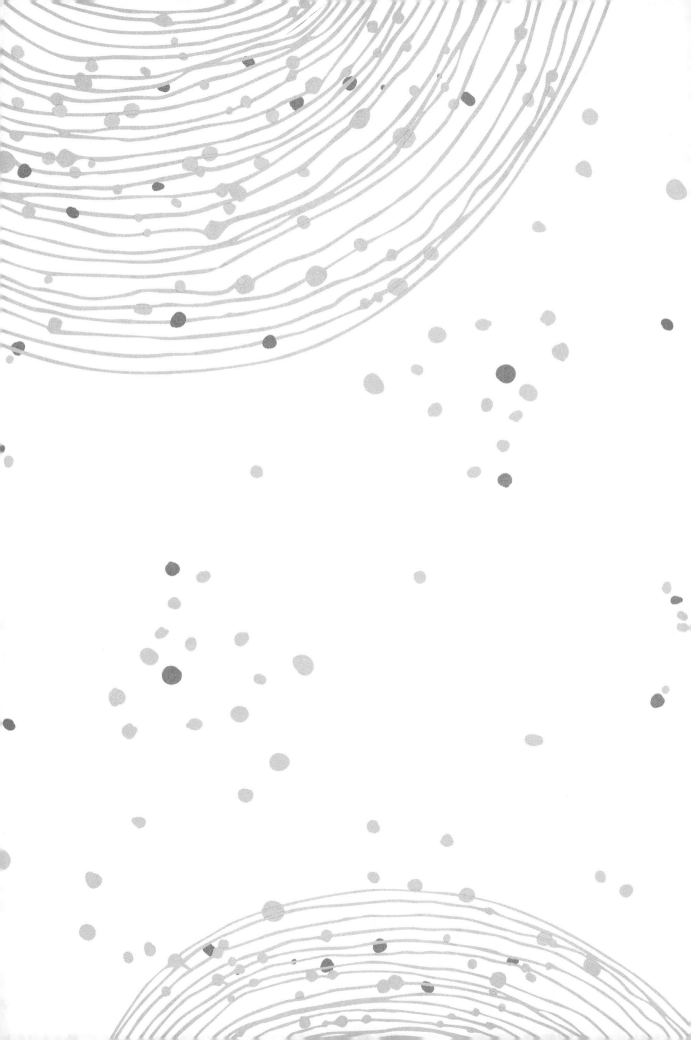

Narrative Writing: Prewriting (B)

Spelling List 5 Activity Bank

Circle any words in the box that you did not spell correctly on your pretest. Choose one activity to do with your circled words. Do as much of the activity as you can in the time given.

Did you spell all the words on the pretest correctly? Do the one activity with as many spelling words as you can.

assign	Friday	lie	quite	supply
blind	inside	lightning	shy	tie
child	island	might	sigh	while
entire	July			

Spelling Activity Choices

Alphabetizing

1. In the left column, write your spelling words in alphabetical order.

2. Correct any spelling errors.

Vowel-Free Words

1. In the left column, write only the consonants in each of your spelling words. Put a dot where each vowel should be.

2. Spell each word aloud, stating which vowels should be in the places with dots.

3. In the right column, rewrite the entire spelling word.

4. Correct any spelling errors.

Rhymes

1. In the left column, write your spelling words.

2. In the right column, write a word that rhymes with each spelling word.

3. Correct any spelling errors.

Uppercase and Lowercase

1. In the left column, write each of your spelling words in all uppercase letters.

2. In the right column, write each of your spelling words in all lowercase letters.

3. Correct any spelling errors.

Complete the activity that you chose.

My chosen activity: _____

1. _____   _____

2. _____   _____

3. _____   _____

4. _____   _____

5. _____   _____

6. _____   _____

7. _____   _____

8. _____   _____

9. _____   _____

10. _____   _____

11. _____   _____

12. _____   _____

13. _____   _____

14. _____   _____

15. _____   _____

16. _____   _____

17. _____   _____

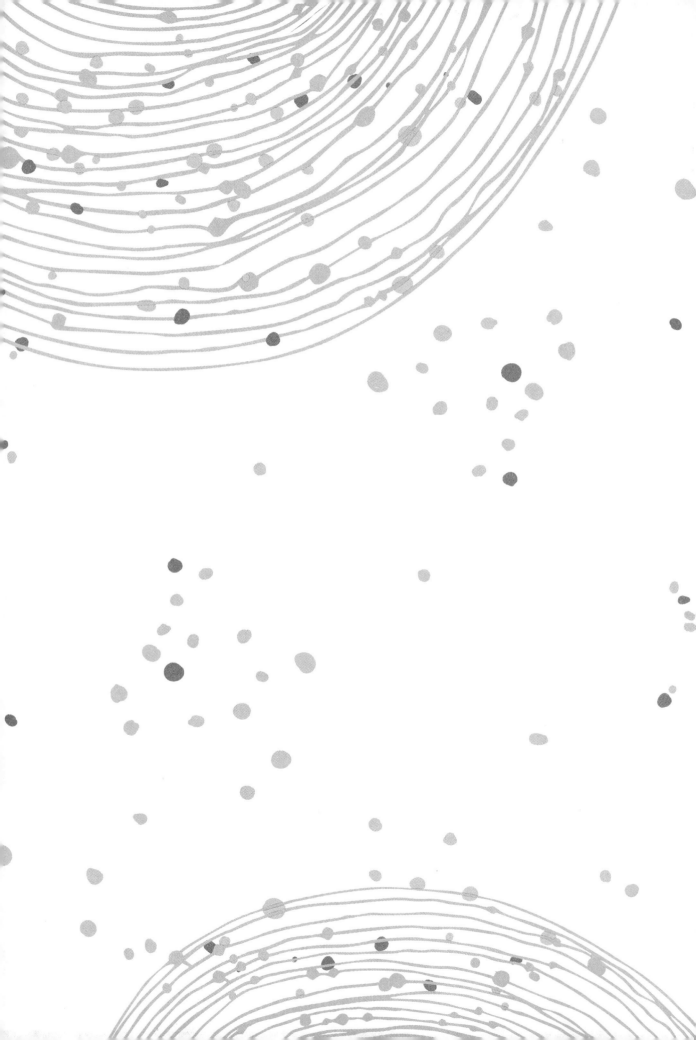

Narrative Writing: Prewriting (B)

Plan Your Short Story

Plan the setting for your short story by answering the questions.

1. When will your story take place? Check one box.

☐ long ago

☐ the present time

☐ the future

2. What time of day will your story take place? Check one box.

☐ morning

☐ afternoon

☐ evening

☐ night

3. Where will each part of your story take place?

    a. Beginning:

_____

_____

    b. Middle:

_____

_____

    c. End:

_____

_____

Plan the characters. Write their names, describe them, and describe how they feel about the other characters.

    4. Character 1

       a. Name: _____

       b. Description: _____

_____

c. How this character feels about other characters:

_____

_____

_____

5. Character 2

    a. Name: _____

    b. Description: _____

    _____

    c. How this character feels about other characters:

    _____

    _____

    _____

6. Character 3

    a. Name: _____

    b. Description: _____

    _____

c. How this character feels about other characters:

_____

_____

_____

Develop the plot. Answer the questions in complete sentences.

7. What problem does the main character face?

_____

_____

8. What causes the problem?

_____

_____

9. How does the main character solve the problem?

_____

_____

_____

Organize the story. Use your answers from Questions 1–9 to describe the setting, characters, and plot events for each part of the story.

Beginning

Setting

Characters

Plot Events (Include the problem.)

Middle

Setting

Characters

Plot Events

End

Setting

Characters

Plot Events (Include the solution.)

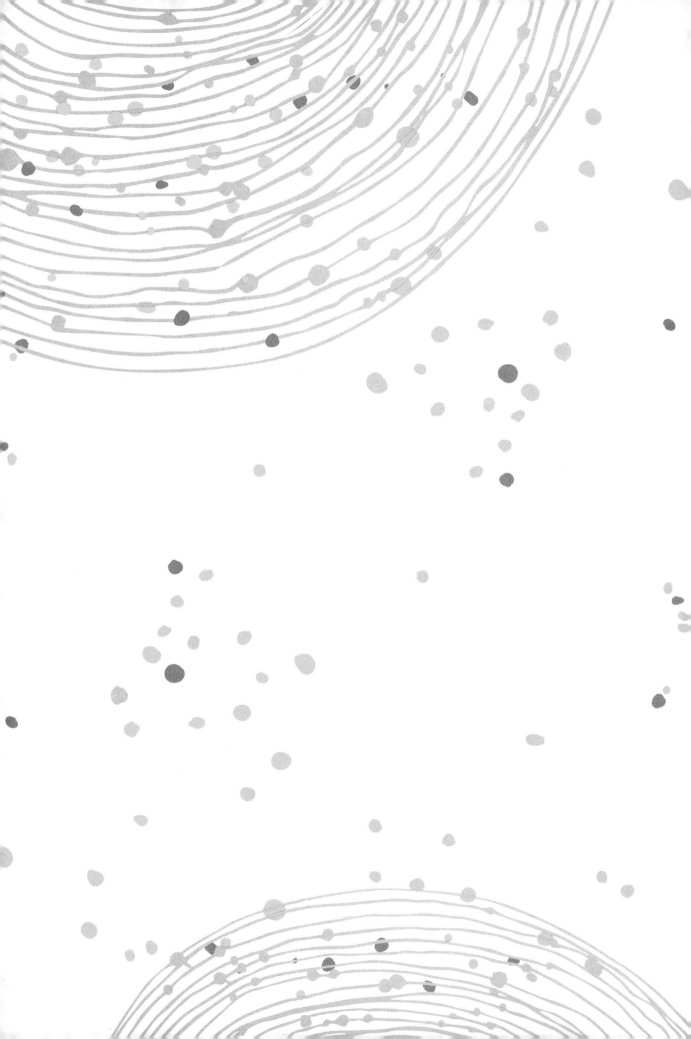

Narrative Writing: Drafting (A)

Draft Your Short Story

Write the first draft of your short story. Write only on the white rows. You will use the purple rows for revisions later.

Title: _____

start here ▶

keep writing ▶

Draft Page 1

keep writing ▶

Draft Page 2

keep writing ►

Draft Page 3

keep writing ▶

Draft Page 4

keep writing ▶

Draft Page 5

Draft Page 6

Nuance and Shades of Meaning

Apply: Nuance and Shades of Meaning

Circle the word that best completes the sentence. Then, explain your choice. Think about the nuances, or small differences in meaning, between the two choices.

1. The detective _____ the cat spilled the milk but needed to gather evidence to be sure.

Choices: *knew* or *suspected*

Explanation:

_____

_____

_____

2. Sally _____ she had a week off from school because she read it in the school newsletter.

Choices: *knew* or *believed*

Explanation:

_____

_____

_____

3. Federico _____ it was unfair that his sister got to go to the movies but he didn't.

Choices: *believed* or *suspected*

Explanation:

_____

_____

_____

Write your own sentence using one of the given words, but leave a blank space where your chosen word belongs. Have someone else read your sentence. Ask this person to choose which word best completes the sentence. Discuss the answer.

4. Choices: *believed* or *knew* or *suspected*

_____

_____

Nuance and Shades of Meaning

Go Write! Look Out the Window

Respond to the prompt. Or, write about a topic of your choice!

Prompt: Look out a window, and write about what you see.
Describe the colors, shapes, and sizes of the things you are
looking at, such as trees, clouds, buildings, people, birds,
or other animals. You may also describe sounds and smells.

My Journal

Words to Show Time and Space

Apply: Words to Show Time and Space

The words *meanwhile*, *during*, and *afterward* show time. Use these words to write a short paragraph that describes your day. Use the sample response as a model.

Sample response: During the morning, I did my schoolwork. Afterward, I had lunch. Now, I'm waiting for my brother to get home. In the meanwhile, I am playing cards with my friend Maria.

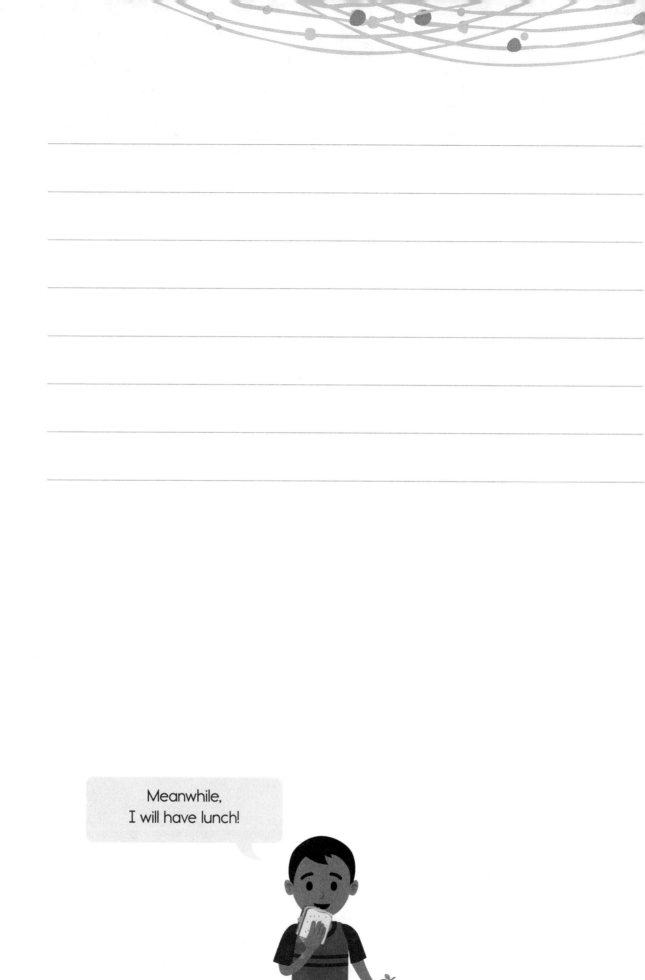

Meanwhile,
I will have lunch!

Words to Show Space and Time

Go Write! Who Gives Good Advice?

Respond to the prompt. Or, write about a topic of your choice!

Prompt: If you had a problem, who is the person you would ask for advice? Why?

My Journal

"The Stone in the Road" (A)

Spelling List 6 Pretest

1. Open the Spelling Pretest activity online. Listen to the first spelling word. Type the word. Check your answer.

2. Write the correct spelling of the word in the Word column of the Spelling Pretest table.

Word	✓	✗
1 blindfold		

3. Put a check mark in the ✓ column if you spelled the word correctly online.

Word	✓	✗
1 blindfold	✓	

Put an X in the ✗ column if you spelled the word incorrectly online.

Word	✓	✗
1 blindfold		✗

4. Repeat Steps 1–3 for the remaining words in the Spelling Pretest.

"The Stone in the Road" (A)

Spelling List 6 Pretest

Write each spelling word in the Word column, making sure to spell it correctly.

	Word	✓	✗
1			
2			
3			
4			
5			
6			
7			
8			
9			

	Word	✓	✗
10			
11			
12			
13			
14			
15			
16			
17			

"The Stone in the Road" (A)

Describe a Sequence of Events

Explain the sequence of events in "The Stone in the Road: A Story." Use signal words and complete sentences.

1. What happens at the beginning of the story?

    _____

    _____

    _____

2. What happens in the middle of the story?

    _____

    _____

    _____

3. What happens after that?

    _____

    _____

    _____

4. What happens at the end of the story?

_____

_____

_____

Spelling List 6 Activity Bank

Circle any words in the box that you did not spell correctly on the pretest. Choose one activity to do with your circled words. Do as much of the activity as you can in the time given.

Did you spell all the words on the pretest correctly? Do the one activity with as many spelling words as you can.

almost	doe	hole	open	sailboat
alone	dough	known	phone	tiptoe
although	focus	locate	rowboat	window
crossroad	follow			

Spelling Activity Choices

Silly Sentences

1. Write a silly sentence for each of your spelling words.

2. Underline the spelling word in each sentence.
   Example: The dog was <u>driving</u> a car.

3. Correct any spelling errors.

Spelling Story

1. Write a very short story using each of your spelling words.

2. Underline the spelling words in the story.

3. Correct any spelling errors.

Riddle Me This

1. Write a riddle for each of your spelling words.
   Example: "I have a trunk, but it's not on my car."

2. Write the answer, which is your word, for each riddle.
   Example: Answer: elephant

3. Correct any spelling errors.

RunOnWord

1. Gather some crayons, colored pencils, or markers. Use a different color to write each of your spelling words. Write the words end to end as one long word.
   Example: dogcatbirdfishturtle

2. Rewrite the words correctly and with proper spacing.

3. Correct any spelling errors.

Complete the activity that you chose.

My chosen activity: _____

_____

_____

_____

_____

_____

_____

_____

_____

_____

_____

_____

_____

_____

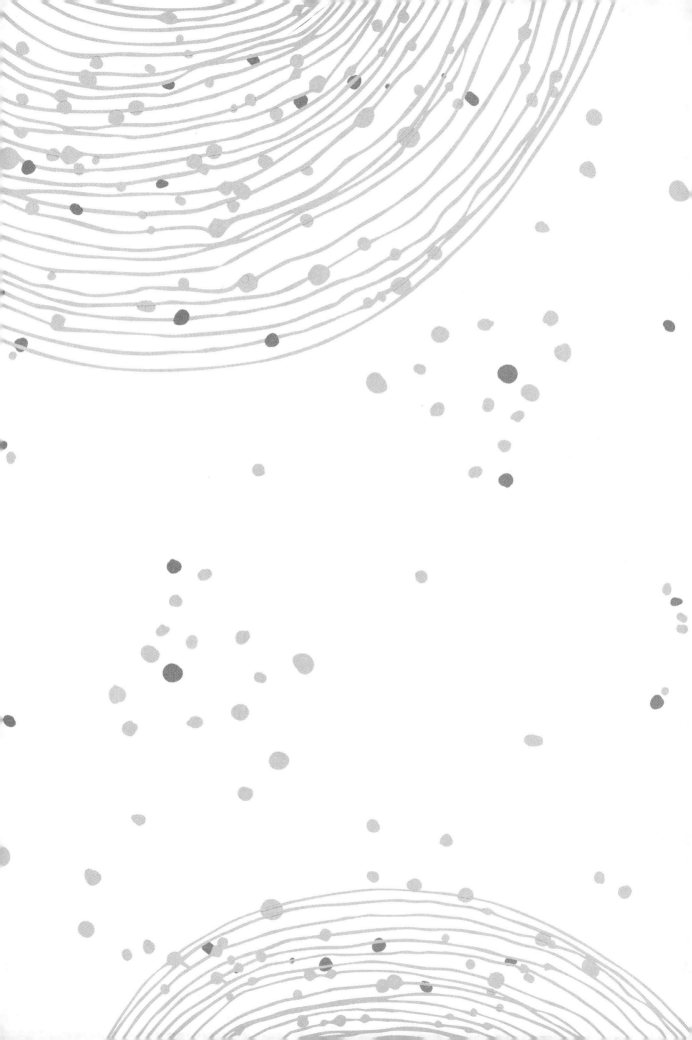

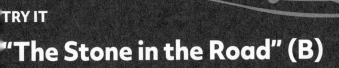

"The Stone in the Road" (B)

Support a Theme

Answer the questions in complete sentences.

1. Identify a theme in "The Stone in the Road: A Play."

_____

_____

_____

Choose two scenes in the play. Record a detail from each scene that supports the theme you identified in Question 1. The detail can be an action or a line of dialogue. Explain how the detail supports the theme.

2. First Scene: _____

a. Detail

_____

_____

_____

b. Explanation

_____

_____

_____

_____

_____

3. Second Scene: _____

a. Detail

_____

_____

_____

b. Explanation

_____

_____

_____

_____

"The Stone in the Road" (C)

Compare a Story and a Play

Fill in the chart to compare "The Stone in the Road: A Story" with "The Stone in the Road: A Play." The first entry in the chart has been completed for you.

Question	"The Stone in the Road: A Story"	"The Stone in the Road: A Play"
Who are the main characters?	king milkmaid	King Alvis Sir Gavin Milkmaid
What is the setting?		
What happens first?		

Question	"The Stone in the Road: A Story"	"The Stone in the Road: A Play"
What happens second?		
What happens next?		
What happens at the end?		

Question	"The Stone in the Road: A Story"	"The Stone in the Road: A Play"
What is the theme?		

Answer the question in complete sentences. Use three details to support your answer.

Which version of "The Stone in the Road" do you like better? Why?

_____

_____

_____

_____

_____

_____

_____

_____

_____

_____

_____

_____

Personally, I think a musical version would be neat.

"The Stone in the Road" Wrap-Up

Plan a Folktale

Complete the table to plan your own folktale.

Title: _____

Question	Notes
What lesson will your folktale teach?	
Describe at least two characters in your folktale.	

Question	Notes
What is the setting for your folktale?	
What is the problem to be solved?	
List at least four plot events in your folktale.	First, Next,

Question	Notes
List at least four plot events in your folktale. *(continued)*	Then, ——————————————— Finally,
How is the problem solved?	

Illustrate one event from your folktale.

Title:

Narrative Writing: Revising

Revise Your Short Story

Read your short story draft. Then, use the checklist to improve your organization and ideas. Make changes to your short story draft.

Ideas

☐ Do I begin by describing the characters and setting, and presenting the problem?

☐ Do I develop the plot in the middle paragraphs?

☐ Do I end by showing how the characters solve the problem?

☐ Do I use dialogue to develop characters and events?

☐ Do I *show* instead of *tell*, when possible?

Organization

☐ Are my ideas in chronological order?

☐ Do I use transitions to show order?

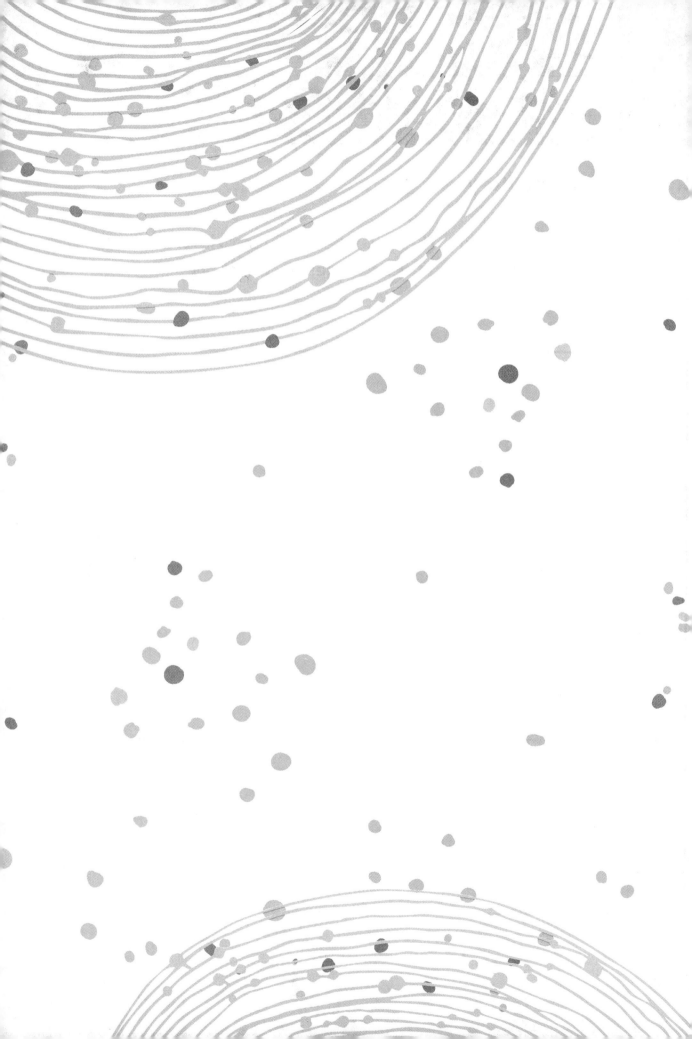

Narrative Writing: Proofreading

Proofread Your Short Story

Read your revised short story draft. Then, use the checklist to improve your grammar, usage, and mechanics. Make changes to your revised short story draft.

Grammar and Usage

☐ Are all sentences complete and correct?

☐ Do I use different types of sentences (simple, compound, complex)?

☐ Are there any missing or extra words?

Mechanics

☐ Is every word spelled correctly?

☐ Does every sentence begin with a capital letter and end with correct punctuation?

☐ Is dialogue punctuated and capitalized correctly?

☐ Do I indent paragraphs?

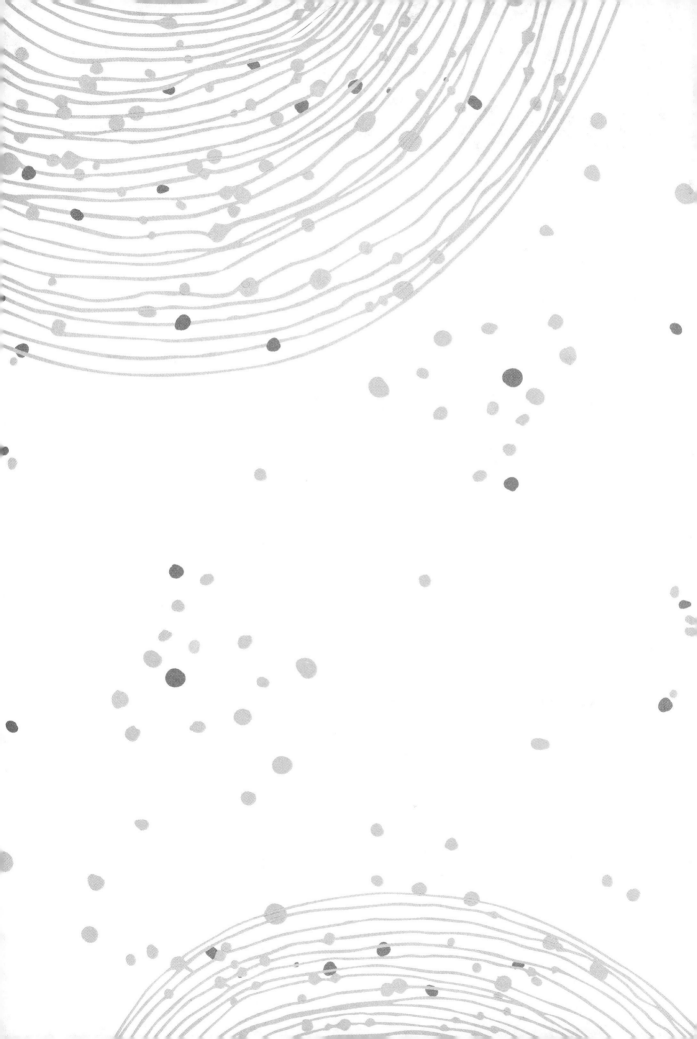

"The Tiger, the Brahman, and the Jackal"

Spelling List 7 Pretest

1. Open the Spelling Pretest activity online. Listen to the first spelling word. Type the word. Check your answer.

2. Write the correct spelling of the word in the Word column of the Spelling Pretest table.

	Word	✓	✗
1	blindfold		

3. Put a check mark in the ✓ column if you spelled the word correctly online.

	Word	✓	✗
1	blindfold	✓	

Put an X in the ✗ column if you spelled the word incorrectly online.

	Word	✓	✗
1	blindfold		X

4. Repeat Steps 1–3 for the remaining words in the Spelling Pretest.

"The Tiger, the Brahman, and the Jackal"

Spelling List 7 Pretest

Write each spelling word in the Word column, making sure to spell it correctly.

	Word	✓	✗
1			
2			
3			
4			
5			
6			
7			
8			
9			

	Word	✓	✗
10			
11			
12			
13			
14			
15			
16			
17			

"The Tiger, the Brahman, and the Jackal"

Retell the Story

Retell "The Tiger, the Brahman, and the Jackal."

- Explain the events in your own words in the order in which they happened.

- Include the main characters, setting, and main plot events.

- End with a sentence that states the theme.

- Use complete sentences.

_____

_____

_____

_____

_____

_____

_____

_____

_____

_____

_____

_____

_____

_____

"The Tiger, the Brahman, and the Jackal" Wrap-Up

Spelling List 7 Activity Bank

Circle any words in the box that you did not spell correctly on your pretest. Choose one activity to do with your circled words. Do as much of the activity as you can in the time given.

Did you spell all the words on the pretest correctly? Do the one activity with as many spelling words as you can.

agreed	chief	field	melody	safety
athlete	complete	least	probably	steel
between	eclipse	leave	real	teaching
body	even			

Spelling Activity Choices

Hidden Words

1. Draw a picture. "Hide" as many of your spelling words as you can inside the picture.

2. See if others can find the words you hid in the picture.

Triangle Spelling

Write each of your spelling words in a triangle.

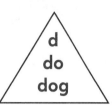

Ghost Words

1. Use a white crayon to write each of your spelling words.

2. Write over the words in white crayon with a colored marker.

Complete the activity that you chose.

My chosen activity: _____

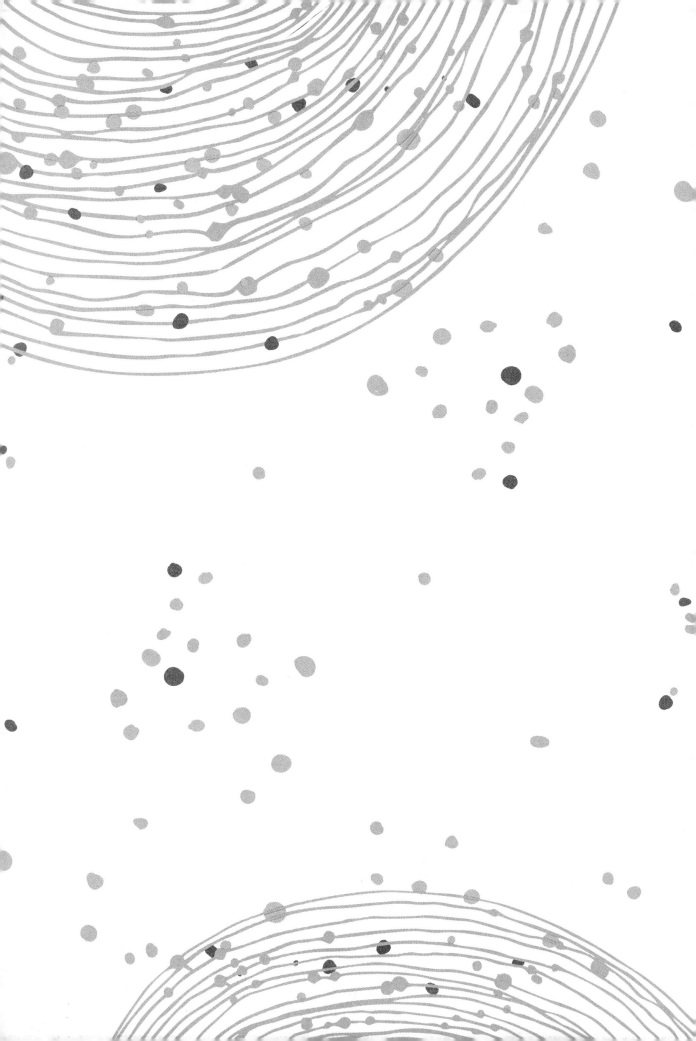

"The Tiger, the Brahman, and the Jackal" Wrap-Up

What Would Change?

Choose a character in "The Tiger, the Brahman, and the Jackal." Complete the sentences and answer the question.

1. The character I chose is:

   _____

2. This character's traits include:

   a. _____

   b. _____

   c. _____

3. How do this character's traits affect the plot events of the story? Write at least two examples.

_____

_____

_____

_____

_____

_____

_____

Imagine that the character you chose had different traits. Give your character three new traits. Then, answer the question.

4. This character's NEW traits include:

a. _____

b. _____

c. _____

5. How would the character's new traits affect the plot of the story? Write an example for each new trait.

_____

_____

_____

_____

_____

_____

_____

I wonder what three traits my friends would say that _I_ have.

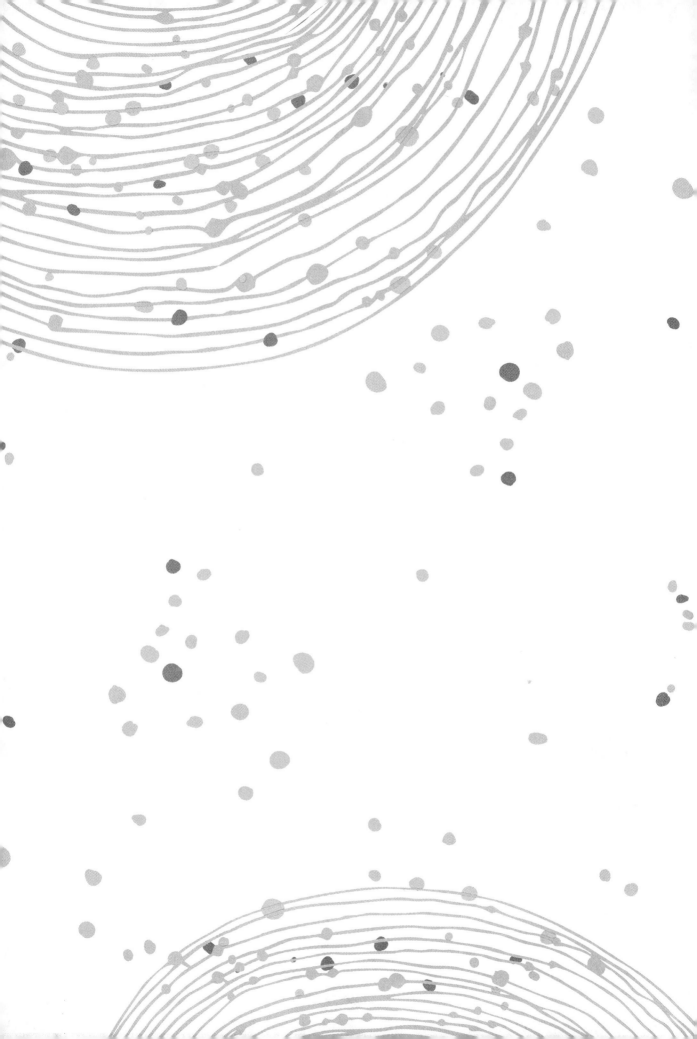

Describe Robert Bruce

Think about the main character in the legend "Bruce and the Spider." Then, answer the questions in complete sentences.

1. Who is the main character?

2. What are some words that describe the main character at the beginning of the legend?

3. What happens to the main character that makes him change?

4. What are some words that describe the main character at the end of the story?

_____

_____

Please do not touch
my web!

"Bruce and the Spider" Wrap-Up

Write About a Lesson Learned

Answer the questions in the graphic organizer.

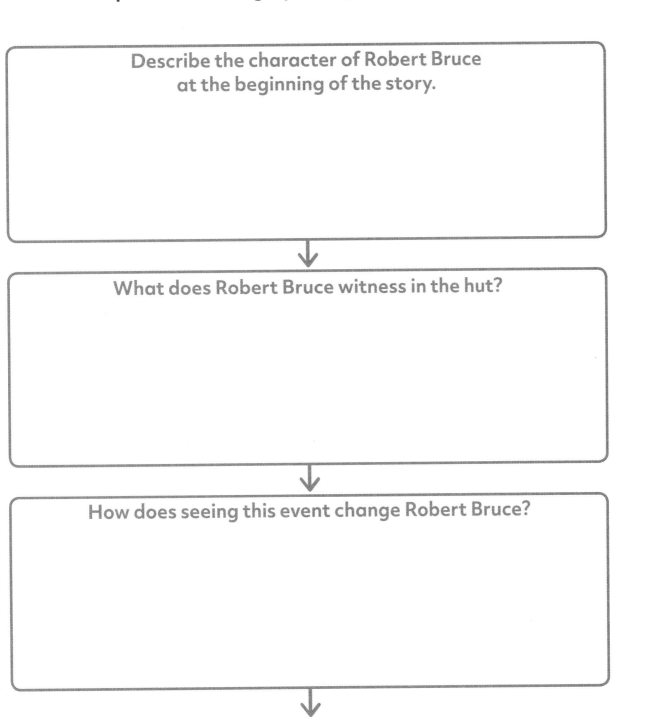

> Describe the character of Robert Bruce
> at the beginning of the story.

> What does Robert Bruce witness in the hut?

> How does seeing this event change Robert Bruce?

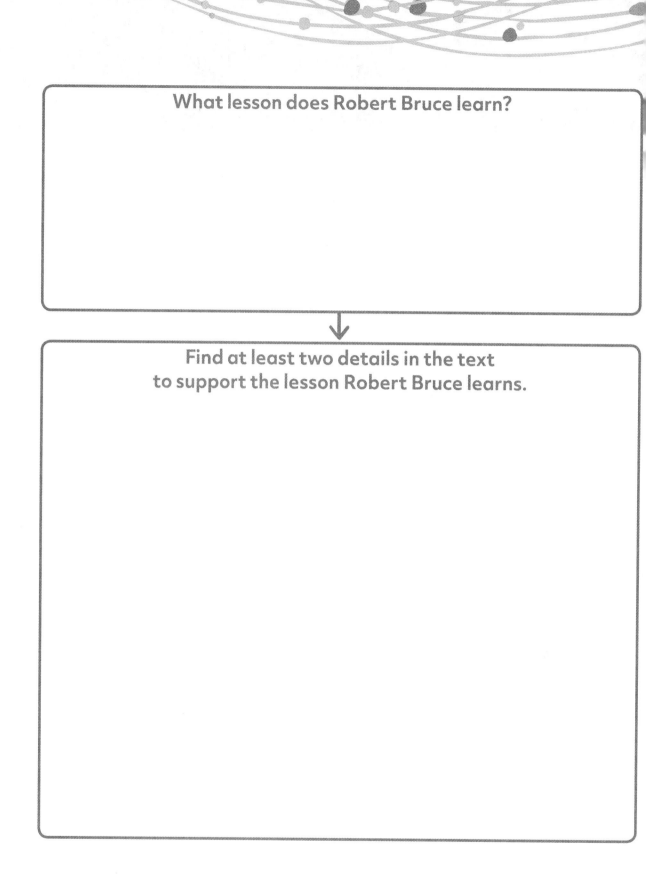

What lesson does Robert Bruce learn?

Find at least two details in the text
to support the lesson Robert Bruce learns.

Use your completed graphic organizer to write a paragraph that explains how Robert Bruce changes from the beginning of the story to the end of the story. Include the lesson he learns and the details from the text that support your ideas.

_____

_____

_____

_____

_____

_____

_____

_____

_____

_____

_____

_____

_____

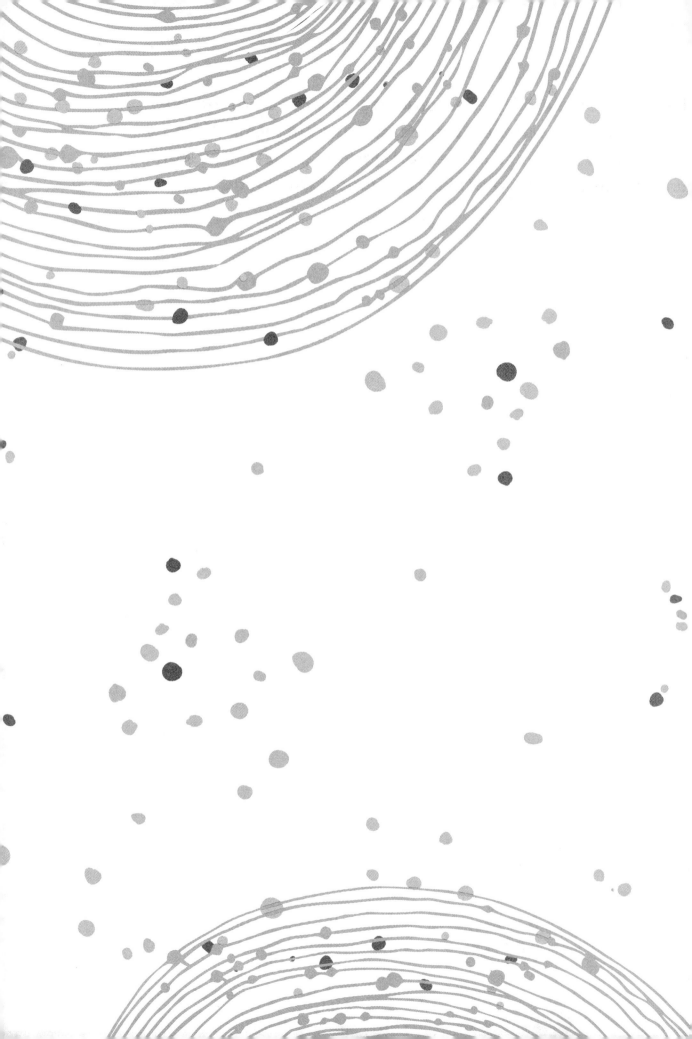

Apply: Dictionary Skills

Alphabetize the words in the Word Bank.

Word Bank

believed	explore	afterward
explain	around	during

1. _____

2. _____

3. _____

4. _____

5. _____

6. _____

Look up the word in a dictionary. Then, write the part of speech and the definition next to each word.

7. celebrate

part of speech: _____

definition: _____

_____

8. gradual

part of speech: _____

definition: _____

_____

9. odor

part of speech: _____

definition: _____

_____

Read the sentences. Then, look up the word *chair* in the dictionary. Write the part of speech and the definition that best match how the word *chair* is used in the sentence.

10. Our recycling club had a big meeting last weekend. We held a vote to decide who would be our club **chair** for the next year. Our previous leader is moving away, so we needed to choose a new one.

chair

part of speech: _____

definition: _____

_____

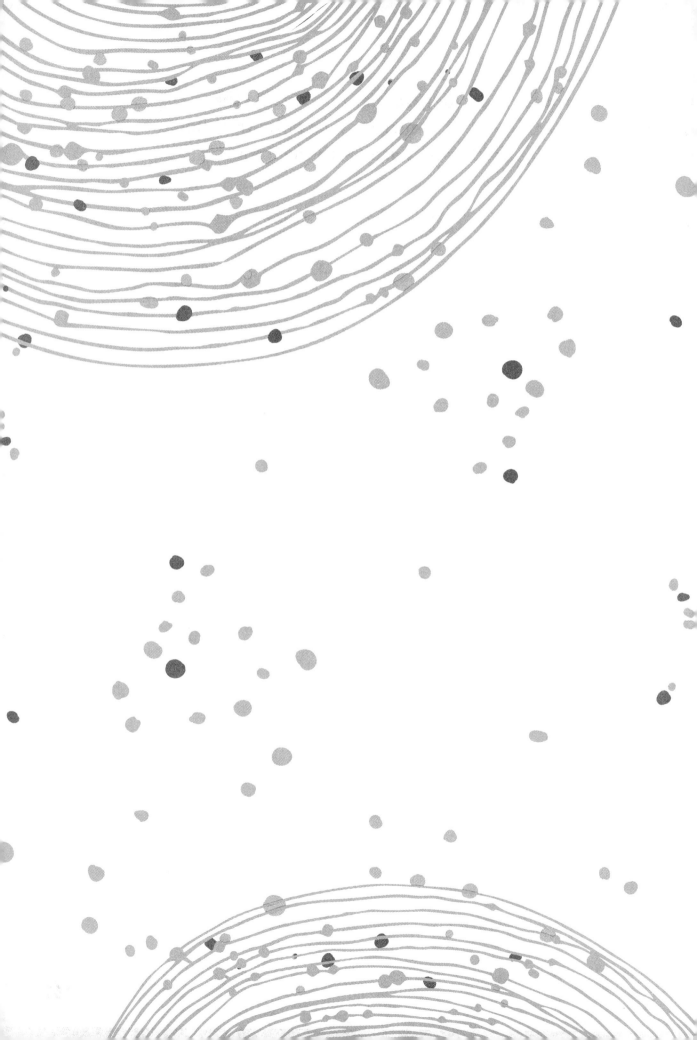

Dictionary Skills

Go Write! What Do You Do Well?

Respond to the prompt. Or, write about a topic of your choice!

Prompt: What is one thing you do well? How did you learn to do it?

My Journal

Snowy Days (A)

Spelling List 8 Pretest

1. Open the Spelling Pretest activity online. Listen to the first spelling word. Type the word. Check your answer.

2. Write the correct spelling of the word in the Word column of the Spelling Pretest table.

Word	✓	✕
1 blindfold		

3. Put a check mark in the ✓ column if you spelled the word correctly online.

Word	✓	✕
1 blindfold	✓	

Put an X in the ✕ column if you spelled the word incorrectly online.

Word	✓	✕
1 blindfold		✕

4. Repeat Steps 1–3 for the remaining words in the Spelling Pretest.

Snowy Days (A)

Spelling List 8 Pretest

Write each spelling word in the Word column, making sure to spell it correctly.

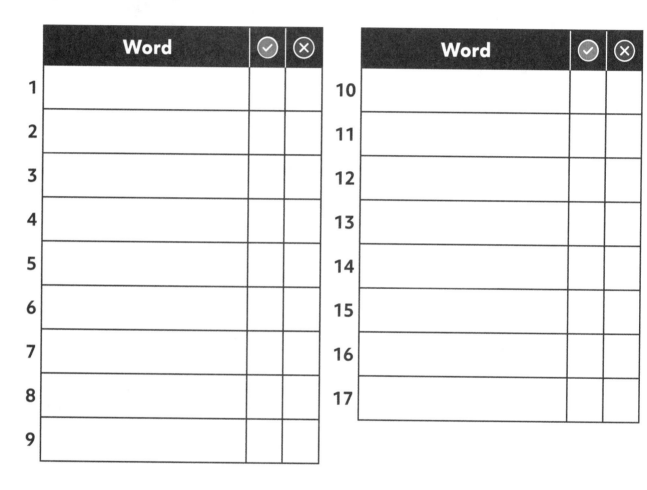

	Word	✓	✗
1			
2			
3			
4			
5			
6			
7			
8			
9			

	Word	✓	✗
10			
11			
12			
13			
14			
15			
16			
17			

Snowy Days (A)

What Do You Know About Snow?

Before you read *Our Wonderful Weather: Snow*, preview the cover, table of contents, and photos in the book. Answer the questions in complete sentences.

1. What do you predict *Our Wonderful Weather: Snow* will be about?

    _____

    _____

    _____

2. What do you know about snow?

    _____

    _____

    _____

After you read *Our Wonderful Weather: Snow*, answer the questions. Use complete sentences.

3. What did you learn from *Our Wonderful Weather: Snow*? List at least three things you learned.

_____

_____

_____

_____

_____

_____

_____

_____

_____

_____

4. What else do you want to learn about snow? List at least
three questions that you hope to find answers for as you read
more about snow.

_____

_____

_____

_____

_____

_____

_____

_____

_____

_____

_____

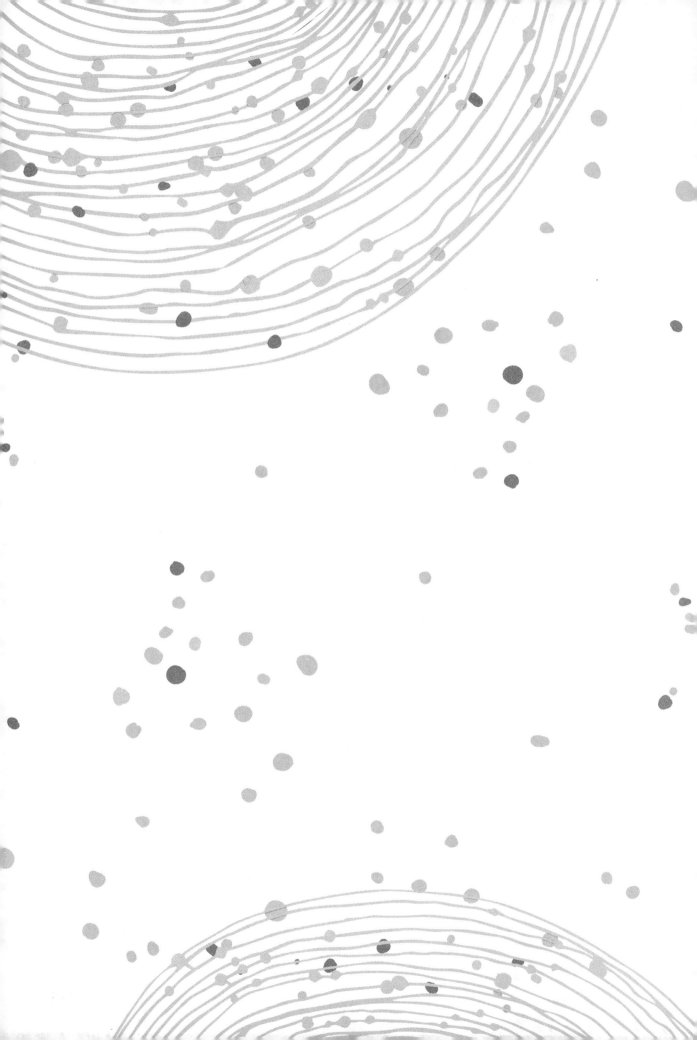

Snowy Days (B)

Spelling List 8 Activity Bank

Circle any words in the box that you did not spell correctly on your pretest. Choose one activity to do with your circled words. Do as much of the activity as you can in the time given.

Did you spell all the words on the pretest correctly? Do the one activity with as many spelling words as you can.

argue	fuel	molecule	pew	use
continue	fumes	music	rescue	value
curfew	human	nephew	unit	view
cute	menu			

Spelling Activity Choices

Create a Crossword

1. Write one of your spelling words going down in the center of the grid.

2. Write another spelling word going across that shares a letter with the first word. See how many words you can connect.

Example:

			p				
		k	i	s	s	e	s
	d		n				
r	o	c	k	s			
	g						
	s						

Word Search Puzzle

1. Draw a box on the grid. The box should be large enough to hold your spelling words.

2. Fill in the grid with your spelling words. Write them across, up and down, and diagonally. You can write them forward and backward.

3. Fill in the rest of the box with random letters.

4. Ask someone to find and circle your words in the puzzle.

Complete the activity that you chose.

My chosen activity: _____

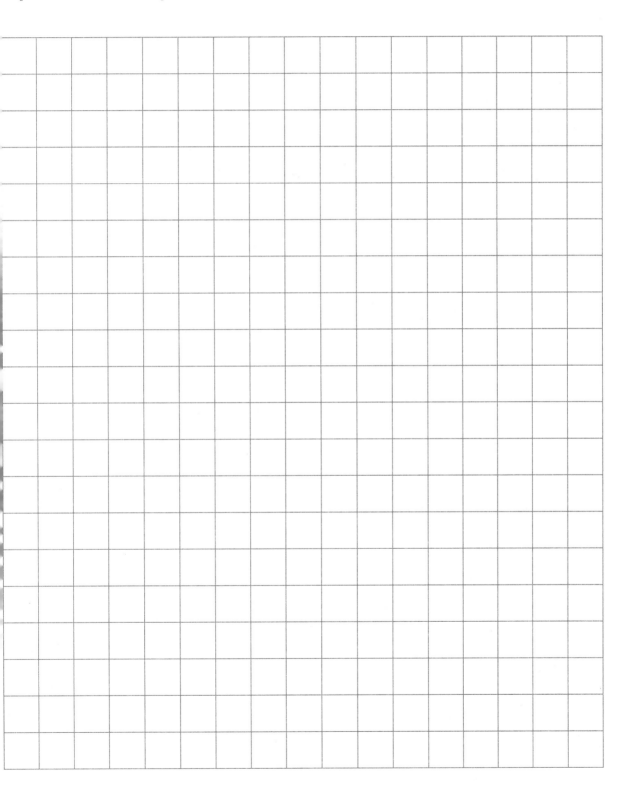

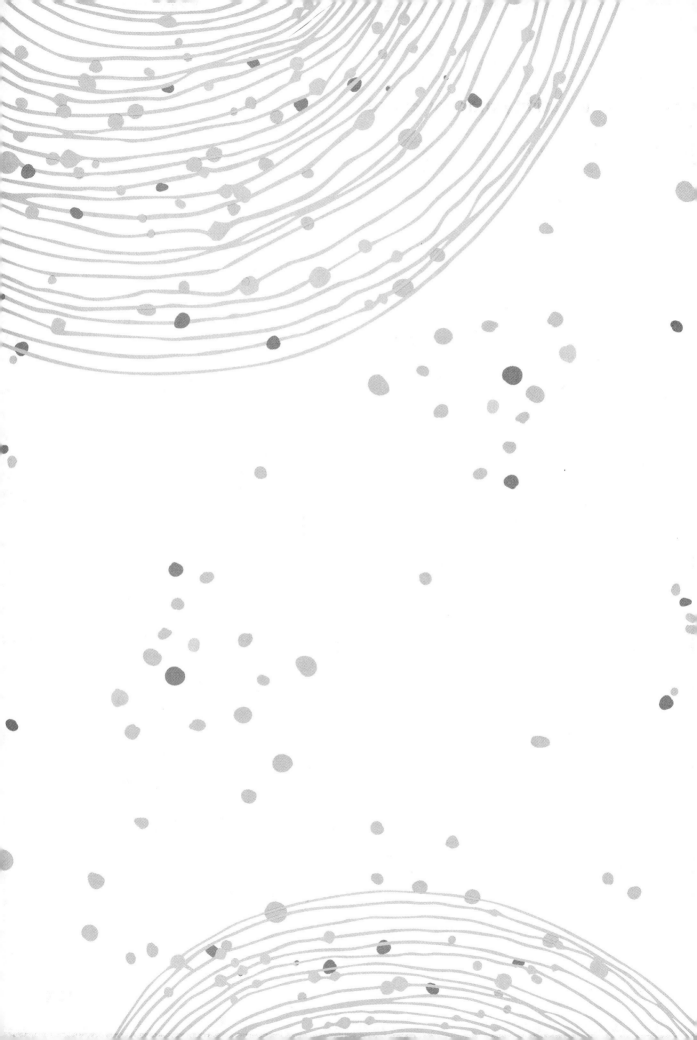

Snowy Days (B)

What Did You Learn from *Curious About Snow*?

Answer the questions in complete sentences.

1. What did you learn from *Curious About Snow*? List at least three things you learned.

_____

_____

_____

_____

_____

_____

_____

_____

Refer to what you wrote for Question 4 on the What Do You Know About Snow? activity page.

2. Did you find the answer to any of your questions about snow in *Curious About Snow*? If so, how would you answer your question(s)?

_____

_____

_____

_____

_____

_____

_____

Snowy Days (C)

What Did You Learn from *Snowflake Bentley*, Part 1?

Answer the questions in complete sentences.

1. What did you learn from Part 1 of the book *Snowflake Bentley*? List at least three things you learned.

_____

_____

_____

_____

_____

_____

_____

Refer to what you wrote for Question 4 on the What Do You Know About Snow? activity page.

2. Did you find the answer to any of your questions about snow in Part 1 of *Snowflake Bentley*? If so, how would you answer your question(s)?

_____

_____

_____

_____

_____

_____

_____

Don't tell my brother, but I hid a snowball in the freezer!

Snowy Days (D)

What Did You Learn from *Snowflake Bentley*, Part 2?

Answer the questions in complete sentences.

1. What did you learn from Part 2 of the book *Snowflake Bentley*? List at least three things you learned.

_____

_____

_____

_____

_____

_____

_____

_____

Refer to what you wrote for Question 4 on the What Do You Know About Snow? activity page.

2. Did you find the answer to any of your questions about snow in Part 2 of *Snowflake Bentley*? If so, how would you answer your question(s)?

_____

_____

_____

_____

_____

_____

_____

Snowy Days (E)

Spelling List 9 Pretest

1. Open the Spelling Pretest activity online. Listen to the first spelling word. Type the word. Check your answer.

2. Write the correct spelling of the word in the Word column of the Spelling Pretest table.

	Word	✓	✗
1	blindfold		

3. Put a check mark in the ✓ column if you spelled the word correctly online.

   Put an X in the ✗ column if you spelled the word incorrectly online.

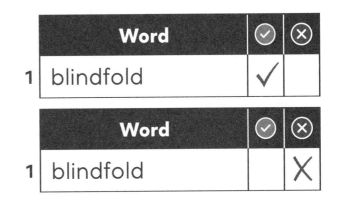

	Word	✓	✗
1	blindfold	✓	

	Word	✓	✗
1	blindfold		✗

4. Repeat Steps 1–3 for the remaining words in the Spelling Pretest.

Snowy Days (E)

Spelling List 9 Pretest

Write each spelling word in the Word column, making sure to spell it correctly.

	Word	✓	✗
1			
2			
3			
4			
5			
6			
7			
8			
9			

	Word	✓	✗
10			
11			
12			
13			
14			
15			
16			
17			

Snowy Days (E)

Illustrations and Setting

Follow the instructions to draw a picture and write about it.

1. Draw a picture of a place you know well.

2. Write one or two sentences that explain why you chose to draw this place.

_____

_____

_____

_____

3. What does your picture show about this place that is not in the sentences you wrote about it?

_____

_____

_____

_____

_____

_____

_____

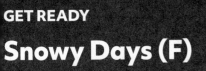

GET READY
Snowy Days (F)

Spelling List 9 Activity Bank

Circle any words in the box that you did not spell correctly on your pretest. Choose one activity to do with your circled words. Do as much of the activity as you can in the time given.

Did you spell all the words on the pretest correctly? Do the one activity with as many spelling words as you can.

bamboo	glue	poof	smooth	suit
bruise	grew	ruby	soup	true
flew	group	rule	student	youth
fruit	include			

Spelling Activity Choices

Alphabetizing

1. In the left column, write your spelling words in alphabetical order.

2. Correct any spelling errors.

Vowel-Free Words

1. In the left column, write only the consonants in each of your spelling words. Put a dot where each vowel should be.

2. Spell each word aloud, stating which vowels should be in the places with dots.

3. In the right column, rewrite the entire spelling word.

4. Correct any spelling errors.

Rhymes

1. In the left column, write your spelling words.

2. In the right column, write a word that rhymes with each spelling word.

3. Correct any spelling errors.

Uppercase and Lowercase

1. In the left column, write each of your spelling words in all uppercase letters.

2. In the right column, write each of your spelling words in all lowercase letters.

3. Correct any spelling errors.

Complete the activity that you chose.

My chosen activity: _____

1. _____   _____

2. _____   _____

3. _____   _____

4. _____   _____

5. _____   _____

6. _____   _____

7. _____   _____

8. _____   _____

9. _____   _____

10. _____   _____

11. _____   _____

12. _____   _____

13. _____   _____

14. _____   _____

15. _____   _____

16. _____   _____

17. _____   _____

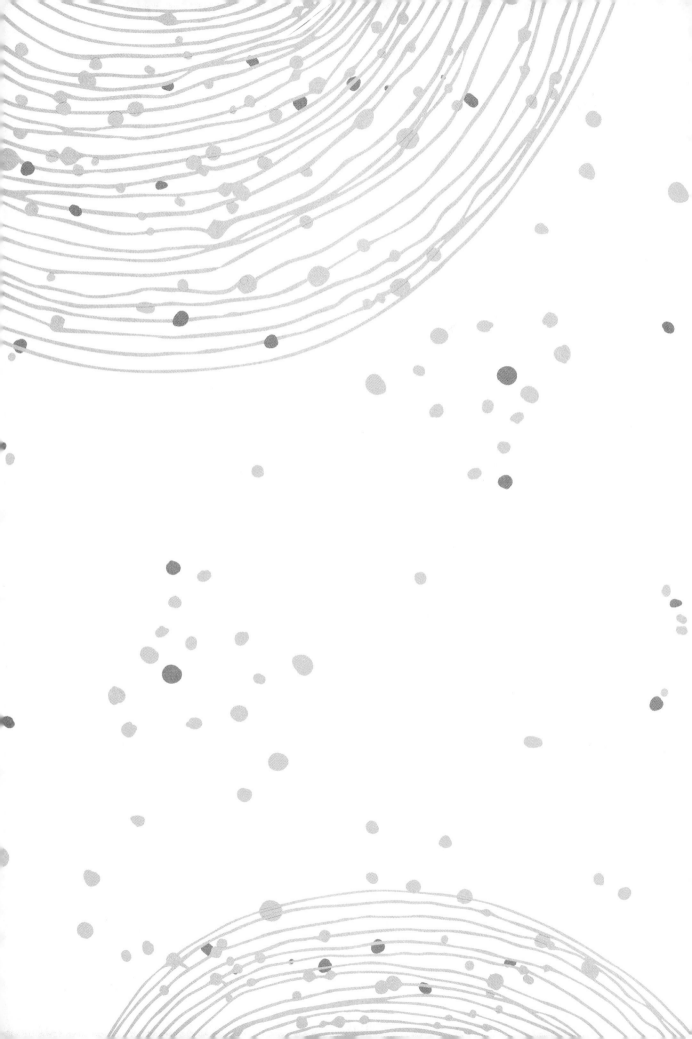

Snowy Days (F)

Prepare to Write a Compare-and-Contrast Essay

Answer the questions in complete sentences.

1. What are some of the topics in *Curious About Snow*? Name at least three.

   _____

   _____

   _____

2. What is the author's purpose for writing *Curious About Snow*?

   _____

   _____

3. What are some of the topics in *Snowflake Bentley*? Name at least two.

   _____

   _____

   _____

4. What is the author's purpose for writing *Snowflake Bentley*?

_____

_____

5. What kind of nonfiction text features are in *Curious About Snow*? What is the purpose of each text feature?

_____

_____

_____

_____

6. What kind of nonfiction text features are in *Snowflake Bentley*? What is the purpose of each text feature?

_____

_____

_____

7. What are some important ideas that appear in both books? Name at least two.

_____

_____

_____

_____

_____

_____

_____

_____

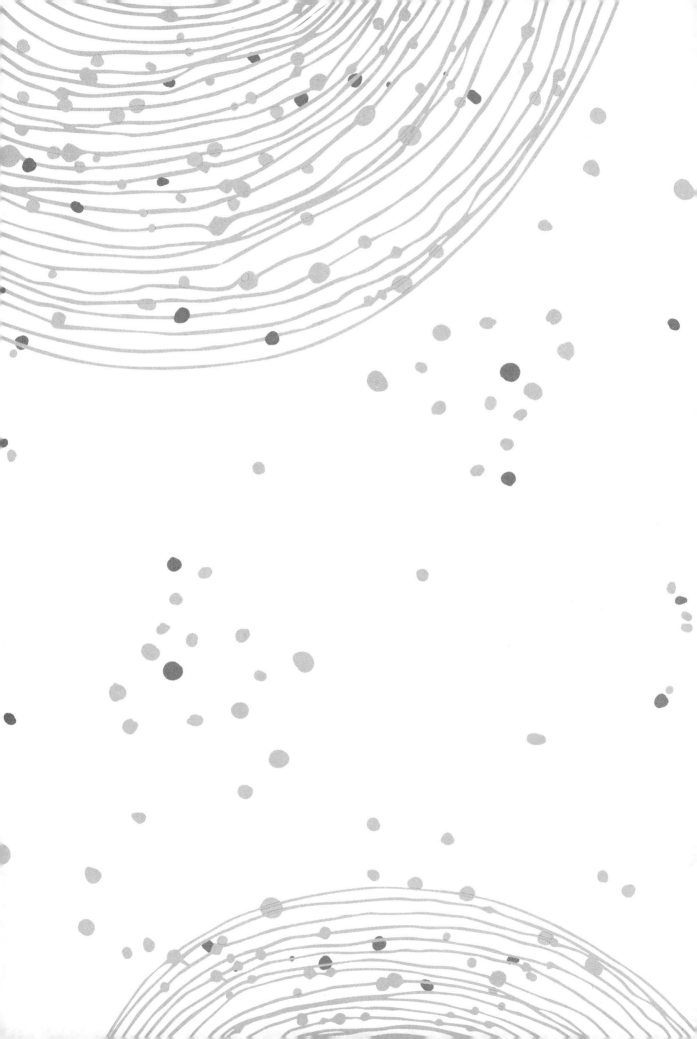

Model Compare-and-Contrast Essay

Use this model as you complete your own compare-and-contrast essay.

Comparing Two Books on Snow

hook — Brrr! Have you ever played in snow? It's cold, but it can be fun. There is a lot to know about snow. You can learn a lot from the books *Our Wonderful Weather: Snow* and *Curious About Snow*. Both books have facts about snow. But, there are things that are alike and things that are — main idea different in the books.

topic sentence — Both books are about snow, so there are many things that are the same. The author's purpose for both books is to teach about snow. The topic for both books is snow and how snowflakes form. Also, both books tell about the dangers of snow. Both books have a glossary — compare paragraph for important words. They also have photographs. In addition, the two books have some important ideas that are the same. One example is that both books say that every snowflake is different, but they all have six sides.

compare paragrap

There are also things that are different in the books. *Our Wonderful Weather: Snow* has a table of contents. *Curious About Snow* does not. The two books also have some topics that are different. For example, *Our Wonderful Weather: Snow* talks about people who study the weather. It also describes some famous snowstorms. *Curious About Snow* does not talk about these things. Instead, it has a section on Wilson Bentley. It tells what he learned about snow. Another difference is that *Curious About Snow* is longer than *Our Wonderful Weather: Snow*. This means that *Curious About Snow* gives a lot more information.

transition

contrast paragrapl

These two books have some facts that are the same and some that are different. You can become an expert on snow by reading both books. You can learn how snowflakes form and all the different shapes they can be. You can even learn about the dangers of snow. So, if you have a chance to visit the snow, try to catch a snowflake.

— conclusion

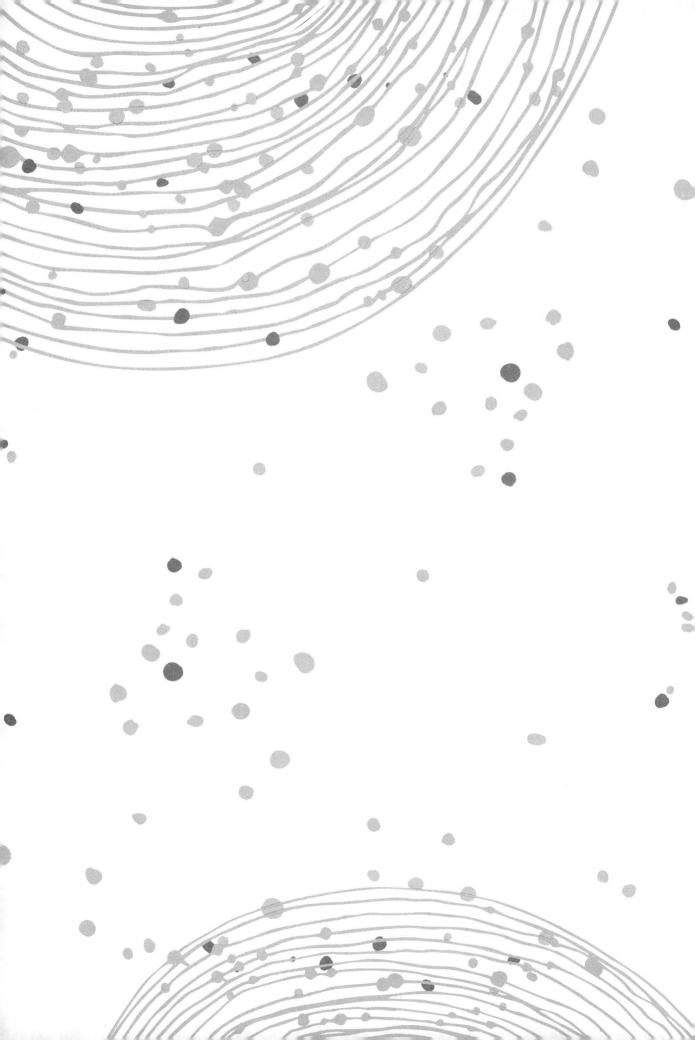

Snowy Days (G)

Write a Compare-and-Contrast Essay

Read the writing prompt.

Prompt: Write an essay that compares and contrasts the books *Curious About Snow* and *Snowflake Bentley*.

- Use a **compare-and-contrast structure**.

- Begin with an **introduction** paragraph that tells the main idea of the essay.

- Include **two body paragraphs** with details and examples that tell what is alike and what is different about the two books.

- Start each body paragraph with a **topic sentence**.

- End with a **conclusion** paragraph.

Respond to the writing prompt.

_____

_____

_____

_____

Snowy Days Wrap-Up

Can You Answer Your Questions?

Refer to what you wrote for Question 4 on the What Do You Know About Snow? activity page. Then, answer the questions in complete sentences.

1. What is the first question you listed that you wanted to find an answer to as you read more about snow?

2. Did you find the answer to your question? If so, write the answer here.

3. What is the second question you listed that you wanted to find an answer to?

4. Did you find the answer to your question? If so, write the answer here.

_____

_____

_____

5. What is the third question you listed that you wanted to find an answer to?

_____

_____

6. Did you find the answer to your question? If so, write the answer here.

_____

_____

_____

Informative Writing Skills (A)

Spelling List 10 Pretest

1. Open the Spelling Pretest activity online. Listen to the first spelling word. Type the word. Check your answer.

2. Write the correct spelling of the word in the Word column of the Spelling Pretest table.

Word	✓	✗
1 blindfold		

3. Put a check mark in the ✓ column if you spelled the word correctly online.

   Put an X in the ✗ column if you spelled the word incorrectly online.

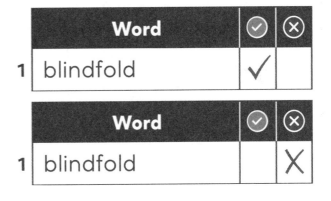

Word	✓	✗
1 blindfold	✓	

Word	✓	✗
1 blindfold		✗

4. Repeat Steps 1–3 for the remaining words in the Spelling Pretest.

Informative Writing Skills (A)

Spelling List 10 Pretest

Write each spelling word in the Word column, making sure to spell it correctly.

	Word	⊘	⊗
1			
2			
3			
4			
5			
6			
7			
8			
9			

	Word	⊘	⊗
10			
11			
12			
13			
14			
15			
16			
17			

Informative Writing Skills (A)

Model Informative Essay

Use the model essay as you complete your own informative essay.

title —[

The Truth About Bats

topic sentence —[

Bats may look scary, but you don't have to be afraid of them. I know

details —[

because I used to be scared of bats. I thought they were ugly and mean. I thought they hurt people. I even had bad dreams about bats. Then I went to the Lincoln County Zoo. That's where I learned what bats are really like.

— introduction

topic sentence —[

At the zoo, I learned that bats are really interesting animals. They cannot

facts —[

see well, but they have great hearing. They sleep during the day and are awake at night. Bats are much smaller than I thought, too. They look like mice with wings. I still think they are ugly,

— body

but they are not mean. They mostly eat insects, and they try to stay away from people. So if you don't bother a bat, it probably won't bother you.

body

topic sentence I am not afraid of bats anymore. I know that real bats are not like bats in stories or movies. Now my dreams about bats are not scary ones. They just make me want to learn more.

conclusion

Informative Writing Skills (A)

Plan Your Informative Essay

Read the writing prompt.

Prompt: Write an informative essay.

- Think about your purpose and audience.

- Begin with an introduction that states your topic and tells why it is important.

- Write information about your topic in the body of the essay.

- Use facts, definitions, and details.

- End with a conclusion that wraps up the essay in an interesting way.

- Include an illustration about your topic.

Follow the instructions to brainstorm a topic.

1. What topics do you know a lot about? List as many topics as
   you can think of for your informative essay.

   _____   _____

   _____   _____

   _____   _____

   _____   _____

   _____   _____

   _____   _____

2. Read your list of topics. Choose your favorite. Then, answer
   Yes or No to each question.

   a. Is this topic really interesting to you?   _____

   b. Will this topic be interesting to your readers?   _____

   c. Do you know enough about the topic?   _____

   d. Is this topic something you can write about in three
      paragraphs (something that is not too simple and
      not too complicated)?   _____

3. Did you answer Yes to Parts a–d of Question 2? If not, answer the question for another topic in your list. Repeat until you find a topic that works.

Informative essay topic:

_____

Follow the instructions to plan your essay.

4. State your audience and purpose.

   a. Audience: _____

   b. Purpose: _____

I am deciding between two topics: dimetrodons or pteranodons.

5. Complete the graphic organizer. You do not need to use complete sentences.

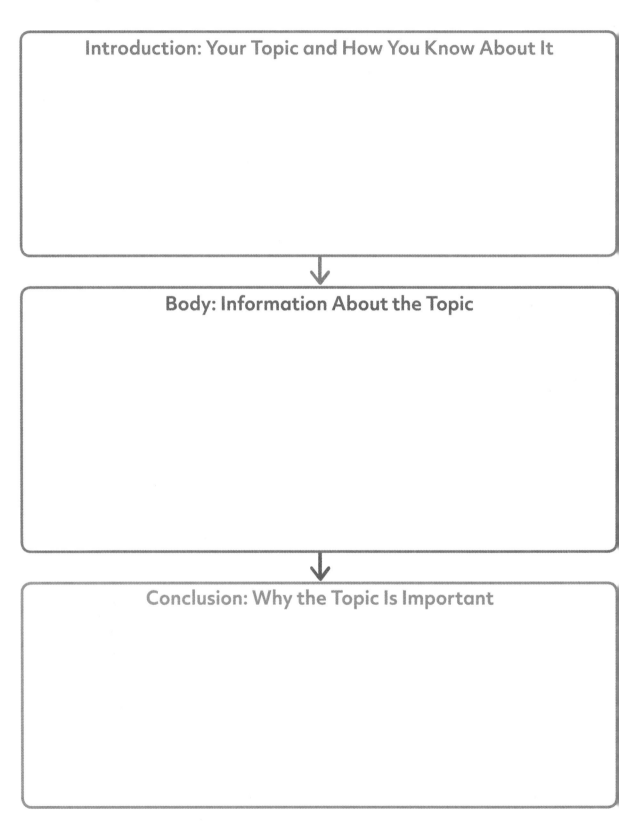

Introduction: Your Topic and How You Know About It

Body: Information About the Topic

Conclusion: Why the Topic Is Important

Informative Writing Skills (B)

Spelling List 10 Activity Bank

Circle any words in the box that you did not spell correctly on the pretest. Choose one activity to do with your circled words. Do as much of the activity as you can in the time given.

Did you spell all the words on the pretest correctly? Do the one activity with as many spelling words as you can.

about	mountain	vowel	destroy	loyal
crown	outline	avoid	enjoy	ploy
downtown	pounce	choice	joint	soil
flowers	thousands			

Spelling Activity Choices

Silly Sentences

1. Write a silly sentence for each of your spelling words.

2. Underline the spelling word in each sentence.
   Example: The dog was <u>driving</u> a car.

3. Correct any spelling errors.

Spelling Story

1. Write a very short story using each of your spelling words.

2. Underline the spelling words in the story.

3. Correct any spelling errors.

Riddle Me This

1. Write a riddle for each of your spelling words.
   Example: "I have a trunk, but it's not on my car."

2. Write the answer, which is your word, for each riddle.
   Example: Answer: elephant

3. Correct any spelling errors.

RunOnWord

1. Gather some crayons, colored pencils, or markers. Use a different color to write each of your spelling words. Write the words end to end as one long word.
   Example: dogcatbirdfishturtle

2. Rewrite the words correctly and with proper spacing.

3. Correct any spelling errors.

Complete the activity that you chose.

My chosen activity: _____

_____

_____

_____

_____

_____

_____

_____

_____

_____

_____

_____

_____

_____

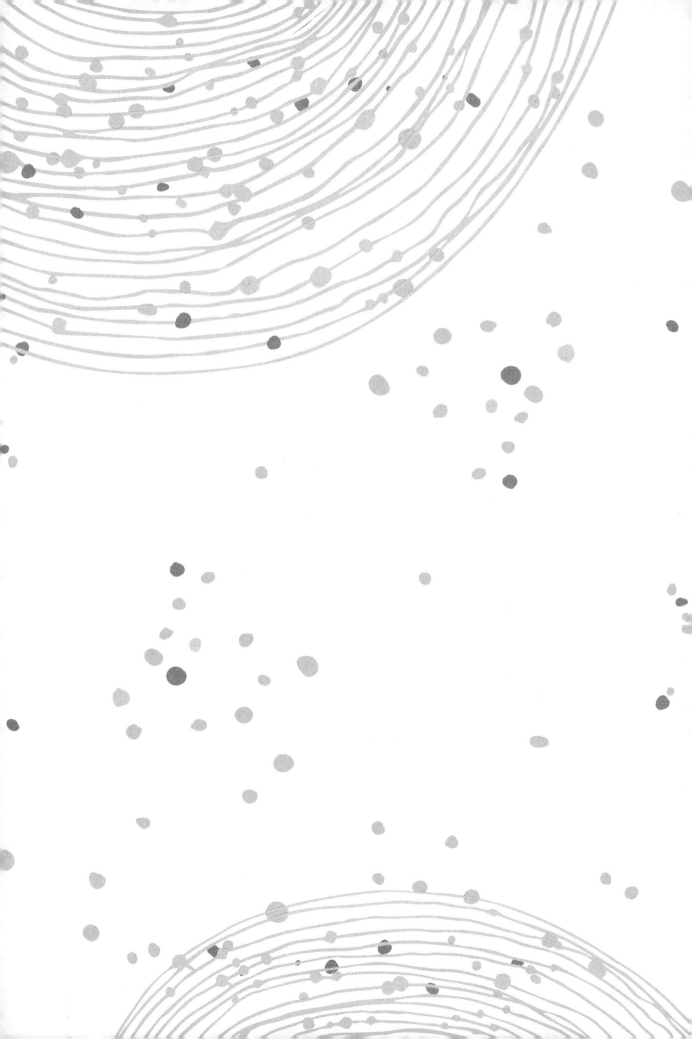

Informative Writing Skills (B)

Write Your Informative Essay

Read the writing prompt.

Prompt: Write an informative essay.

- Think about your purpose and audience.

- Begin with an introduction that states your topic and tells why it is important.

- Write information about your topic in the body of the essay.

- Use facts, definitions, and details.

- End with a conclusion that wraps up the essay in an interesting way.

- Include an illustration about your topic.

Respond to the writing prompt.

_____

_____

_____

_____

Draw a picture that illustrates an important part of your informative essay, such as a fact or idea. Write a short caption under your picture that describes or explains it.

Informative Writing Skills Wrap-Up

Reflect on Your Informative Essay

Read your informative essay. Then, answer the questions in complete sentences.

1. A strong informative essay begins with a clear introduction.

   a. Does your introduction clearly tell what your essay is about? Explain your answer.

   _____

   _____

   b. What do you think you could improve?

   _____

   _____

2. The body of an informative essay includes facts and details that develop the topic.

   a. List two facts or details from your essay.

   _____

   _____

   _____

   b. Explain why each fact or detail is important to your audience and purpose.

   _____

   _____

   _____

3. Good writers use transitions to connect ideas.

   a. List one sentence that includes a transition.

   _____

   _____

b. Rewrite one sentence that you could clarify by adding a transition.

_____

_____

4. A strong informative essay ends with a conclusion.

a. What sentence or sentences from your conclusion explain why the topic is important to you?

_____

_____

_____

b. What additional thoughts could you add to your conclusion?

_____

_____

5. Illustrations can add meaning to an informative essay.

    a. What is the purpose of the illustration you made?

_____

_____

    b. How does your caption support that purpose?

_____

_____

6. What is your favorite part of your essay? Explain.

_____

_____

_____

My favorite part of my informative essay about snowflakes is my illustration.

Roots and Affixes

Apply: Roots and Affixes

The suffix –*able* means "can" or "able to."

- Read the definition of the word.
- Add –*able* to the word to form a new word.
- Define the new word.

The first one has been done for you.

1. **enjoy: to like or get pleasure from**

   New word: enjoyable

   Definition: able to get pleasure from

2. **break: to separate into pieces or parts**

   New word: _____

   Definition: _____

   _____

3. **explain: to make something known**

   New word: _____

   Definition: _____

   _____

4. **understand: to comprehend or know**

New word: _____

Definition: _____

_____

The suffix *–ible* means "can" or "able to."
• Read the definition of the word.
• Add *–ible* to the word to form a new word.
• Define the new word.
The first one has been done for you.

5. **erode: to wear away**

New word: erodible

Definition: able to be worn away

6. **collapse: to break down or fold**

New word: _____

Definition: _____

_____

7. **reverse: to turn in the opposite direction**

New word: _____

Definition: _____

_____

Go Write! Your Favorite Place

Respond to the prompt. Or, write about a topic of your choice!

Prompt: **Places are important to people. What is your favorite place in the world? Describe it. Explain why you like that place so much and how you feel when you are there.**

My Journal

The Glory of Greece (A)

Spelling List 11 Pretest

1. Open the Spelling Pretest activity online. Listen to the first spelling word. Type the word. Check your answer.

2. Write the correct spelling of the word in the Word column of the Spelling Pretest table.

	Word	✓	✗
1	blindfold		

3. Put a check mark in the ✓ column if you spelled the word correctly online.

Put an X in the ✗ column if you spelled the word incorrectly online.

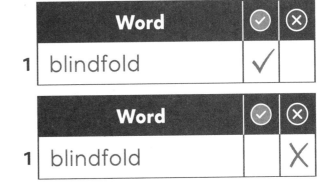

	Word	✓	✗
1	blindfold	✓	

	Word	✓	✗
1	blindfold		✗

4. Repeat Steps 1–3 for the remaining words in the Spelling Pretest.

The Glory of Greece (A)

Spelling List 11 Pretest

Write each spelling word in the Word column, making sure to spell it correctly.

	Word	✓	✗
1			
2			
3			
4			
5			
6			
7			
8			
9			
10			
11			

	Word	✓	✗
12			
13			
14			
15			
16			
17			
18			
19			
20			
21			

The Glory of Greece (A)

Practice Using Text Features

Use the text features in Chapters 1 and 2 of *The Glory of Greece* to answer the questions. Use complete sentences.

1. Where would you find the definitions of words in bold type?

_____

_____

_____

2. What does a heading tell readers?

_____

_____

_____

_____

_____

_____

3. Look at the time line on page vi. When was ancient Greece at its height?

_____

_____

Use the map to answer the questions. Use complete sentences.

4. Which city-state is farthest east on the map?

_____

5. Explain how you determined your answer.

_____

_____

_____

_____

_____

I wonder what other
questions I could answer
using this map.

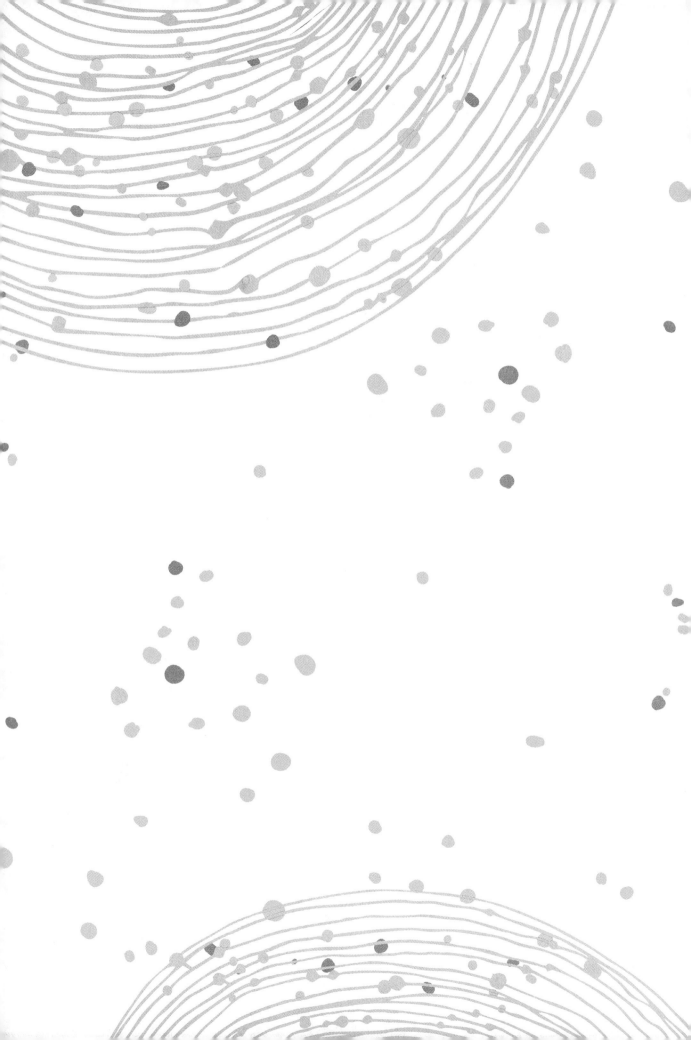

Spelling List 11 Activity Bank

Circle any words in the box that you did not spell correctly on your pretest. Choose one activity to do with your circled words. Do as much of the activity as you can in the time given.

Did you spell all the words on the pretest correctly? Do the one activity with as many spelling words as you can.

chirp	doctor	earth	pattern	together
circle	dollar	forward	return	turkey
collar	early	learn	Saturday	western
color	earn	numeral	third	worth
curtain				

Spelling Activity Choices

Hidden Words

1. Draw a picture. "Hide" as many of your spelling words as you can inside the picture.

2. See if others can find the words you hid in the picture.

Triangle Spelling

Write each of your spelling words in a triangle.

```
    d
   do
  dog
```

Ghost Words

1. Use a white crayon to write each of your spelling words.

2. Write over the words in white crayon with a colored marker.

Complete the activity that you chose.

My chosen activity: _____

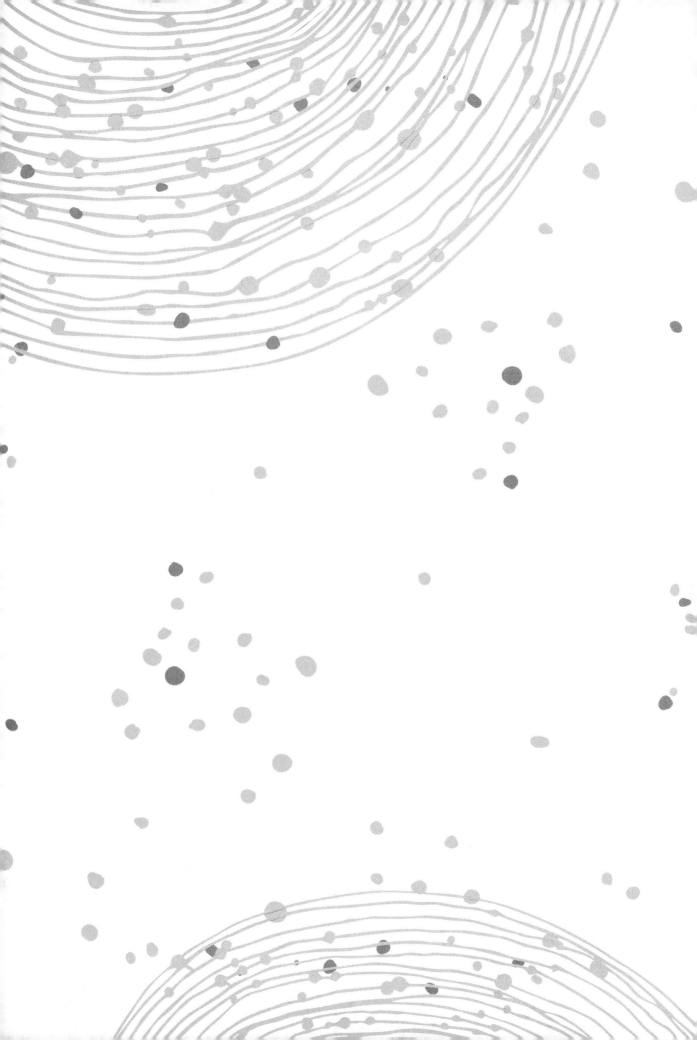

The Glory of Greece (B)

Paraphrase, Compare, and Contrast

Read the excerpt from *The Glory of Greece* by Beth Zemble and John Holdren.

Democracy in Athens was not perfect. It did not include all the people. In Athens, the citizens voted to choose their leaders. But only free adult men were citizens. Women and slaves were not citizens.

Even though democracy in Athens was not perfect, it was still a bold new idea. In most ancient lands, the people were ruled by kings or by the strongest soldiers or by a few rich men. But in Athens, the citizens could finally rule themselves.

Answer the question in complete sentences.

1. Paraphrase the information about democracy and voting from the passage.

_____

_____

_____

_____

_____

_____

_____

_____

_____

_____

_____

Read pages 17 and 19 of *The Glory of Greece*.

2. Fill in the Venn diagram to show how Sparta and Athens were alike and different.

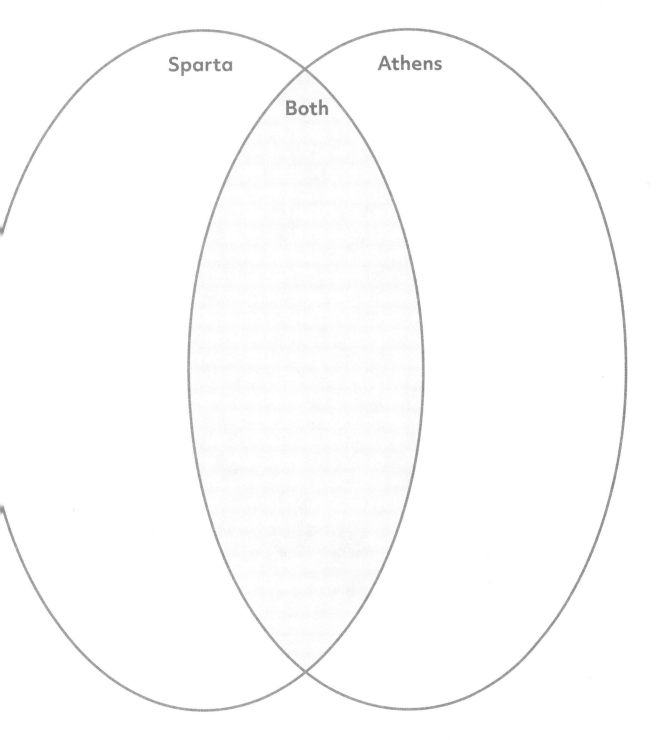

Sparta

Both

Athens

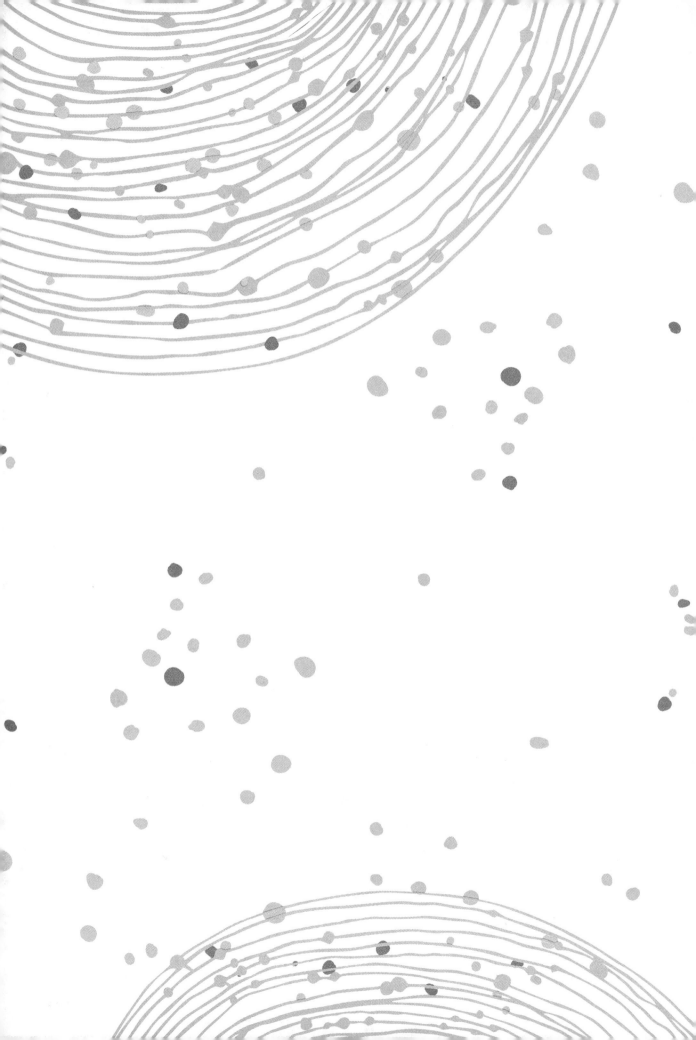

TRY IT

The Glory of Greece (C)

They Came from Ancient Greece

Many ideas and events that were born in ancient Greece still exist and happen today. Choose three ideas or events from the list. Brainstorm how those ideas or events affect our lives today.

Olympic Games	art and architecture	trial by jury
going to plays	democracy	

Event/Idea 1: _____

_____

_____

_____

_____

_____

_____

_____

Event/Idea 2: _____

_____

_____

_____

_____

_____

_____

Event/Idea 3: _____

_____

_____

_____

_____

_____

_____

The Glory of Greece (D)

Draw a Conclusion

Refer to the They Came from Ancient Greece activity page. Answer the question in complete sentences.

How do the three events or ideas that you chose affect our lives today? Draw a conclusion.

_____

_____

_____

_____

_____

_____

_____

_____

_____

_____

_____

_____

_____

_____

_____

_____

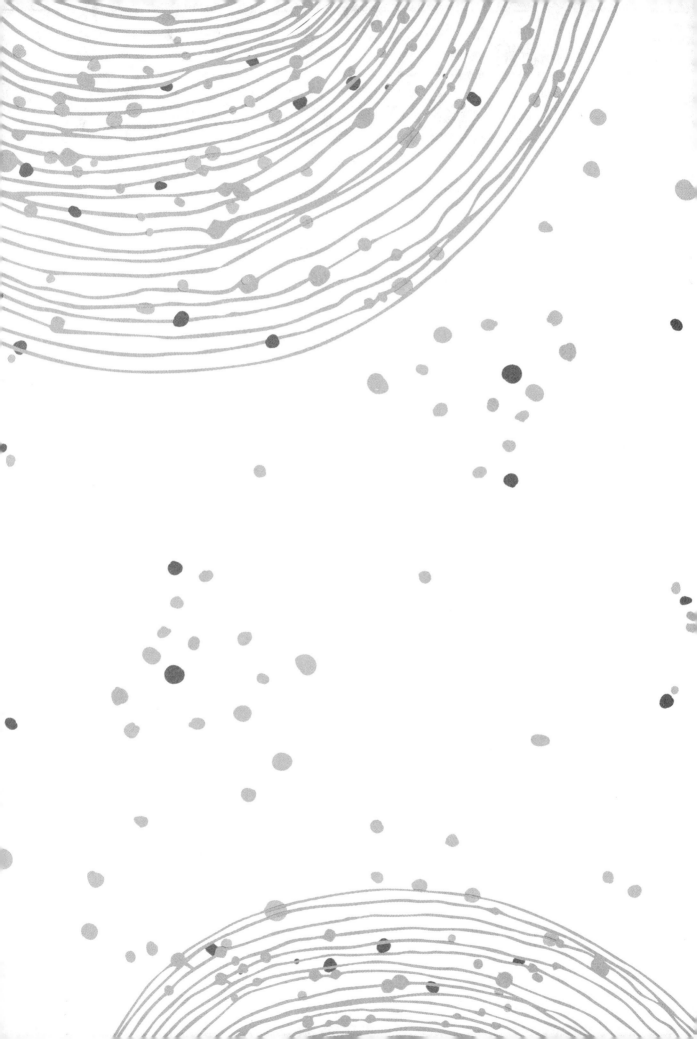

TRY IT
The Glory of Greece Wrap-Up

Ancient Greece and Modern Life

Read the writing prompt.

Prompt: **Write an essay about ancient Greece and modern life.
Include the following:**

- An introduction

- A body that describes your three ideas or events from the
  They Came from Ancient Greece activity page

- Your conclusion from the Draw a Conclusion activity page

- Transitions such as *for example* and *also*

Respond to the writing prompt.

_____

_____

_____

_____

_____

_____

_____

_____

_____

_____

_____

_____

_____

_____

_____

_____

_____

_____

_____

_____

_____

Informative Writing: Prewriting (A)

Spelling List 12 Pretest

1. Open the Spelling Pretest activity online. Listen to the first spelling word. Type the word. Check your answer.

2. Write the correct spelling of the word in the Word column of the Spelling Pretest table.

Word	✓	✗
1 blindfold		

3. Put a check mark in the ✓ column if you spelled the word correctly online.

Word	✓	✗
1 blindfold	✓	

Put an X in the ✗ column if you spelled the word incorrectly online.

Word	✓	✗
1 blindfold		✗

4. Repeat Steps 1–3 for the remaining words in the Spelling Pretest.

Informative Writing: Prewriting (A)

Spelling List 12 Pretest

Write each spelling word in the Word column, making sure to spell it correctly.

	Word	✓	✗
1			
2			
3			
4			
5			
6			
7			
8			
9			
10			
11			

	Word	✓	✗
12			
13			
14			
15			
16			
17			
18			
19			
20			
21			

Informative Writing: Prewriting (A)

Model Research Report

Use this model to help you as you complete your own research report.

title ─[**Pennsylvania**

hook ─[Do you know that just about every state has a nickname? Pennsylvania's nickname is the Keystone State, and it comes from a long time ago. Early settlers knew that Pennsylvania was in the middle of the 13 original states, just as a keystone ─ introduction

main idea ─[is in the middle of an arch. Of course, Pennsylvania is not in the middle of the United States anymore, but it is still an important and interesting state.

Pennsylvania is in the northeastern part of the United States. This area is known as the Mid-Atlantic region. ─ body
Six states touch Pennsylvania. Ohio, West Virginia, Maryland, and Delaware

touch Pennsylvania on its west and its south. New Jersey and New York are to the east and the north of Pennsylvania. Pennsylvania is cold in the winter and hot in the summer. People put on coats, hats, and gloves when it is chilly. The chilly weather lets them ski and snowboard in the Pocono Mountains. People go hiking and camping when the weather is warm. They wear shorts in the summer and go swimming in pools and ponds.

Philadelphia and Lancaster County are two popular places to visit in Pennsylvania. Philadelphia is a big city. It has great museums and parks. The city also has many historical sites to see. For example, the Liberty Bell is in Philadelphia. Lancaster County has farms and fields. Many Amish people live there. Amish people do not drive cars. They use horses and buggies. Amish people do not have electricity in their homes, either. So they do not have televisions, radios, computers, or lights.

body

There are so many remarkable things about Pennsylvania. One of the most important battles of the Civil War was fought in the town of Gettysburg, Pennsylvania. People in Pennsylvania made a lot of the steel that built America's railroads and buildings, too. Today, products such as crayons, candy, and ketchup are made in Pennsylvania.

William Penn founded Pennsylvania. In 1683, he described the state by writing, "The air is sweet and clear, and the heavens serene." Pennsylvania's location, along with its cold winters and warm summers, means that there are always some fun outdoor activities for people to do. Places like Philadelphia and Lancaster County are great for visitors, and Pennsylvania's importance to American history and American business is unmatched. Even today, Pennsylvania remains one of the nation's key states.

body

conclusion

statement
main idea

My Sources

"PA Pennsylvania" www.state.pa.us.model

"Pennsylvania History" http://www.legis.state.pa.us/wu01/vc/ visitor_info/pa_history/pa_history.model

"Pennsylvania – Visit PA" http://www.visitpa.model

"Pennsylvania" World Book Encyclopedia. Scott Fetzer Company, 2015.

Pennsylvania: Birthplace of a Nation by Sylvester K. Stevens. Random House, 1967.

Classic World Atlas for maps

Informative Writing: Prewriting (A)

Brainstorm for Your Research Report

Read the assignment. You will complete the assignment in steps over multiple lessons.

Prompt: Write a research report about a U.S. state.

Requirements:

Your research report should have the following:

- A **title**

- An **introduction** that has a **hook** and states the **topic** and **main idea**

- Three organized **body paragraphs** that use **facts**, **details**, and **definitions** to develop the topic

- A **conclusion** that includes a **summary** of the report's facts and details and **restates the main idea** in different words than the introduction

- **Transitions** that connect ideas

- A list of the **research sources** where you found the information for your report. You must use at least one print source (such as a book or magazine) and one online source. Books that you read in the digital library or on an e-reader count as print sources.

- Correct **grammar, punctuation, capitalization**, and **spelling**

Audience: Your teacher, peers, and Learning Coach

Purpose: Inform readers about a U.S. state.

Length: 300–450 words long, approximately 5–7 handwritten drafting pages or $1\frac{1}{2}$–2 pages typed and double spaced

Answer the questions to choose a state as the topic of your research report.

1. Have you visited any states other than your own? If so, list them.

_____

_____

_____

2. Which states would you visit if you could? Why?

_____

_____

_____

3. Do you have family members or friends who live in other states? If so, which states?

_____

_____

_____

4. Think about the characters in stories and books you've read, and in TV shows and movies you've seen. Which states do these characters live in?

_____

_____

_____

_____

5. Review your answers to Questions 1–4. Which state would you like to learn more about for your research report?

_____

_____

6. Why did you choose this state?

Why do so many state names start with *New?*

Informative Writing: Prewriting (B)

Spelling List 12 Activity Bank

Circle any words in the box that you did not spell correctly on your pretest. Choose one activity to do with your circled words. Do as much of the activity as you can in the time given.

Did you spell all the words on the pretest correctly? Do the one activity with as many spelling words as you can.

copy	hungry	story	apply	notify
country	hurry	study	crybaby	pry
empty	many	sturdy	deny	reply
fluffy	penny	windy	myself	spy
fuzzy				

Spelling Activity Choices

Create a Crossword

1. Write one of your spelling words going down in the center of the grid.

2. Write another spelling word going across that shares a letter with the first word. See how many words you can connect.

Example:

				p				
			k	i	s	s	e	s
	d			n				
r	o	c	k	s				
	g							
	s							

Word Search Puzzle

1. Draw a box on the grid. The box should be large enough to hold your spelling words.

2. Fill in the grid with your spelling words. Write them across, up and down, and diagonally. You can write them forward and backward.

3. Fill in the rest of the box with random letters.

4. Ask someone to find and circle your words in the puzzle.

Complete the activity that you chose.

My chosen activity: _____

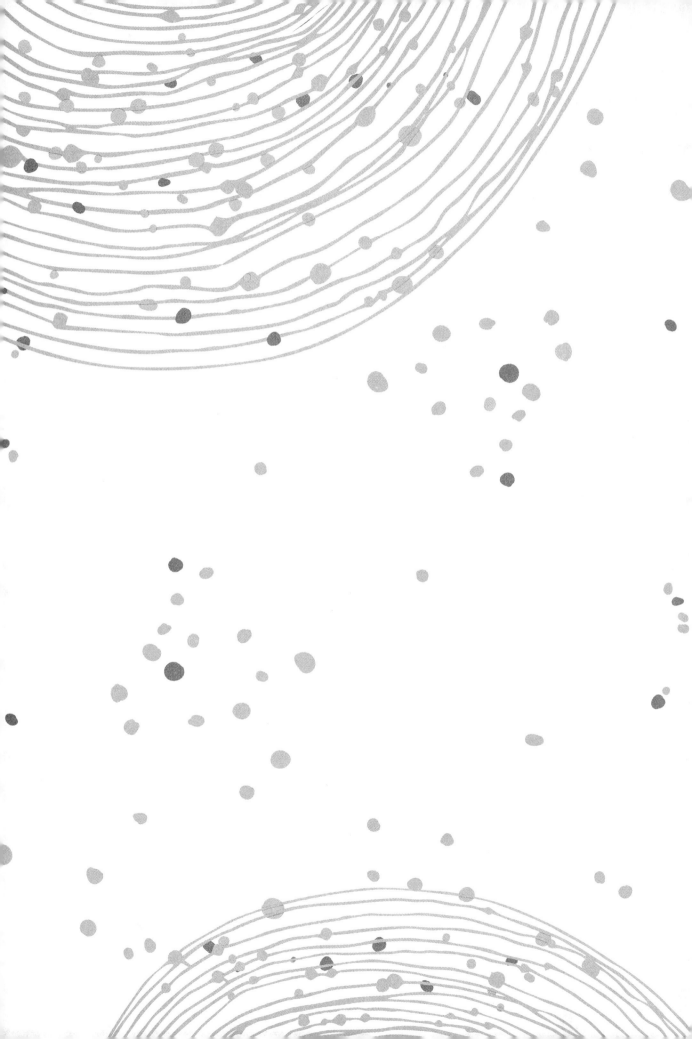

Conduct Your Research

Search for sources of information about the state you chose for your research report.

Use the Internet and go to a library. For each source you find, fill out one section on the form as follows:

- For print sources (a book, an entry in an encyclopedia, an atlas, a magazine, or newspaper article), write the title, author, publisher, year of publication, and notes about each source.

- For online sources (websites), write the name, URL, and notes about each source.

Example

Online or Print: online

Name or Title: PA Pennsylvania

URL or Author: www.state.pa.us.model

Publisher/Year of Publication: ——

Notes: lots of info about state history and things to do for fun

---

Source 1

Online or Print: _____

Name or Title: _____

URL or Author: _____

Publisher/Year of Publication: _____

_____

Notes: _____

_____

Source 2

Online or Print: _____

Name or Title: _____

URL or Author: _____

Publisher/Year of Publication: _____

_____

Notes: _____

_____

Source 3

Online or Print: _____

Name or Title: _____

URL or Author: _____

Publisher/Year of Publication: _____

_____

Notes: _____

_____

Source 4

Online or Print: _____

Name or Title: _____

URL or Author: _____

Publisher/Year of Publication: _____

_____

Notes: _____

_____

Source 5

Online or Print: _____

Name or Title: _____

URL or Author: _____

Publisher/Year of Publication: _____

_____

Notes: _____

_____

Source 6

Online or Print: _____

Name or Title: _____

URL or Author: _____

Publisher/Year of Publication: _____

_____

Notes: _____

_____

Follow the instructions to take notes about your research topic.

1. Gather index cards. Write each of the following labels at the top of three index cards. Label three cards "General Information," three cards "Location and Climate," and so on.

   - General Information
   - Location and Climate
   - Outdoor Activities

   - Popular Places to Visit
   - Interesting Facts

2. Pick a source from your list and read about your state. As you read, look for information that relates to the labels on your cards.

3. When you read something important, find the correct note card and write down the key information. Write information from just one source per card.

4. For each card that you complete, write down the number of the source you used to find the information. If it is a print source, write down chapter or page numbers, too.

5. Continue to read and take notes from all of your sources. Make more cards when you need to. Keep your cards together in a safe place.

Sample card for an online source

Outdoor Activities

- skiing and snowboarding in the Pocono Mountains
- hiking and camping
- swimming in pools and ponds
- polka dancing
- boating and fishing

Source #1

Sample card for a print source

Location and Climate

- Mid-Atlantic region
- PA bordered by NY, NJ, DE, MD, WV, and OH
- looks like a rectangle
- has lots of rivers

Source #6, pages 60 and 71

Informative Writing: Prewriting (C)

Organize Your Research Report

Use your notes to create an outline for your research report.

Paragraph 1: Introduction

A. Main idea of research report

_____

_____

B. General information

_____

_____

_____

_____

_____

_____

Paragraph 2: Location and climate

A. Region of the United States and bordering states

_____

_____

_____

_____

B. Winter weather _____

   1. Clothing _____

   2. Outdoor activities _____

_____

_____

C. Summer weather _____

   1. Clothing _____

   2. Outdoor activities _____

_____

_____

Paragraph 3: Popular places to visit

A. Name of first place to visit _____

    1. Description _____

    _____

    _____

    2. Reason for being popular _____

    _____

    _____

B. Name of second place to visit _____

    1. Description _____

    _____

    _____

    2. Reason for being popular _____

    _____

    _____

Paragraph 4: Other interesting facts

A. Historical facts about the state _____

_____

_____

_____

_____

B. Current facts about the state _____

_____

_____

_____

_____

Did you know that Tennessee's nickname is "The Volunteer State"?

Paragraph 5: Conclusion

A. Short summary _____

_____

_____

_____

_____

_____

B. Restatement of main idea _____

_____

_____

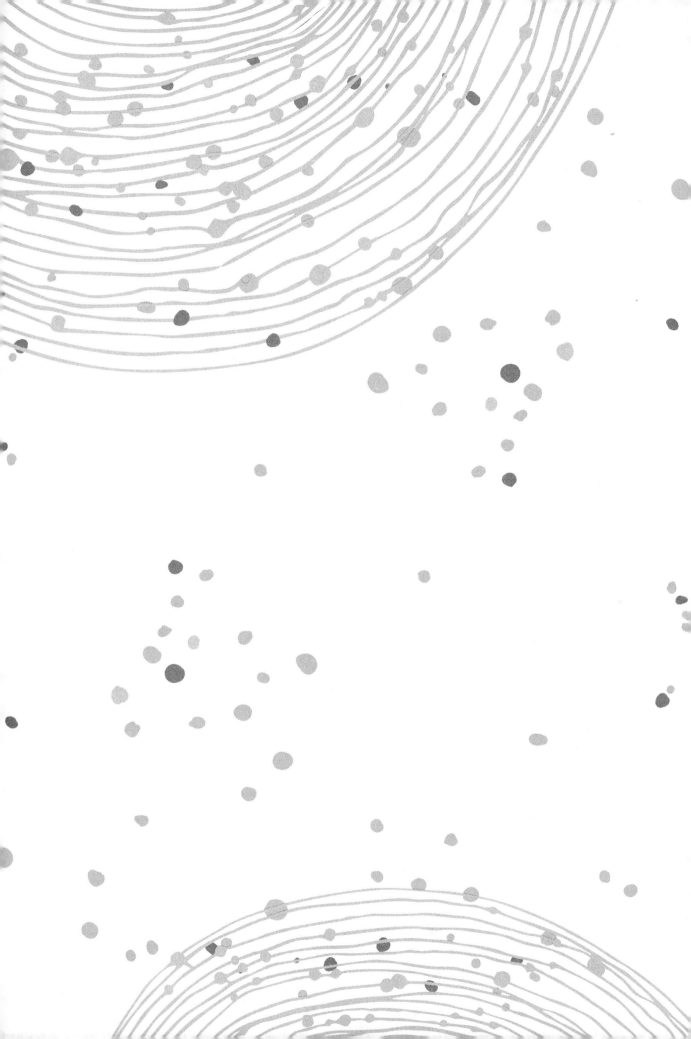

Informative Writing: Drafting (A)

Draft Your Research Report

Write the first draft of your research report. Write only on the white rows. You will use the purple rows for revisions later.

Title: _____

start here ▶

keep writing ▶

Draft Page 1

keep writing ▶

Draft Page 2

keep writing ►

Draft Page 3

keep writing ▸

Draft Page 4

keep writing ▶

Draft Page 5

keep writing ▶

Draft Page 6

keep writing ▸

Draft Page 7

Draft Page 8

Apply: Multiple-Meaning Words

Choose the word from the Word Bank that best completes the sentence. Use context clues and the part of speech of the missing word to help you.

Word Bank

grave	match	meal	rank

1. My little cousin loves pickles so much that she eats them at

   every _____ .

2. The _____ look on Pablo's face told me he

   was not joking.

3. Many people take flowers when they visit the

   _____ of someone they love.

4. I covered my nose to avoid the _____ smell

   coming from the garbage can.

5. April made sure to keep the last _____ dry so she could use it to start a campfire that night.

6. We couldn't find rice _____ in the store, so we decided to grind some ourselves.

7. At our first book club meeting, we are going to _____ the books on the list from our favorite to our least favorite.

8. Mike's parents are going to _____ the amount of money he saves to help him buy a new violin.

My dad says that he's in a pickle. I don't think that's possible!

Multiple-Meaning Words

Go Write! Under Water or in the Air

Respond to the prompt. Or, write about a topic of your choice!

Prompt: **Would you rather be able to breathe under water or fly in the air? Why?**

My Journal

Myths (A)

Spelling List 13 Pretest

1. Open the Spelling Pretest activity online. Listen to the first spelling word. Type the word. Check your answer.

2. Write the correct spelling of the word in the Word column of the Spelling Pretest table.

Word	✓	✗
1 blindfold		

3. Put a check mark in the ✓ column if you spelled the word correctly online.

Word	✓	✗
1 blindfold	✓	

Put an X in the ✗ column if you spelled the word incorrectly online.

Word	✓	✗
1 blindfold		✗

4. Repeat Steps 1–3 for the remaining words in the Spelling Pretest.

Myths (A)

Spelling List 13 Pretest

Write each spelling word in the Word column, making sure to spell it correctly.

Word	✓	✗
1		
2		
3		
4		
5		
6		
7		
8		
9		
10		
11		

Word	✓	✗
12		
13		
14		
15		
16		
17		
18		
19		
20		
21		

Myths (A)

Retell a Myth

Retell the myth "Tangled Webs" by filling in the story map.
Use complete sentences.

<table>
<tr><td>

Who are the main characters?

</td><td>

What is the setting?

</td></tr>
</table>

What happens first?

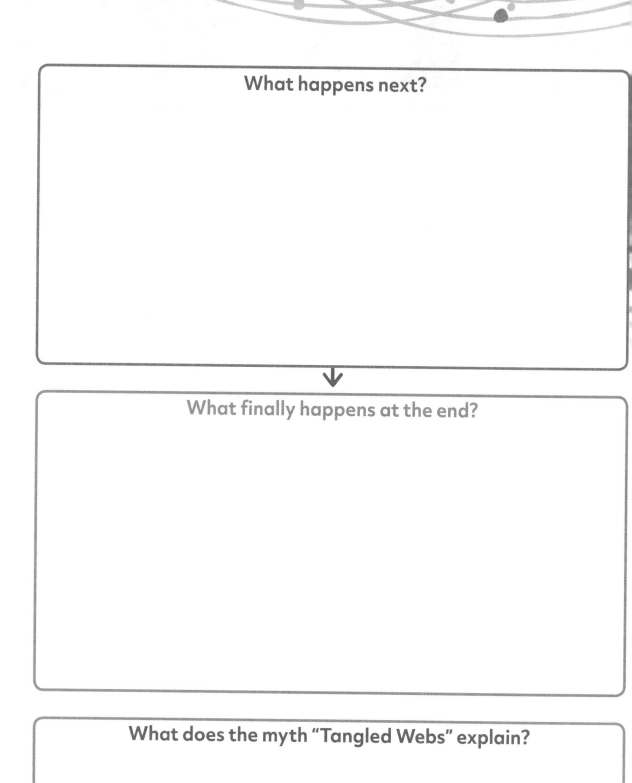

What happens next?

What finally happens at the end?

What does the myth "Tangled Webs" explain?

Spelling List 13 Activity Bank

Circle any words in the box that you did not spell correctly on your pretest. Choose one activity to do with your circled words. Do as much of the activity as you can in the time given.

Did you spell all the words on the pretest correctly? Do the one activity with as many spelling words as you can.

annoying	crazier	grouchier	marries	spies
berries	cried	happier	ponies	stickier
bunnies	easier	hurried	prettier	studying
burying	flies	ladies	replies	trying
carrying				

Spelling Activity Choices

Alphabetizing

1. In the left column, write your spelling words in alphabetical order.

2. Correct any spelling errors.

Vowel-Free Words

1. In the left column, write only the consonants in each of your spelling words. Put a dot where each vowel should be.

2. Spell each word aloud, stating which vowels should be in the places with dots.

3. In the right column, rewrite the entire spelling word.

4. Correct any spelling errors.

Rhymes

1. In the left column, write your spelling words.

2. In the right column, write a word that rhymes with each spelling word.

3. Correct any spelling errors.

Uppercase and Lowercase

1. In the left column, write each of your spelling words in all uppercase letters.

2. In the right column, write each of your spelling words in all lowercase letters.

3. Correct any spelling errors.

Complete the activity that you chose.

My chosen activity: _____

1. _____   _____

2. _____   _____

3. _____   _____

4. _____   _____

5. _____   _____

6. _____   _____

7. _____   _____

8. _____   _____

9. _____   _____

10. _____   _____

11. _____   _____

12. _____   _____

13. _____   _____

14. _____   _____

15. _____   _____

16. _____   _____

17. _____ _____

18. _____ _____

19. _____ _____

20. _____ _____

21. _____ _____

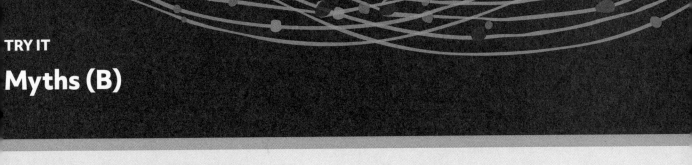

Compare Two Goddesses

Review the stories "Repeat After Me, Me, Me..." and "Tangled Webs."

1. Fill in the diagram to show how the goddesses Hera and Athena are alike and different.

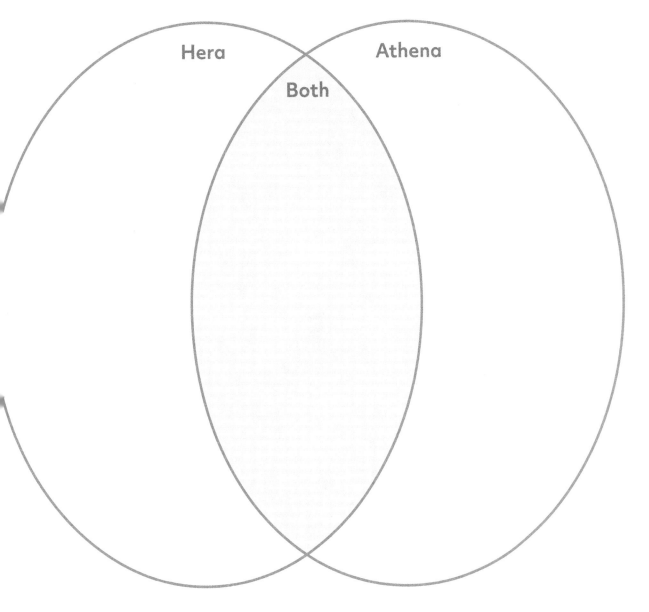

Hera

Athena

Both

Answer the question in complete sentences. Refer to your completed Venn diagram from Question 1.

2. How are Hera and Athena alike? Use examples from the myths.

_____

_____

_____

_____

_____

_____

_____

_____

_____

_____

_____

_____

_____

What's That Character Like?

Think about the characters in the myth "A Flight Through the Sky."

1. Match each character to the **two** traits that best describe him.

Characters	Traits
Daedalus	selfish
	careful
	clever
King	adventurous
	cruel
Icarus	foolish

2. Choose Daedalus, the king, or Icarus. Explain how the character shows the traits you matched him with. Use complete sentences.

_____

_____

_____

_____

_____

_____

_____

Do you share any character traits with Daedalus, the king, or Icarus?

Myths (D)

Prepare to Compare Two Myths

Answer the questions about characters and events in "Roll, Roll, Roll That Rock" and "Tangled Webs." Use complete sentences.

1. What is Sisyphus like in "Roll, Roll, Roll That Rock"?

_____

_____

_____

2. What is Arachne like in "Tangled Webs"?

_____

_____

_____

3. What do people warn both Sisyphus and Arachne about?

_____

_____

_____

4. What does Sisyphus do that makes Zeus notice him? Why do Sisyphus's actions make Zeus angry?

_____

_____

_____

_____

_____

_____

_____

5. How does Zeus punish Sisyphus?

_____

_____

_____

_____

_____

6. What does Arachne do that makes Athena notice her? Why do Arachne's actions make Athena angry?

_____

_____

_____

_____

_____

_____

_____

7. How does Athena punish Arachne?

_____

_____

_____

_____

_____

_____

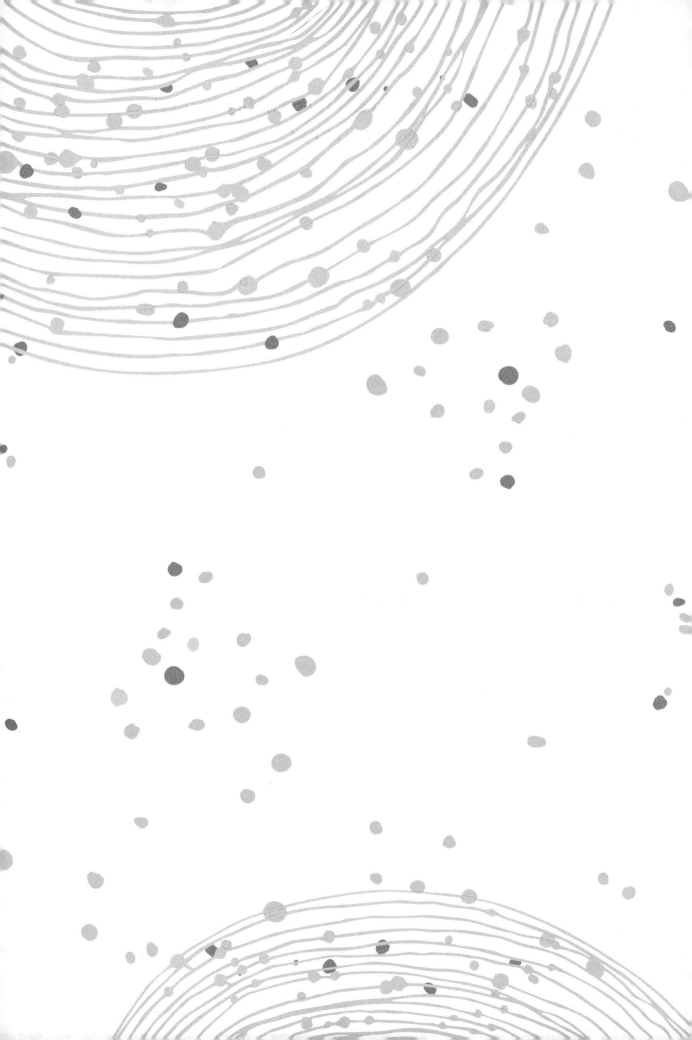

Myths Wrap-Up

Compare Two Myths

Answer the questions to compare the myths "Roll, Roll, Roll That Rock" and "Tangled Webs." Use complete sentences.

1. How are the characters Sisyphus and Arachne alike?

_____

_____

_____

_____

_____

_____

2. How are Sisyphus and Arachne different?

_____

_____

_____

3. What is similar about the events in the middle of each myth? Gives examples from each myth.

_____

_____

_____

_____

_____

_____

_____

4. What is similar about how the myths end?

_____

_____

5. What is different about how the myths end?

_____

_____

6. Think about how Zeus punished Sisyphus and how Athena punished Arachne. Based on the punishments, do you think that Zeus and Athena are more alike or different? Explain why you think that.

_____

_____

_____

_____

_____

_____

_____

7. Ancient Greeks used myths to teach important lessons about their gods. What is a lesson that is found in both "Roll, Roll, Roll That Rock" and "Tangled Webs"?

_____

_____

_____

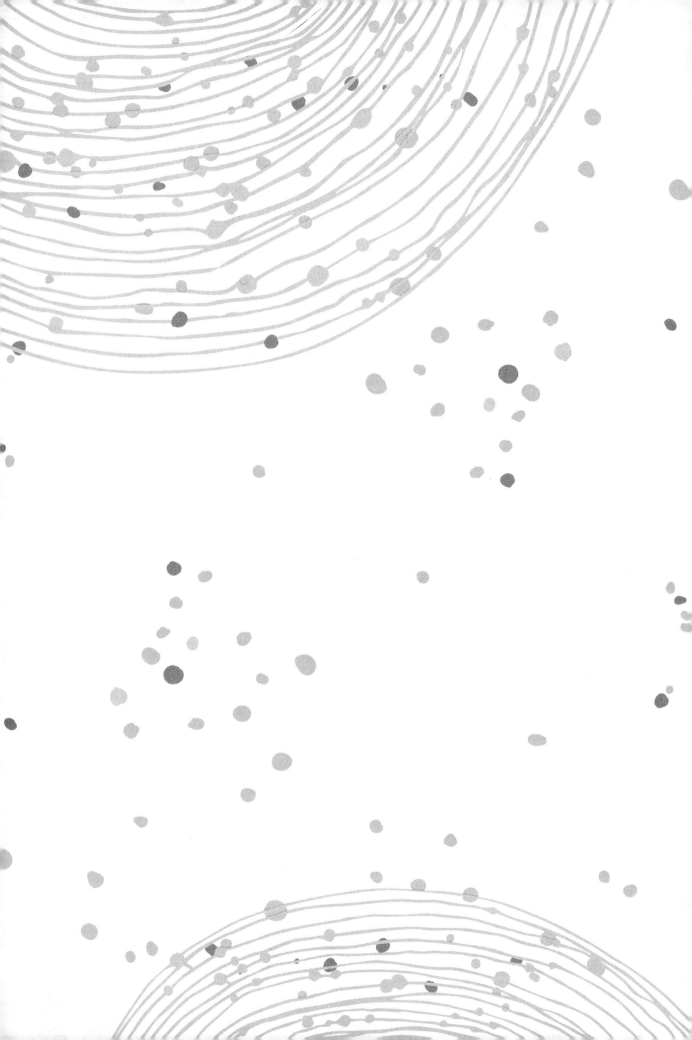

Informative Writing: Revising

Revise Your Research Report

Read your research report draft. Then, use the checklist to improve your organization and ideas. Make changes on your research report draft.

Ideas

☐ Does my introduction have a hook?

☐ Does my introduction clearly state the topic and main idea?

☐ Does each body paragraph begin with a topic sentence?

☐ Does each body paragraph have facts and details that develop the paragraph's topic?

☐ Does my report include information from research? Did I write this information in my own words?

☐ Does my conclusion state my main idea differently than I stated it in the introduction?

Organization

☐ Does each body paragraph contain related ideas? Are any facts or details in the wrong paragraph?

☐ Do I use transitions to connect ideas?

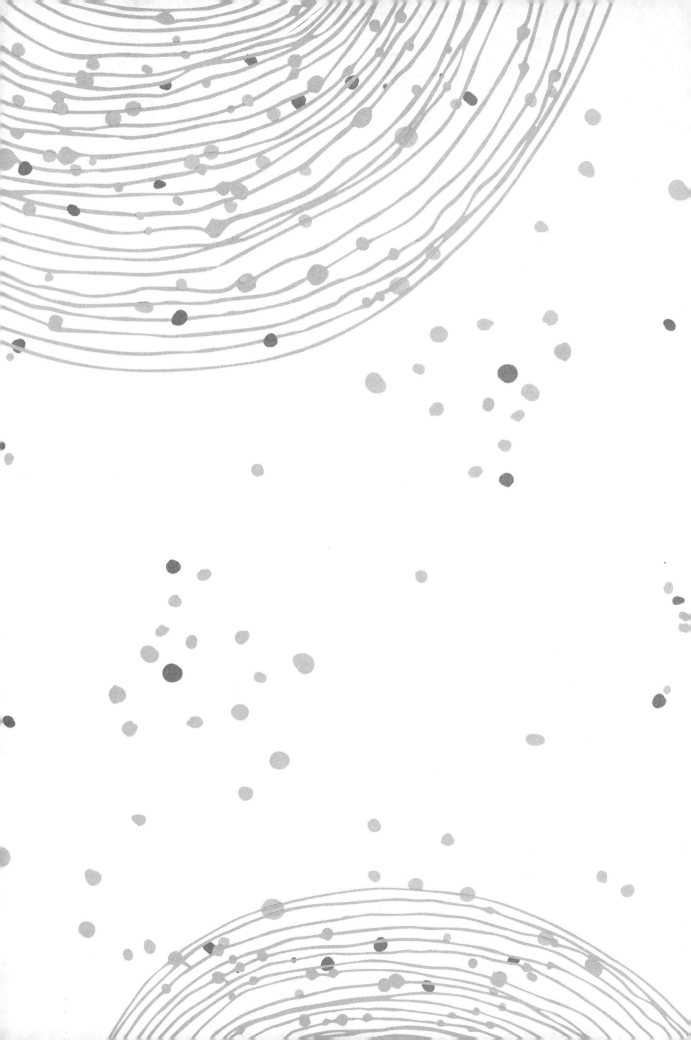

Informative Writing: Proofreading

Proofread Your Research Report

Read your revised research report draft. Then, use the checklist to improve your grammar, usage, and mechanics. Make changes on your revised research report draft.

Grammar and Usage

☐ Are all sentences complete and correct?

☐ Do I use nouns correctly, including abstract, plural, and possessive nouns?

☐ Are there any missing or extra words?

Mechanics

☐ Is every word spelled correctly?

☐ Does every sentence begin with a capital letter and end with correct punctuation?

☐ Are proper nouns capitalized and common nouns lowercased?

(continued)

☐ Are plural and possessive nouns formed correctly?

☐ Are titles of works capitalized correctly?

☐ Are quotations punctuated and capitalized correctly?

☐ Do I indent paragraphs?

I loved writing about Florida's beautiful beaches.

Utility Wires (A)

Spelling List 14 Pretest

1. **Open the Spelling Pretest activity online. Listen to the first spelling word. Type the word. Check your answer.**

2. **Write the correct spelling of the word in the Word column of the Spelling Pretest table.**

Word	✓	✗
1 blindfold		

3. **Put a check mark in the ✓ column if you spelled the word correctly online.**

Word	✓	✗
1 blindfold	✓	

   Put an X in the ✗ column if you spelled the word incorrectly online.

Word	✓	✗
1 blindfold		X

4. **Repeat Steps 1–3 for the remaining words in the Spelling Pretest.**

Utility Wires (A)

Spelling List 14 Pretest

Write each spelling word in the Word column, making sure to spell it correctly.

	Word	✓	✗
1			
2			
3			
4			
5			
6			
7			
8			
9			
10			
11			
12			
13			

	Word	✓	✗
14			
15			
16			
17			
18			
19			
20			
21			
22			
23			
24			
25			

Write About Main Idea and Supporting Details

Answer the questions in complete sentences.

1. What is the main idea of "Bury All Utility Wires"?

   _____

   _____

2. Find and record three details in the text that support the main idea. Explain how the details support the main idea.

   a. First Supporting Detail:

   _____

   _____

   _____

   _____

   _____

b. Second Supporting Detail:

_____

_____

_____

_____

_____

_____

c. Third Supporting Detail:

_____

_____

_____

_____

_____

_____

Utility Wires (B)

Spelling List 14 Activity Bank

Circle any words in the box that you did not spell correctly on the pretest. Choose one activity to do with your circled words. Do as much of the activity as you can in the time given.

Did you spell all the words on the pretest correctly? Do the one activity with as many spelling words as you can.

braces	center	excite	police	space
celebrate	cereal	fancy	recess	spruce
celery	decide	lettuce	sentence	surface
cell	decimal	office	since	trace
cent	except	piece	sincere	voice

Spelling Activity Choices

Silly Sentences

1. Write a silly sentence for each of your spelling words.

2. Underline the spelling word in each sentence.
   Example: The dog was <u>driving</u> a car.

3. Correct any spelling errors.

Spelling Story

1. Write a very short story using each of your spelling words.

2. Underline the spelling words in the story.

3. Correct any spelling errors.

Riddle Me This

1. Write a riddle for each of your spelling words.
   Example: "I have a trunk, but it's not on my car."

2. Write the answer, which is your word, for each riddle.
   Example: Answer: elephant

3. Correct any spelling errors.

RunOnWord

1. Gather some crayons, colored pencils, or markers. Use a different color to write each of your spelling words. Write the words end to end as one long word.
   Example: dogcatbirdfishturtle

2. Rewrite the words correctly and with proper spacing.

3. Correct any spelling errors.

Complete the activity that you chose.

My chosen activity: _____

_____

_____

_____

_____

_____

_____

_____

_____

_____

_____

_____

_____

_____

_____

_____

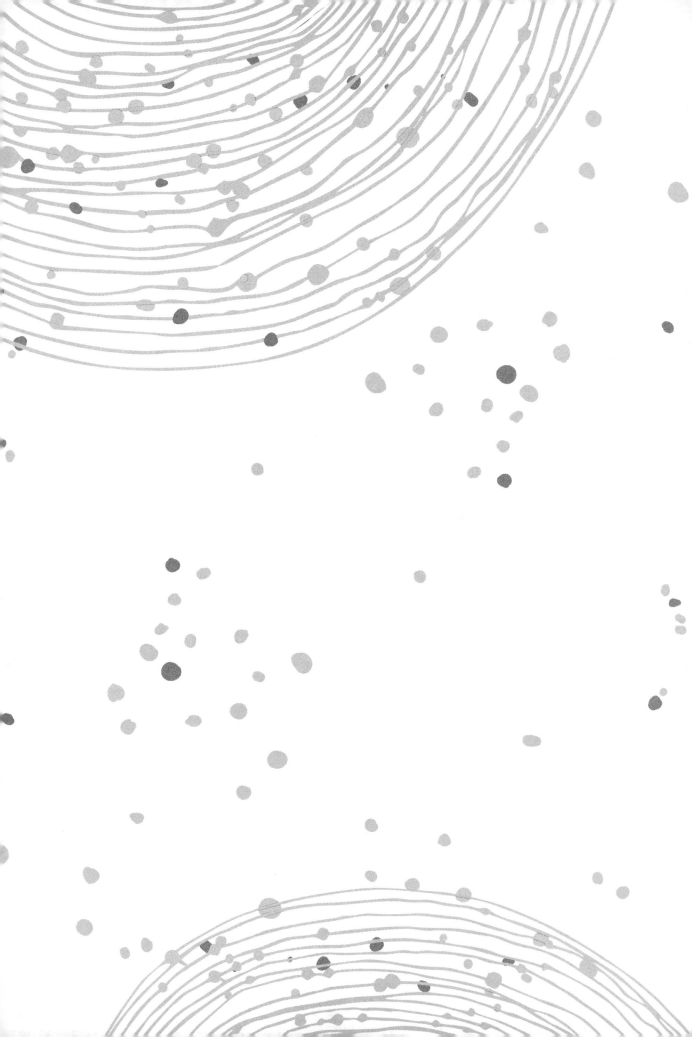

Utility Wires (B)

Write About Main Idea, Supporting Details, and Your Opinion

Answer the questions in complete sentences.

1. What is the main idea of "Keep Our Wires High in the Sky"?

2. Find and record three details in the text that support the main idea. Explain how the details support the main idea.

   a. First Supporting Detail:

b. Second Supporting Detail:

_____

_____

_____

_____

_____

_____

c. Third Supporting Detail:

_____

_____

_____

_____

_____

_____

3. What is your opinion about utility wires?

_____

_____

_____

4. Find and record three details in the text to support your opinion. Explain how the details support your opinion.

   a. First Supporting Detail:

   _____

   _____

   _____

   _____

   _____

   _____

b. Second Supporting Detail:

_____

_____

_____

_____

_____

_____

c. Third Supporting Detail:

_____

_____

_____

_____

_____

_____

Utility Wires Wrap-Up

Compare and Contrast Points of View

Create two characters: one who wants to bury utility wires and one who wants to keep them above the ground. Give each character a name, and state each character's point of view.

Character 1

Name: _____

Point of view: _____

_____

_____

Character 2

Name: _____

Point of view: _____

_____

_____

Write a dialogue between your two characters. Remember to use quotation marks and commas. Characters should state their point of view and three supporting details. Use the articles and your completed Write About Main Idea and Supporting Details and Write About Main Idea, Supporting Details, and Your Opinion activity pages.

_____

_____

_____

_____

_____

_____

_____

_____

_____

_____

_____

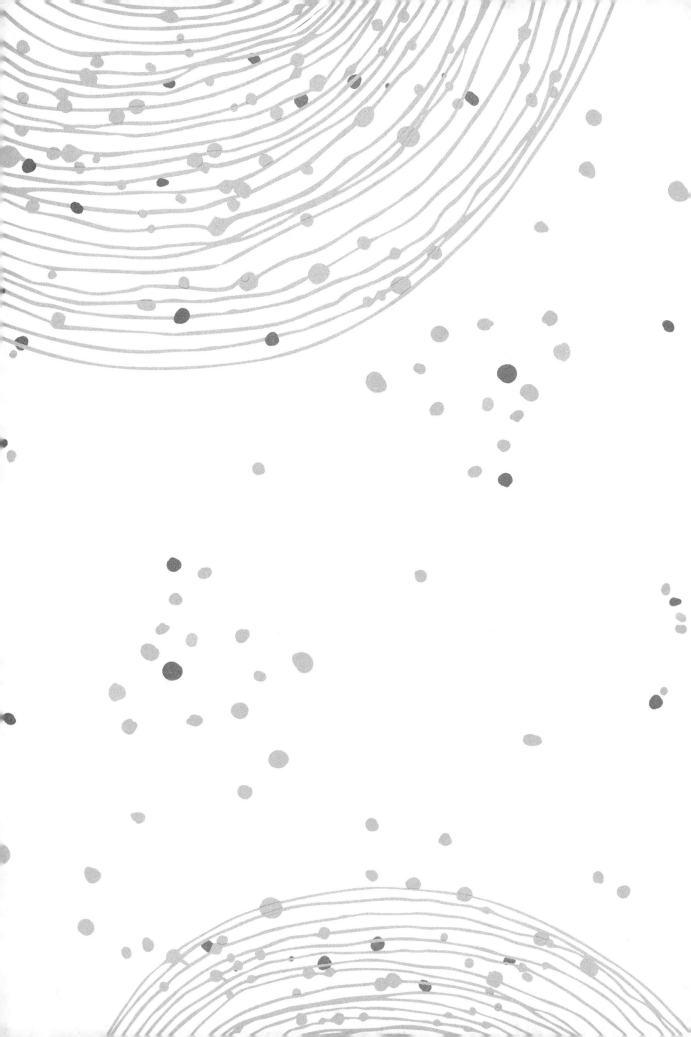

TRY IT

Fast Food (A)

Write About Points of View

Answer the questions in complete sentences.

1. What is the author's point of view in "Down with Fast Food"?

   _____

   _____

   _____

2. Find and record three pieces of evidence in the text that support the author's point of view. Explain how the evidence supports the author's point of view.

   a. First Piece of Evidence:

   _____

   _____

   _____

   _____

   _____

b. Second Piece of Evidence:

_____

_____

_____

_____

_____

c. Third Piece of Evidence:

_____

_____

_____

_____

_____

3. What is your point of view about eating fast food?

_____

_____

_____

4. Find and record three pieces of evidence in the text that support your point of view. Explain how the evidence supports your point of view.

    a. First Piece of Evidence:

_____

_____

_____

_____

_____

b. Second Piece of Evidence:

_____

_____

_____

_____

_____

_____

c. Third Piece of Evidence:

_____

_____

_____

_____

_____

_____

Fast Food (B)

Compare Points of View

Answer the questions in complete sentences.

1. What is the author's point of view in "In Favor of Fast Food"?

_____

_____

_____

2. Find and record three pieces of evidence in the text that support the author's point of view. Explain how the evidence supports the author's point of view.

   a. First Piece of Evidence:

   _____

   _____

   _____

   _____

   _____

b. Second Piece of Evidence:

_____

_____

_____

_____

_____

c. Third Piece of Evidence:

_____

_____

_____

_____

_____

3. Did your point of view about eating fast food change after reading "In Favor of Fast Food"?

_____

_____

4. Explain three ways your point of view is either similar to or different than the point of view of the author of "In Favor of Fast Food."

a. First Way:

_____

_____

_____

_____

_____

b. Second Way:

_____

_____

_____

_____

_____

c. Third Way:

_____

_____

_____

_____

_____

Create a Mini-Book

Write a mini-book about fast food. Use the articles and your completed Write About Points of View and Compare Points of View activity pages.

To create your mini-book, tear out page 337. Fold the page in half. Use your best cursive handwriting to add your title and name to your mini-book.

Use the lines inside your mini-book to write two paragraphs.

- The first paragraph should explain your opinion about fast food. Include examples to support your opinion.

- The second paragraph should compare the author's opinion in one of the articles you read to your own opinion.

Use the boxes inside your mini-book to illustrate your opinion.

What's a frog's favorite fast food? French flies!

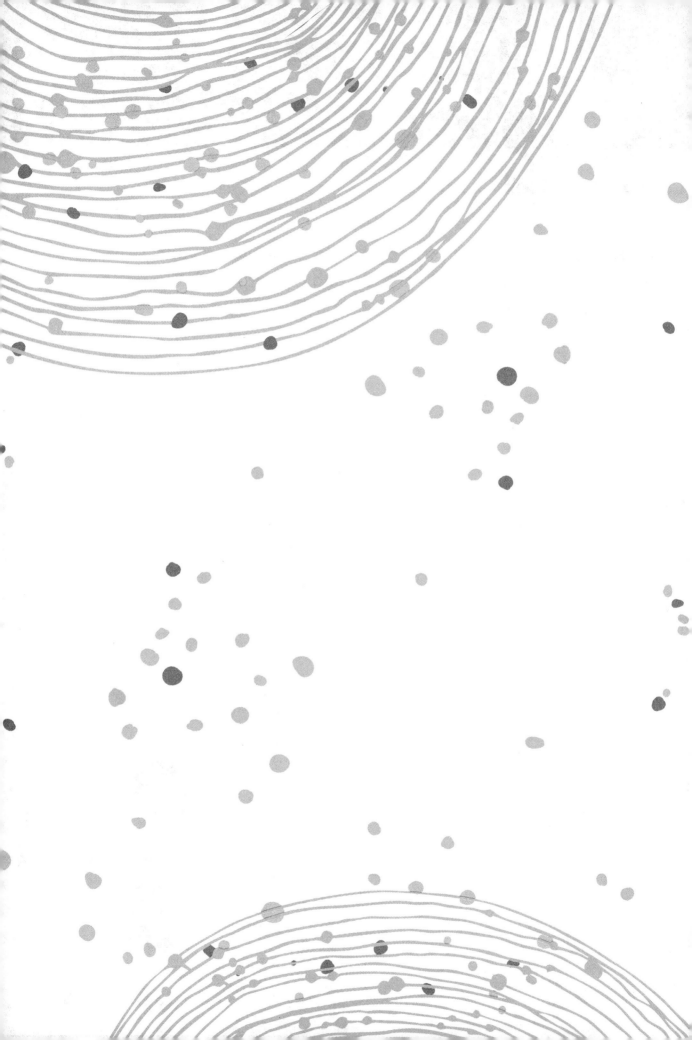

Title:

Author:

fold

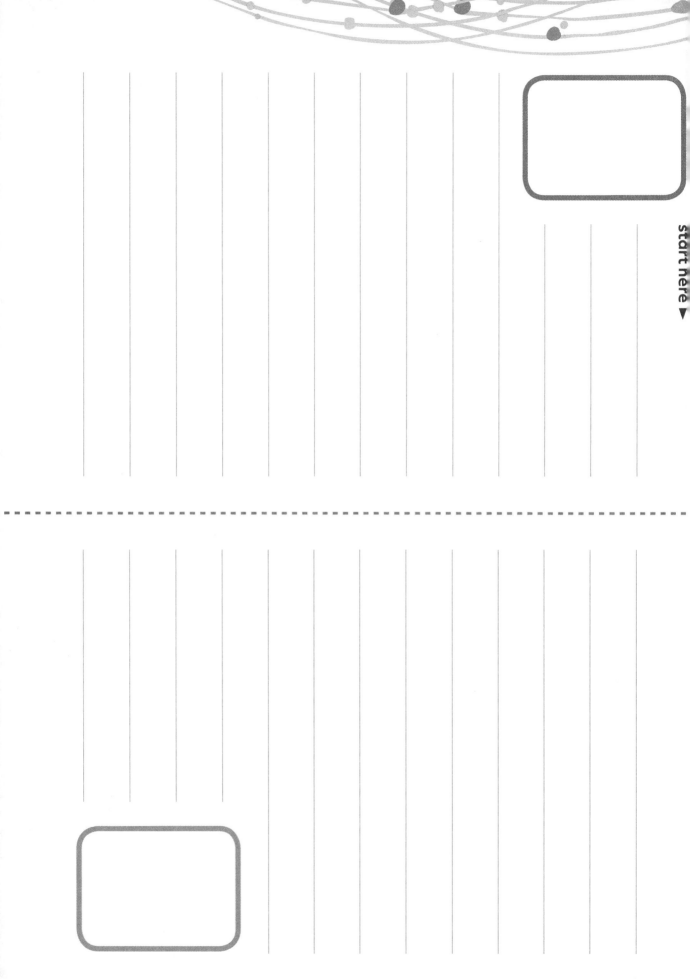

start here ▶

Opinion Writing Skills (A)

Spelling List 15 Pretest

1. Open the Spelling Pretest activity online. Listen to the first spelling word. Type the word. Check your answer.

2. Write the correct spelling of the word in the Word column of the Spelling Pretest table.

	Word	✓	✗
1	blindfold		

3. Put a check mark in the ✓ column if you spelled the word correctly online.

   Put an X in the ✗ column if you spelled the word incorrectly online.

	Word	✓	✗
1	blindfold	✓	

	Word	✓	✗
1	blindfold		✗

4. Repeat Steps 1–3 for the remaining words in the Spelling Pretest.

Opinion Writing Skills (A)

Spelling List 15 Pretest

Write each spelling word in the Word column, making sure to spell it correctly.

	Word	✓	✗
1			
2			
3			
4			
5			
6			
7			
8			
9			

	Word	✓	✗
10			
11			
12			
13			
14			
15			
16			
17			

Opinion Writing Skills (A)

Model Opinion Essay

Use this model as you complete your own opinion essay.

Kickball

Imagine you are playing baseball. You hit the ball and sprint around first base. What a thrill! Now, imagine you are playing soccer. You kick the ball from midfield with a loud smack. There is a game that combines the best parts of baseball and soccer. The game is played on a baseball field, but there are no gloves, bat, or baseball. Instead, a pitcher tosses a large rubber ball from the pitcher's mound, and the player who is "at bat" kicks the ball. This game is kickball. Kickball is a fun sport that everyone should try.

— introduction

pinion
atement

topic sentence

There are many reasons that kickball is a fun sport. First, it is fun because many

supporting reasons

people can play at the same time. There are so many roles in kickball. For example, there are people in the field and at each base. There is a pitcher and a catcher. And, there are the people kicking the ball and running the bases. Almost everyone is active the whole game, so kickball is never dull. Next, players get to do different things while they play. Players switch between the field and kicking often. During a game, players get to throw, catch, run, tag, and kick.

body

topic sentence

Kickball is a game that everyone should try. Kickball is easy to play

supporting reasons

because you only need a ball, a field, and some friends. Players don't need helmets or mouth guards either. Kickball is also a great way to get exercise since it involves a lot of running. Everyone needs exercise! Therefore, everyone should give kickball a try.

Kickball is an entertaining sport. It does not use a lot of special equipment, and it is a great way to get exercise. — conclusion

statement opinion

There are a lot of ways to spend a sunny day, but kickball is the best way.

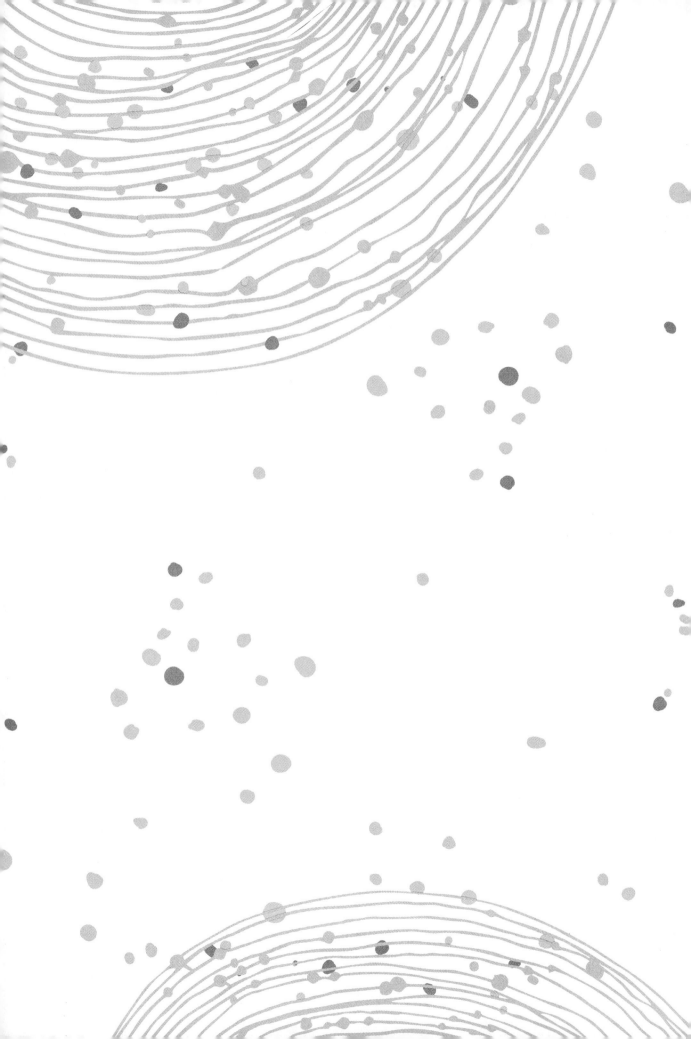

Opinion Writing Skills (A)

Choose Your Topic and State Your Opinion

Read the writing prompt.

Prompt: Write an essay that expresses your opinion on a topic.

- Write an **introduction** that gives information about your topic and clearly states your opinion.

- Write **one or two body paragraphs** that give reasons that support your opinion. Use transitions such as *because* and *for example* to connect your reasons and opinion.

- Write a **conclusion** that restates your opinion in a new way.

In my opinion, polka dots match everything!

In my opinion. . .

Follow the instructions to choose a topic and state your opinion.

1. List as many possible topics for your opinion essay as you can think of. You should have an opinion about the topics.

2. Read your list of topics. State an opinion about each topic. If you don't have an opinion about a topic, cross it off! Cross off any topics you are not excited to write about. Keep crossing off topics until you have one left. Circle that topic.

3. Write the opinion that you will support in your essay.

Sample answers:
Watermelon is the perfect summer dessert.
All kids should learn about ancient Egypt.
The voting age should be changed to 10 years old.

GET READY

Opinion Writing Skills (B)

Spelling List 15 Activity Bank

Circle any words in the box that you did not spell correctly on your pretest. Choose one activity to do with your circled words. Do as much of the activity as you can in the time given.

Did you spell all the words on the pretest correctly? Do the one activity with as many spelling words as you can.

danced	grading	liking	used	wasting
dancer	hoped	smiled	using	write
dancing	hoping	smiling	wasted	writing
graded	liked			

Spelling Activity Choices

Hidden Words

1. Draw a picture. "Hide" as many of your spelling words as you can inside the picture.

2. See if others can find the words you hid in the picture.

Triangle Spelling

Write each of your spelling words in a triangle.

d
do
dog

Ghost Words

1. Use a white crayon to write each of your spelling words.

2. Write over the words in white crayon with a colored marker.

Complete the activity that you chose.

My chosen activity: _____

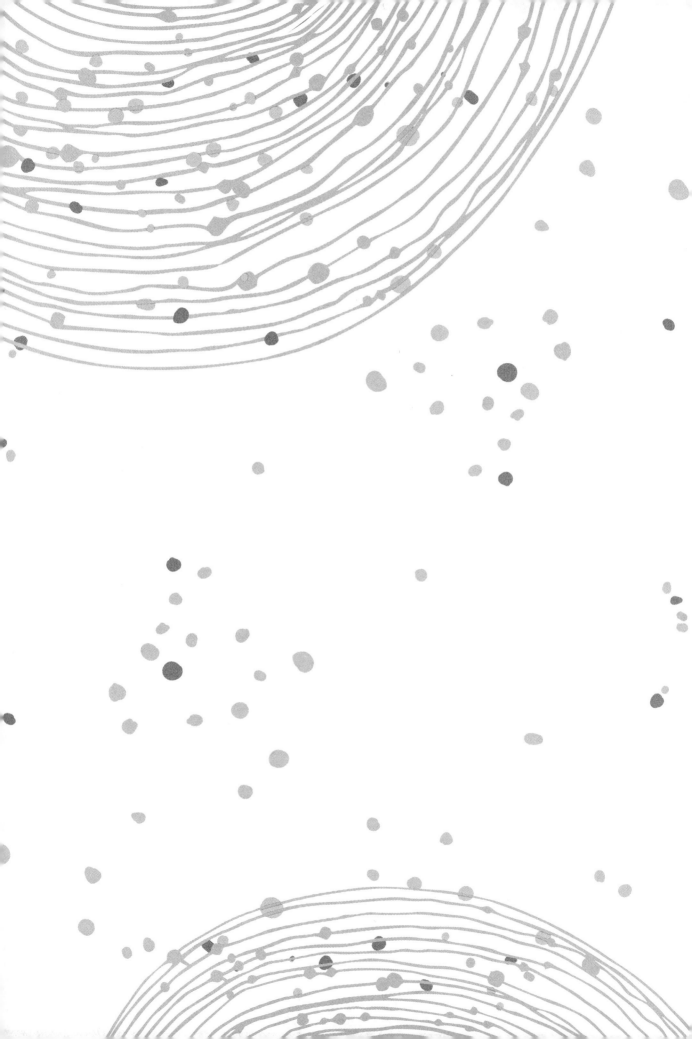

Opinion Writing Skills (B)

Support Your Opinion with Reasons

Read the writing prompt.

Prompt: **Write an essay that expresses your opinion on a topic.**

- Write an **introduction** that gives information about your topic and clearly states your opinion.

- Write **one or two body paragraphs** that give reasons that support your opinion. Use transitions such as *because* and *for example* to connect your reasons and opinion.

- Write a **conclusion** that restates your opinion in a new way.

Complete the chart to plan your opinion essay. Make sure your reasons are clear. Add details to support your reasons.

Introduce Topic
Opinion

Reason

Reason

Reason

Reason

Restate Opinion

Opinion Writing Skills (C)

Write Your Opinion Essay

Read the writing prompt.

Prompt: **Write an essay that expresses your opinion on a topic.**

- Write an **introduction** that gives information about your topic and clearly states your opinion.

- Write **one or two body paragraphs** that give reasons that support your opinion. Use transitions such as *because* and *for example* to connect your reasons and opinion.

- Write a **conclusion** that restates your opinion in a new way.

Respond to the writing prompt. Use your prewriting work to help you.

_____

_____

_____

_____

_____

_____

Reflect on Your Opinion Essay

Read your opinion essay. Then, answer the questions in complete sentences.

1. A strong opinion essay begins with information about the topic and a clear opinion statement.

   a. What did you tell readers about your topic? How will that information help readers understand your opinion?

   _____

   _____

   _____

   b. Is there anything else about your topic you should tell readers?

   _____

   _____

c. Write one way you could make your opinion statement stronger. For example, you might change a vague word or add a detail.

_____

_____

2. The body of an opinion essay includes reasons that support the writer's opinion.

    a. Which of your reasons is the strongest? Why?

_____

_____

_____

    b. Rewrite one sentence from your body to improve it. Explain how your revision makes that sentence stronger.

    Revised sentence:

_____

_____

    Explanation:

_____

_____

3. Transitions like *because*, *since*, and *for example* can connect an opinion and reason.

    a. Write one sentence from your essay that has a transition.

      _____

      _____

    b. Rewrite one sentence from your essay so that it has a transition.

      _____

      _____

4. A strong opinion essay ends with a conclusion.

    a. Which sentence or sentences from your conclusion restate your opinion?

      _____

      _____

    b. If you did not restate your opinion in a new way, revise the sentences you wrote in Part a.

      _____

      _____

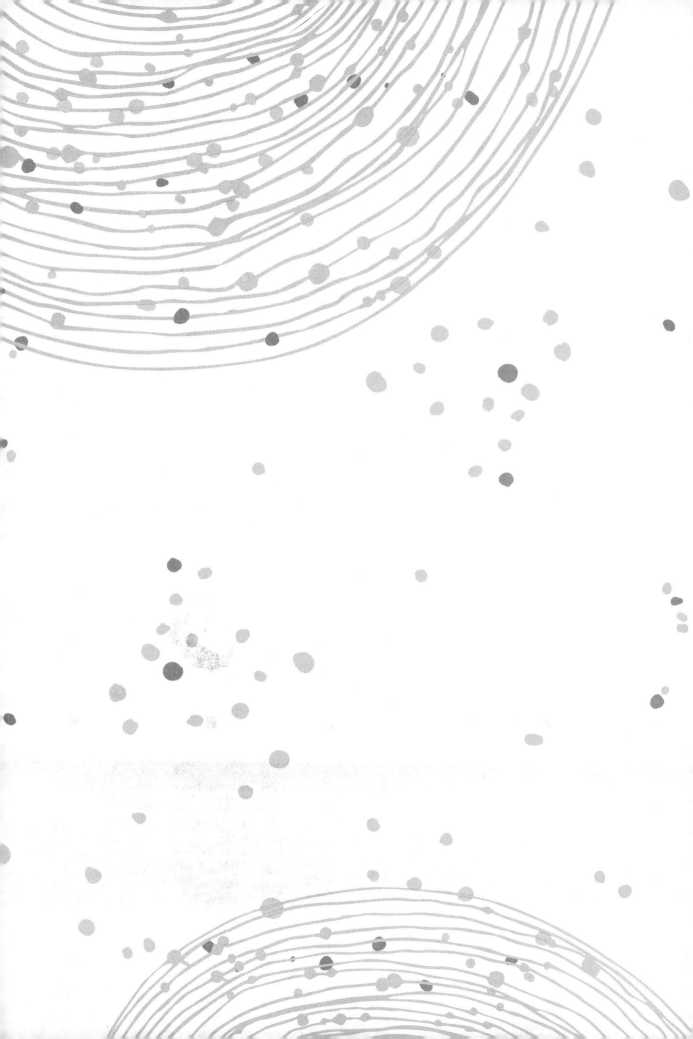

Apply: Figurative Language

Circle the phrase that best completes the passage. Define the phrase. Explain what context clues led you to choose that phrase.

1. Clara was all set to sing her first solo with her choir. She had practiced for weeks. But when it came time to perform, Clara _____ . She got so nervous when she saw the audience that she couldn't open her mouth.

   Choices: *dropped the ball* or *got cold feet*

   Definition:

   _____

   _____

   Context Clues:

   _____

   _____

   _____

2. My family likes to eat at a restaurant by the harbor. We enjoy watching the ships. We go there so often that we're now friends of the owner, Marco. Last week, Marco would not let us pay for our desserts. He gave them to us _____ because we're such good customers.

Choices: *on the house* or *in the same boat*

Definition:

_____

_____

Context Clues:

_____

_____

_____

Write your own short passage using one of the given phrases. Leave a blank space where your chosen phrase belongs. Have someone else read your passage. Ask this person to choose which phrase best completes the passage. Discuss the answer.

3. **Choices:** *cough up* or *stick together*

_____

_____

Go Write! The Best Book or Movie

Respond to the prompt. Or, write about a topic of your choice!

Prompt: **Which book or movie do you think is the best?**
Why do you think it is the best?

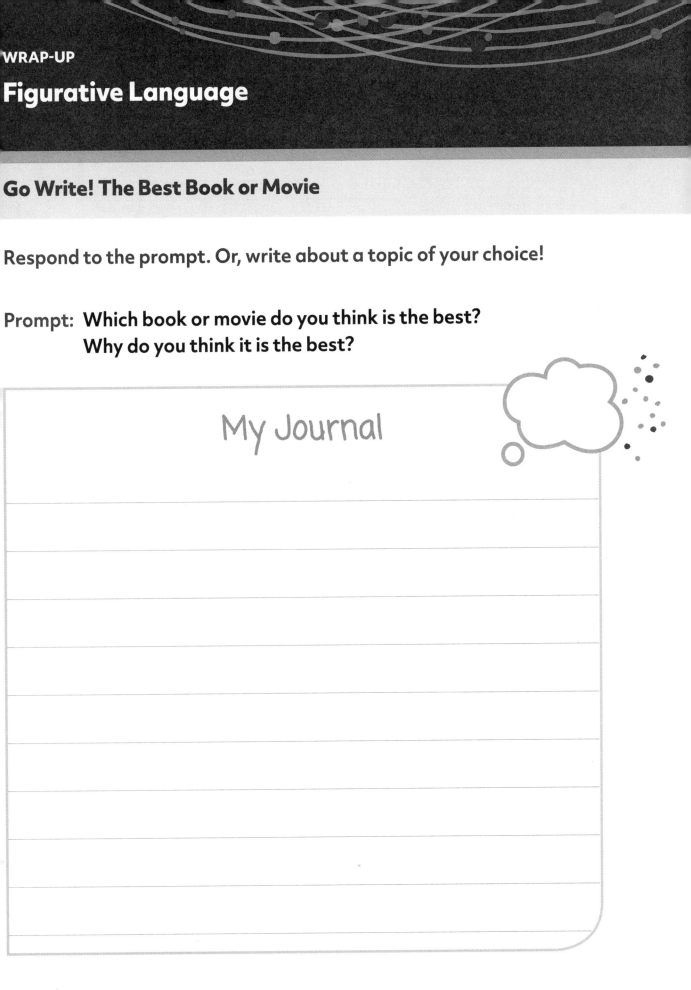

My Journal

The Tale of Despereaux (A)

Spelling List 16 Pretest

1. Open the Spelling Pretest activity online. Listen to the first spelling word. Type the word. Check your answer.

2. Write the correct spelling of the word in the Word column of the Spelling Pretest table.

	Word	✓	✗
1	blindfold		

3. Put a check mark in the ✓ column if you spelled the word correctly online.

   Put an X in the ✗ column if you spelled the word incorrectly online.

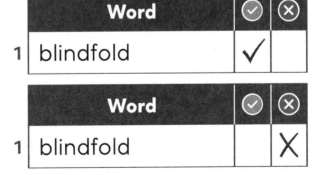

	Word	✓	✗
1	blindfold	✓	

	Word	✓	✗
1	blindfold		X

4. Repeat Steps 1–3 for the remaining words in the Spelling Pretest.

The Tale of Despereaux (A)

Spelling List 16 Pretest

Write each spelling word in the Word column, making sure to spell it correctly.

	Word	✓	✗
1			
2			
3			
4			
5			
6			
7			
8			
9			
10			
11			

	Word	✓	✗
12			
13			
14			
15			
16			
17			
18			
19			
20			
21			

Describe Despereaux

Describe Despereaux using evidence from the text.

It can be inferred that Despereaux is not like other mice. Write
a paragraph that describes at least two ways that Despereaux
is different from other mice. Use quotations from the text as
evidence to support your description.

_____

_____

_____

_____

_____

_____

_____

_____

_____

_____

_____

_____

I found evidence to support my idea!

Spelling List 16 Activity Bank

Circle any words in the box that you did not spell correctly on your pretest. Choose one activity to do with your circled words. Do as much of the activity as you can in the time given.

Did you spell all the words on the pretest correctly? Do the one activity with as many spelling words as you can.

asked	founded	melting	quitting	speaker
beginning	heaped	mixed	runner	stopped
boating	hunter	mopping	shouted	trapped
crashed	looking	pinching	sleeping	warming
dotted				

Spelling Activity Choices

Create a Crossword

1. Write one of your spelling words going down in the center of the grid.

2. Write another spelling word going across that shares a letter with the first word. See how many words you can connect.

Example:

			p			
	k	i	s	s	e	s
d		n				
r	o	c	k	s		
g						
s						

Word Search Puzzle

1. Draw a box on the grid. The box should be large enough to hold your spelling words.

2. Fill in the grid with your spelling words. Write them across, up and down, and diagonally. You can write them forward and backward.

3. Fill in the rest of the box with random letters.

4. Ask someone to find and circle your words in the puzzle.

Complete the activity that you chose.

My chosen activity: _____

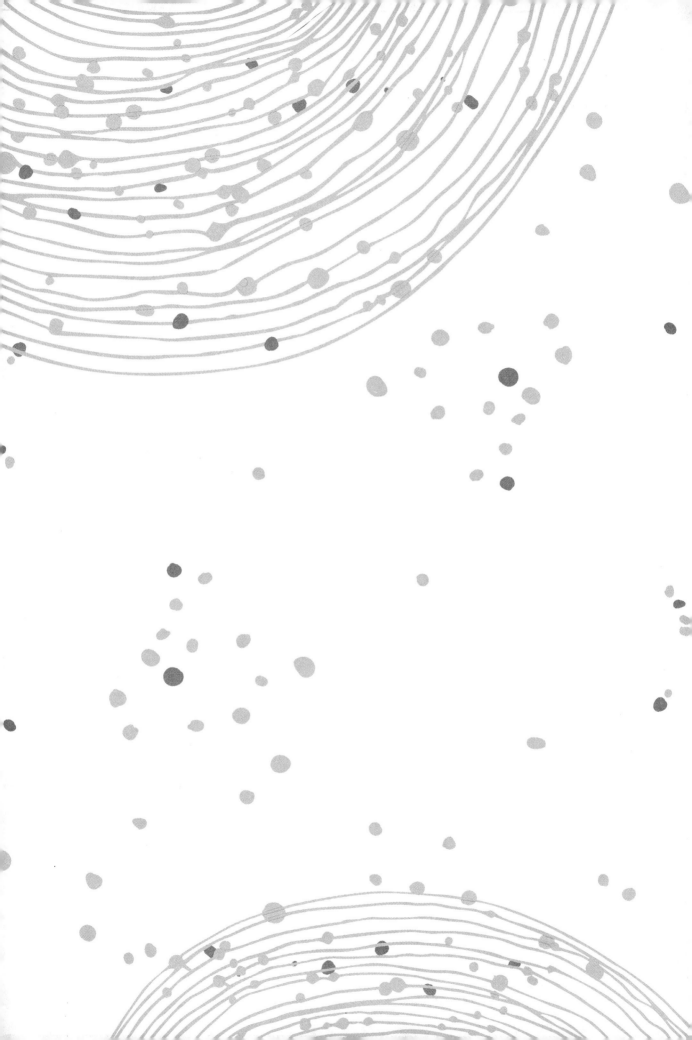

The Tale of Despereaux (B)

Describe the Castle

Describe what you imagine the inside of the castle is like.

Write a paragraph that describes what the inside of the castle is like. Base your description on details directly stated in the story and inferences you make from the details. Use at least three examples from the text to support your description.

_____

_____

_____

_____

_____

_____

_____

_____

_____

_____

The Tale of Despereaux (C)

Create a Scene

Read the excerpt from *The Tale of Despereaux* by Kate DiCamillo.

The rat waltzed happily from room to room until he found himself at the door to the banquet hall. He looked inside and saw gathered there King Phillip, Queen Rosemary, the Princess Pea, twenty noble people, a juggler, four minstrels, and all the king's men. This party, reader, was a sight for a rat's eyes. Roscuro had never seen happy people. He had known only the miserable ones. Gregory the jailer and those who were consigned to his domain did not laugh or smile or clink glasses with the person sitting next to them.

Follow the instructions to draw a picture and write about it.

1. Draw a picture that shows the setting of the banquet hall.
    Add details from your imagination that may not be described
    in the passsage.

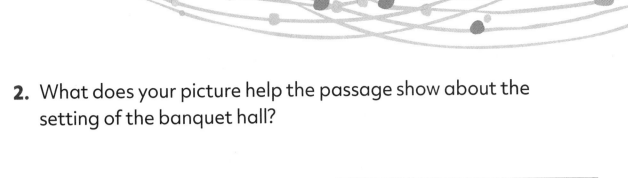

2. What does your picture help the passage show about the setting of the banquet hall?

_____

_____

_____

_____

_____

_____

_____

I imagine lots of singing.

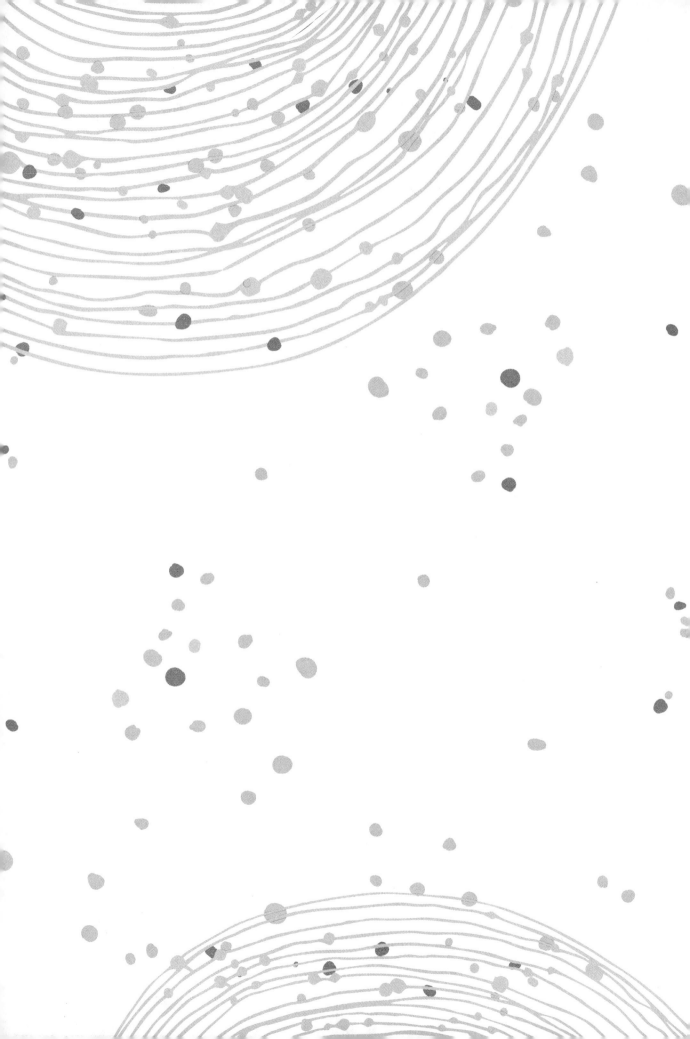

Describe a Chapter's Events

Answer the questions in complete sentences.

1. What is the definition of a chapter?

   _____

   _____

2. Describe the events of Chapter Twenty "a view from a chandelier" from *The Tale of Despereaux*. Tell the events in order.

   _____

   _____

   _____

   _____

   _____

   _____

Literal Versus Nonliteral

Follow the instructions to illustrate the literal and nonliteral meanings of figurative language.

1. Choose a phrase from the list.

   - Raining cats and dogs

   - Under the weather

   - Head in the clouds

2. Write the phrase you chose and the nonliteral meaning of the phrase.

   _____

   _____

   _____

3. Draw a picture that shows the literal, or actual, meaning of the phrase you chose. Then, write a sentence to go with your picture that includes the phrase.

4. Draw a picture that shows the nonliteral meaning of the same phrase. Then, write a sentence to go with your picture that includes the phrase.

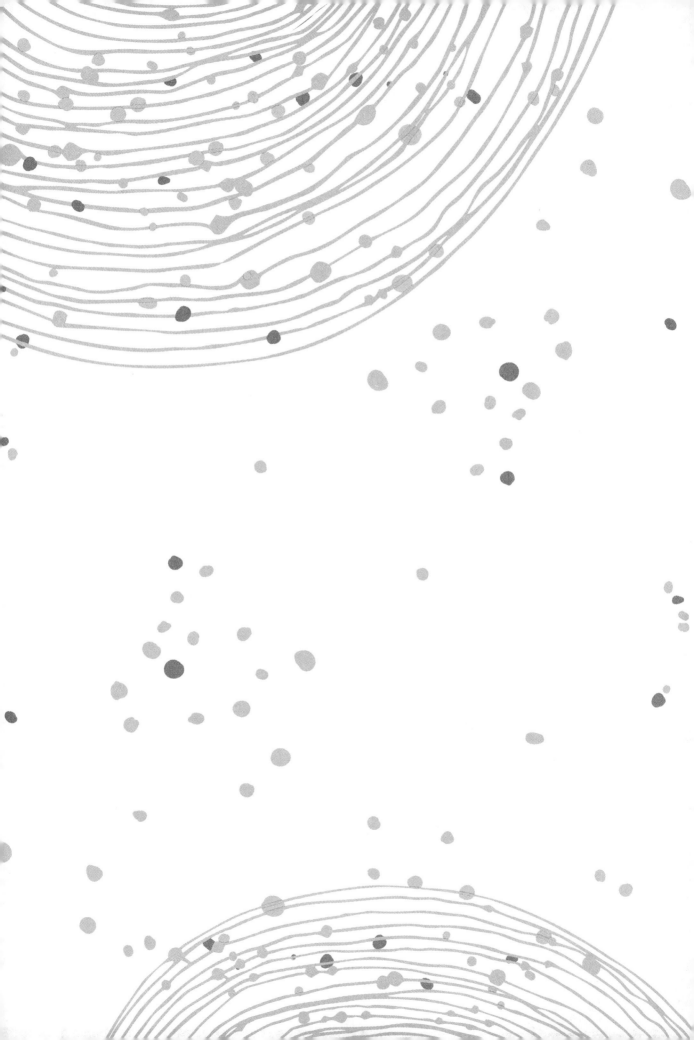

The Tale of Despereaux (F)

Spelling List 17 Pretest

1. Open the Spelling Pretest activity online. Listen to the first spelling word. Type the word. Check your answer.

2. Write the correct spelling of the word in the Word column of the Spelling Pretest table.

Word	✓	✗
1 blindfold		

3. Put a check mark in the ✓ column if you spelled the word correctly online.

   Put an X in the ✗ column if you spelled the word incorrectly online.

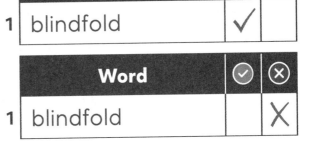

Word	✓	✗
1 blindfold	✓	

Word	✓	✗
1 blindfold		✗

4. Repeat Steps 1–3 for the remaining words in the Spelling Pretest.

The Tale of Despereaux (F)

Spelling List 17 Pretest

Write each spelling word in the Word column, making sure to spell it correctly.

	Word	✓	✗
1			
2			
3			
4			
5			
6			
7			
8			
9			
10			
11			

	Word	✓	✗
12			
13			
14			
15			
16			
17			
18			
19			
20			
21			

The Tale of Despereaux (F)

What Are the Results?

Read the excerpt from *The Tale of Despereaux* by Kate DiCamillo.

> In Cook's kitchen, Mig dropped eggshells in the pound cake batter; she scrubbed the kitchen floor with cooking oil instead of cleanser; she sneezed directly on the king's pork chop moments before it was to be served to him.

Answer the questions in complete sentences.

1. What does Cook do because of Mig's actions in the kitchen?

2. What are the results of Mig going to the dungeon? Include at least three events.

_____

_____

_____

_____

_____

_____

_____

Personally, I think that cooking with Mig sounds like a lot of fun.

Spelling List 17 Activity Bank

Circle any words in the box that you did not spell correctly on your pretest. Choose one activity to do with your circled words. Do as much of the activity as you can in the time given.

Did you spell all the words on the pretest correctly? Do the one activity with as many spelling words as you can.

breeze	easy	praise	rise	those
cheese	elbows	prison	rosebush	Thursday
chose	hose	raise	suppose	Tuesday
details	means	raisin	surprise	Wednesday
disease				

Spelling Activity Choices

Alphabetizing

1. In the left column, write your spelling words in alphabetical order.

2. Correct any spelling errors.

Vowel-Free Words

1. In the left column, write only the consonants in each of your spelling words. Put a dot where each vowel should be.

2. Spell each word aloud, stating which vowels should be in the places with dots.

3. In the right column, rewrite the entire spelling word.

4. Correct any spelling errors.

Rhymes

1. In the left column, write your spelling words.

2. In the right column, write a word that rhymes with each spelling word.

3. Correct any spelling errors.

Uppercase and Lowercase

1. In the left column, write each of your spelling words in all uppercase letters.

2. In the right column, write each of your spelling words in all lowercase letters.

3. Correct any spelling errors.

Complete the activity that you chose.

My chosen activity: _____

1. _____   _____

2. _____   _____

3. _____   _____

4. _____   _____

5. _____   _____

6. _____   _____

7. _____   _____

8. _____   _____

9. _____   _____

10. _____   _____

11. _____   _____

12. _____   _____

13. _____   _____

14. _____   _____

15. _____   _____

16. _____   _____

17. _____ _____

18. _____ _____

19. _____ _____

20. _____ _____

21. _____ _____

The Tale of Despereaux (G)

Events Affect Future Events

Read the excerpt from *The Tale of Despereaux* by
Kate DiCamillo.

> He looked back.
>
> And he saw that the princess was glaring at him. Her
> eyes were filled with disgust and anger.
>
> "Go back to the dungeon" was what the look she gave
> him said. "Go back into the darkness where you belong."
>
> This look, reader, broke Roscuro's heart.

Answer the questions in complete sentences.

1. The passage describes events after Roscuro falls into the
   queen's soup and the queen dies. What does Roscuro do right
   after these events?

   _____

   _____

   _____

2. What does Roscuro do in the future because of the events in the passage?

_____

_____

_____

_____

_____

_____

_____

The Tale of Despereaux (H)

Describe Interactions Among Characters

Read the excerpt from *The Tale of Despereaux* by Kate DiCamillo.

"Mouse," said Cook, "would you like some soup?"...

"Come closer," she said. "I don't aim to hurt you. I promise."

Despereaux sniffed. The soup smelled wonderful, incredible. Keeping one eye on Cook, he stepped out from behind the spool of thread and crept closer.

"Go on," said Cook, "taste it."

Despereaux stepped onto the saucer....He sipped. Oh, it was lovely....

"How is it?" asked Cook anxiously.

"Wonderful," said Despereaux....

Cook smiled. "See?" she said. "There ain't a body, be it mouse or man, that ain't made better by a little soup."

Answer the questions in complete sentences.

1. Think back to when Despereaux escaped from the dungeon and Cook saw him in the kitchen. Describe the interaction between Cook, Mig, and Despereaux at that point in the story.

    _____

    _____

    _____

    _____

    _____

    _____

    _____

2. Is the relationship between Cook, Mig, and Despereaux positive or negative?

    _____

3. The events of the excerpt happen right before Despereaux enters the dungeon to rescue Princess Pea. How do Cook and Despereaux act toward each other in the excerpt?

_____

_____

_____

_____

_____

_____

_____

4. How has the relationship between Cook and Despereaux changed?

_____

_____

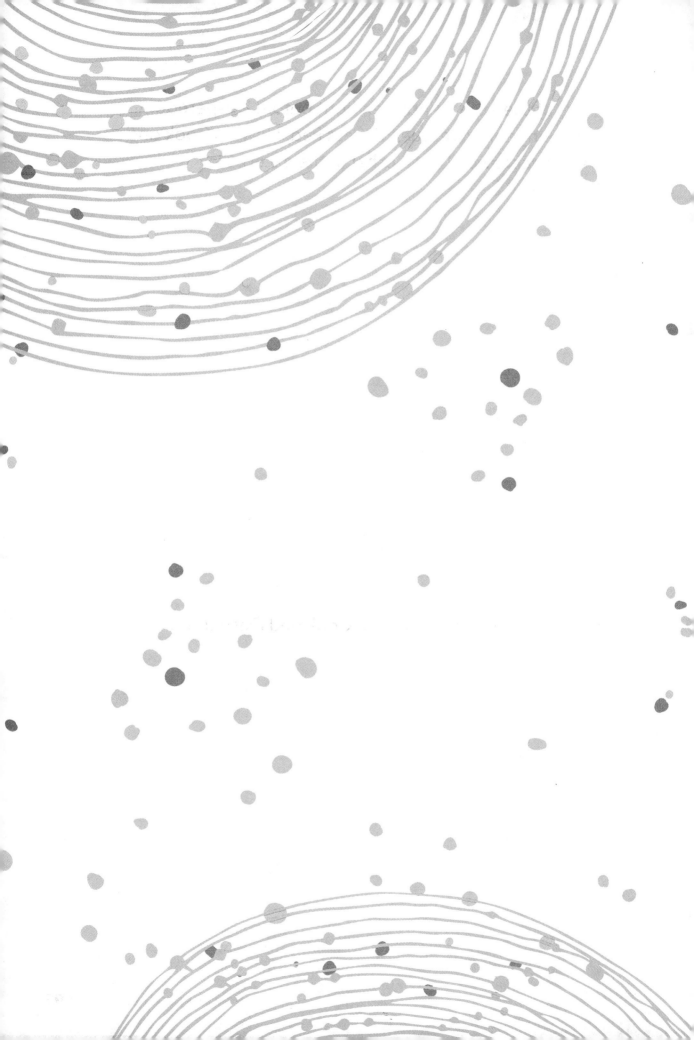

The Tale of Despereaux (I)

Write About a Theme

Follow the instructions to support a theme in *The Tale of Despereaux*.

1. Choose one of the following characters:

   • Despereaux

   • Lester, Despereaux's father

   • Miggery Sow

2. One theme in the book is "Think before you act because actions have serious consequences." How do the actions of the character you chose develop that theme? Write a paragraph that gives and explains an example.

_____

_____

_____

_____

_____

_____

_____

_____

_____

_____

_____

_____

_____

_____

_____

This theme applies to my own life, too.

Reflect on Overcoming Obstacles

Answer the questions in complete sentences.

1. The idea of overcoming obstacles is throughout *The Tale of Despereaux*. Think of a time that you had to overcome an obstacle. What was the obstacle?

_____

_____

2. How did you overcome that obstacle?

_____

_____

_____

_____

_____

_____

_____

3. What did you learn from your experience?

_____

_____

_____

_____

_____

_____

Apply: Prefixes

Write the definition for each prefix.

1. *dis–* _____   *pre–* _____

  in– _____   *re–* _____

  mis– _____   *un–* _____

Form new words with prefixes, and then use one of the new words in a sentence.

2. Add prefixes from Question 1 to the word *placed* to form words that match the definitions.

_____ placed: put in the wrong place

_____ placed: put something in its place again

_____ placed: moved people or things so they are not in their usual place

3. Choose a word from Question 2. Write 1–2 sentences that show the meaning of the word.

_____

_____

_____

4. Add prefixes from Question 1 to the word *cooked* to form words that match the definitions.

_____ cooked: not cooked

_____ cooked: cooked again

_____ cooked: cooked before or ahead of time

5. Choose a word from Question 4. Write 1–2 sentences that show the meaning of the word.

_____

_____

_____

Answer the question.

6. Which word correctly completes the sentence? Circle the word.

pretest   inequality   dislike

Nico said it was a case of _____ when his brother got a bigger piece of cake than he did.

Go Write! Why Read a Book?

Respond to the prompt. Or, write about a topic of your choice!

Prompt: **What makes you want to read a book? How can you convince someone else to read the same book?**

My Journal

Opinion Writing: Prewriting (A)

Spelling List 18 Pretest

1. Open the Spelling Pretest activity online. Listen to the first spelling word. Type the word. Check your answer.

2. Write the correct spelling of the word in the Word column of the Spelling Pretest table.

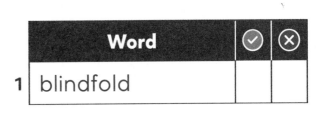

	Word	✓	✗
1	blindfold		

3. Put a check mark in the ✓ column if you spelled the word correctly online.

   Put an X in the ✗ column if you spelled the word incorrectly online.

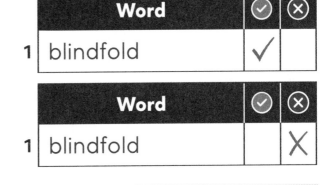

	Word	✓	✗
1	blindfold	✓	

	Word	✓	✗
1	blindfold		✗

4. Repeat Steps 1–3 for the remaining words in the Spelling Pretest.

Opinion Writing: Prewriting (A)

Spelling List 18 Pretest

Write each spelling word in the Word column, making sure to spell it correctly.

	Word	✓	✗
1			
2			
3			
4			
5			
6			
7			
8			
9			
10			
11			

	Word	✓	✗
12			
13			
14			
15			
16			
17			
18			
19			
20			
21			

Model Persuasive Essay

Use this model to help you as you complete your own persuasive essay.

title —[

Tennis, Anyone?

Cedar Park is a nice place. It has a pond and lots of grass. There are swings, jungle gyms, soccer fields, and basketball courts. There is a lot to do in Cedar Park. Yet, Cedar Park does not have a tennis court. This must change. The city should build a tennis court in Cedar Park.

opinion statement

— introduction

Cedar Park should have a tennis court because playing tennis is fun. It is a great way to stay in shape, too. Also, Cedar Park is the only park with room for a tennis court. A tennis court would fit perfectly on the patch of grass behind the soccer fields. In addition, Cedar Park is a good place for a tennis court because it is in the middle of town. People can take a bus or walk to Cedar Park.

— body

The city should build a tennis court in Cedar Park because tennis is a great sport. The park has room for a court, and the park is easy to get to. Cedar Park is already good, but a tennis court would make it great! — conclusion

Opinion Writing: Prewriting (A)

Brainstorm for Your Persuasive Essay

Read the assignment. You will complete the assignment in steps over multiple lessons.

Prompt: **Write a persuasive essay about a way to improve your city, town, or neighborhood.**

Requirements:

Your persuasive essay should have the following:

- A **title**

- An **introduction** that that gives information about your topic and clearly states your opinion

- At least two **body** paragraphs that have well-developed supporting reasons that are facts or reasonable opinions

- A **conclusion** that restates your opinion in a new way and summarizes your reasons

- **Transitions** such as *because* and *for example* that connect your opinion and reasons

- Words and phrases that are chosen for effect

- Correct **grammar**, **punctuation**, **capitalization**, and **spelling**

Audience: You will choose an audience based on your topic and opinion.

Purpose: Persuade your audience to agree with your opinion.

Length: 350–450 words long, approximately 5–7 handwritten drafting pages or $1\frac{1}{2}$–2 pages typed and double spaced

Answer the questions to choose a topic for your persuasive essay.

1. Think about topics you care about. Examples are *pets*, *reading*, and *recycling*. List as many topics as you can.

    _____   _____

    _____   _____

    _____   _____

    _____   _____

    _____   _____

2. Which topics on your list do you care most about?

    _____

    _____

3. Which topics are good ones for a persuasive essay about improving your community? Choose two topics, and restate them as opinions.

_____

_____

_____

_____

4. Choose the opinion you most want to write about.

Topic: _____

5. Based on your topic, choose the audience for your essay. Choose one person, business, or group of people.

Audience: _____

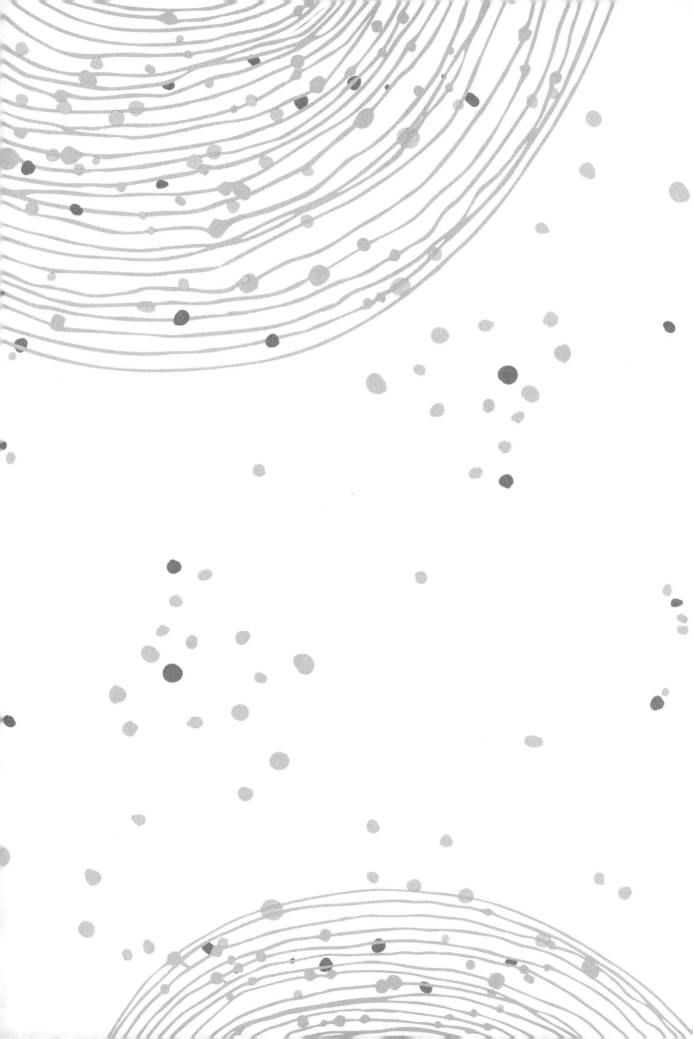

Opinion Writing: Prewriting (B)

Spelling List 18 Activity Bank

Circle any words in the box that you did not spell correctly on the pretest. Choose one activity to do with your circled words. Do as much of the activity as you can in the time given.

Did you spell all the words on the pretest correctly? Do the one activity with as many spelling words as you can.

scrap	splice	spring	squeak	strap
scrape	split	sprout	squeeze	straw
scream	sprain	squash	squint	strength
splash	spray	squat	stranger	stress
splendid				

Spelling Activity Choices

Silly Sentences

1. Write a silly sentence for each of your spelling words.

2. Underline the spelling word in each sentence.

   Example: The dog was <u>driving</u> a car.

3. Correct any spelling errors.

Spelling Story

1. Write a very short story using each of your spelling words.

2. Underline the spelling words in the story.

3. Correct any spelling errors.

Riddle Me This

1. Write a riddle for each of your spelling words.
   Example: "I have a trunk, but it's not on my car."

2. Write the answer, which is your word, for each riddle.
   Example: Answer: elephant

3. Correct any spelling errors.

RunOnWord

1. Gather some crayons, colored pencils, or markers. Use a different color to write each of your spelling words. Write the words end to end as one long word.
   Example: dogcatbirdfishturtle

2. Rewrite the words correctly and with proper spacing.

3. Correct any spelling errors.

Complete the activity that you chose.

My chosen activity: _____

_____

_____

_____

_____

_____

_____

_____

_____

_____

_____

_____

_____

_____

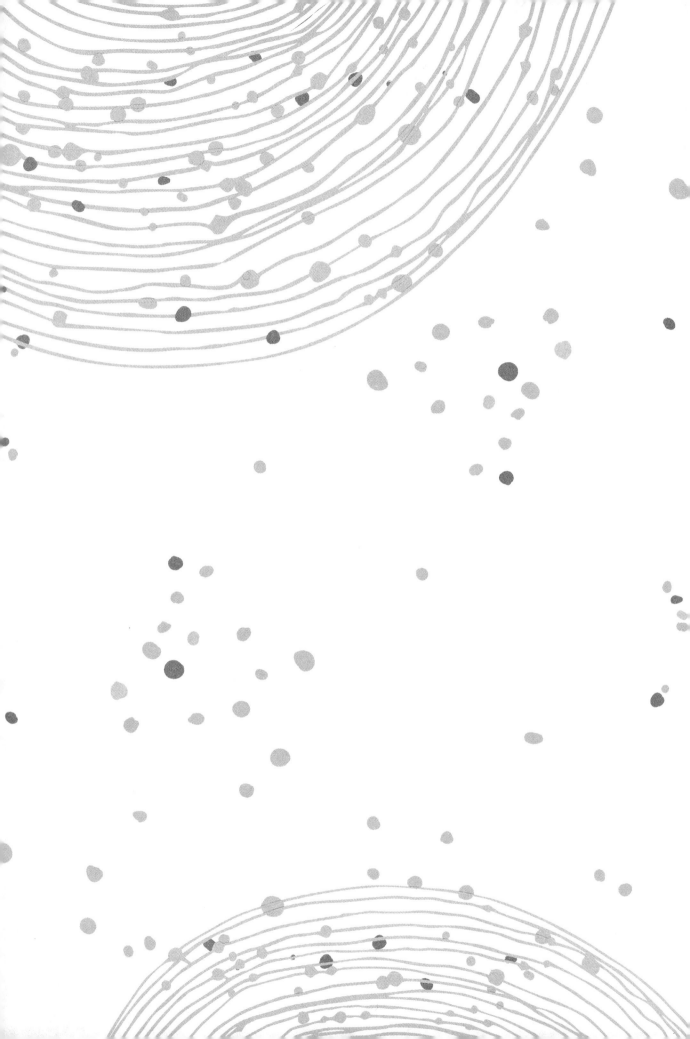

Opinion Writing: Prewriting (B)

Plan Your Persuasive Essay

Write the topic for your persuasive essay. List reasons that support your opinion. Next to each reason, write an *F* if the reason is a fact or an *O* if the reason is an opinion.

My topic is _____

Reasons	Fact or Opinion

Complete the graphic organizer to plan your persuasive essay.

Topic _____

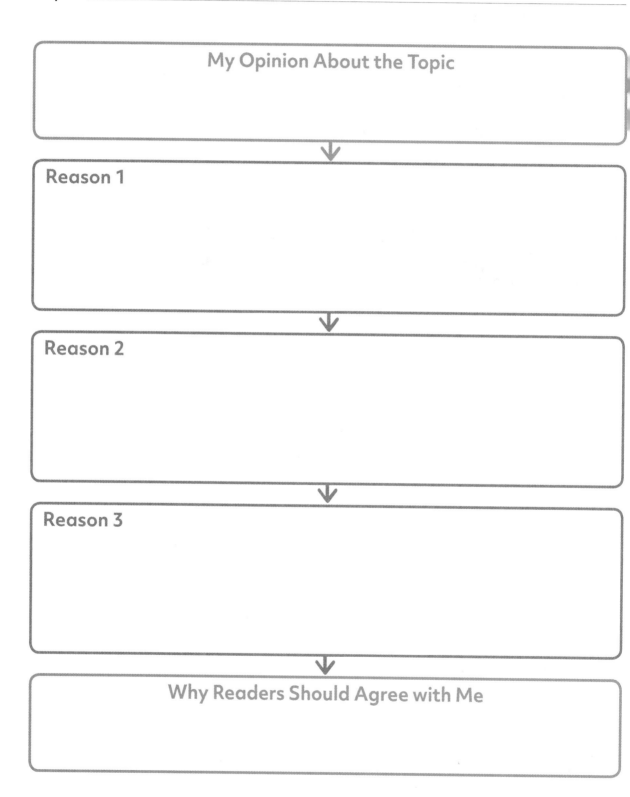

My Opinion About the Topic

↓

Reason 1

↓

Reason 2

↓

Reason 3

↓

Why Readers Should Agree with Me

Opinion Writing: Drafting (A)

Draft Your Persuasive Essay

Write the first draft of your persuasive essay. Write only on the white rows. You will use the purple rows for revisions later.

Title: _____

start here ►

keep writing ►

Draft Page 1

keep writing ▶

Draft Page 2

keep writing ►

Draft Page 3

keep writing ▶

Draft Page 4

keep writing ▶

Draft Page 5

keep writing ▶

Draft Page 6

keep writing ▶

Draft Page 7

Draft Page 8

Opinion Writing: Drafting (C)

Model Business Letter

Use this model to help you as you complete your own business letter.

heading

> 88 Lincoln Lane
> Lexington, VA 24450
> August 11, 2020

inside address

> Ms. Mary Hall
> Town Council
> 15 Main Street
> Lexington, VA 24450

salutation

> Dear Ms. Hall:

body

> Cedar Park is a nice place. It has a pond and lots of grass. There are swings, jungle gyms, soccer fields, and basketball courts. There is a lot to do in Cedar Park. Yet, Cedar Park does not have a tennis court. This must change. The city should build a tennis court in Cedar Park.
>
> Cedar Park should have a tennis court because playing tennis is fun. It is a great way to stay in shape, too. Also, Cedar Park is the only park with room for a tennis court. A tennis court would fit perfectly on the patch of grass behind the soccer fields. In addition, Cedar Park is a good place for a tennis court because it is in the middle of town. People can take a bus or walk to Cedar Park.

body —
⌈ The city should build a tennis court in Cedar Park
| because tennis is a great sport. The park has room for
| a court, and the park is easy to get to. Cedar Park is
⌊ already good, but a tennis court would make it great!

closing —
⌈ Sincerely,

signature —
⌈ *Johnny*
⌊ Johnny

Opinion Writing: Drafting (C)

Turn Your Persuasive Essay into a Business Letter

Think about the audience for your persuasive essay.

1. If your audience is one person, write that person's name. If your audience is a group of people, narrow down that group to one person whose opinion you would like to change.

You will turn your persuasive essay into a business letter to your audience. Follow the instructions to write the parts you will need to add to your essay. You will add these parts in a later lesson.

2. Write the heading. This is your address and the date. Put a comma between the city and state and between the day and year.

    Model heading:

    > 88 Lincoln Lane
    > Lexington, VA 24450
    > August 11, 2020

    Your heading:

    _____

    _____

    _____

3. Write the inside address. This is the address of your audience. Put a comma between the city and state.

Model inside address:

> Ms. Mary Hall
>
> Town Council
>
> 15 Main Street
>
> Lexington, VA 24450

Your inside address:

_____

_____

_____

_____

4. Write the salutation. Put a colon after the name.

Model salutation:

> Dear Ms. Hall:

Your salutation:

_____

5. Write the closing. Put a comma after the closing.

Model closing:

Sincerely,

Your closing:

_____

6. Write the signature. Sign your first and last names in cursive. Below that, clearly print your first and last names. (Johnny doesn't have a last name, but *you* do!)

Model signature:

Johnny

Johnny

Your signature:

_____

_____

It's a good thing I have been practicing cursive handwriting!

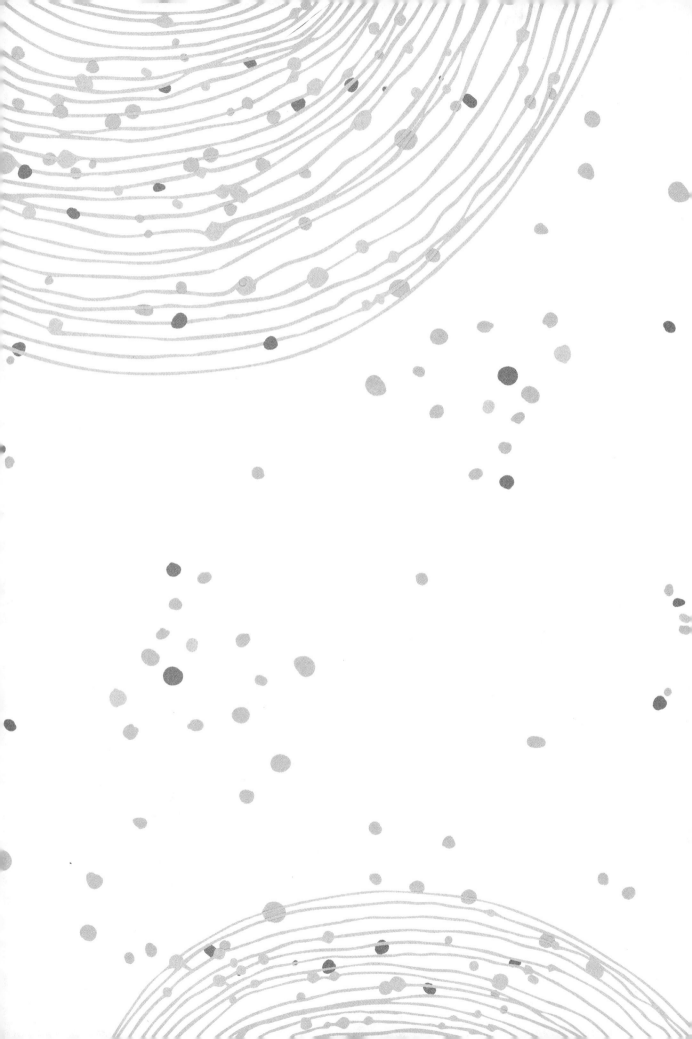

"Forecasting the Weather"

Spelling List 19 Pretest

1. Open the Spelling Pretest activity online. Listen to the first spelling word. Type the word. Check your answer.

2. Write the correct spelling of the word in the Word column of the Spelling Pretest table.

	Word	✓	✗
1	blindfold		

3. Put a check mark in the ✓ column if you spelled the word correctly online.

   Put an X in the ✗ column if you spelled the word incorrectly online.

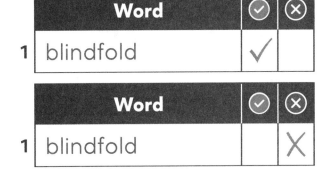

	Word	✓	✗
1	blindfold	✓	

	Word	✓	✗
1	blindfold		✗

4. Repeat Steps 1–3 for the remaining words in the Spelling Pretest.

"Forecasting the Weather"

Spelling List 19 Pretest

Write each spelling word in the Word column, making sure to spell it correctly.

	Word	✓	✗
1			
2			
3			
4			
5			
6			
7			
8			
9			
10			
11			
12			
13			

	Word	✓	✗
14			
15			
16			
17			
18			
19			
20			
21			
22			
23			
24			
25			

"Forecasting the Weather"

Write About Text Features

Use *K12 World: Weather, Weather Everywhere* to answer the questions. Use complete sentences.

1. Answer the question in the caption with the picture of the girl and outdoor thermometer on page 4.

_____

_____

2. Answer the question with the picture of the groundhog on page 10.

_____

_____

3. Look at the pictures on page 5. What do they show?

_____

_____

4. Use the sidebar on page 6 to explain how supercomputers are used to predict the weather.

_____

_____

_____

_____

The forecast calls for sunshine. I'm ready for it!

"Forecasting the Weather" Wrap-Up

Spelling List 19 Activity Bank

Circle any words in the box that you did not spell correctly on your pretest. Choose one activity to do with your circled words. Do as much of the activity as you can in the time given.

Did you spell all the words on the pretest correctly? Do the one activity with as many spelling words as you can.

branch	lunch	shadow	thrill	kitchen
brothers	paragraph	shower	throne	match
bunch	phonics	shred	blotch	scratch
chatter	phrase	shrimp	catch	stretch
health	refresh	telephone	ketchup	watch

Spelling Activity Choices

Hidden Words

1. Draw a picture. "Hide" as many of your spelling words as you can inside the picture.

2. See if others can find the words you hid in the picture.

Triangle Spelling

Write each of your spelling words in a triangle.

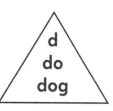

d
do
dog

Ghost Words

1. Use a white crayon to write each of your spelling words.

2. Write over the words in white crayon with a colored marker.

Complete the activity that you chose.

My chosen activity: _____

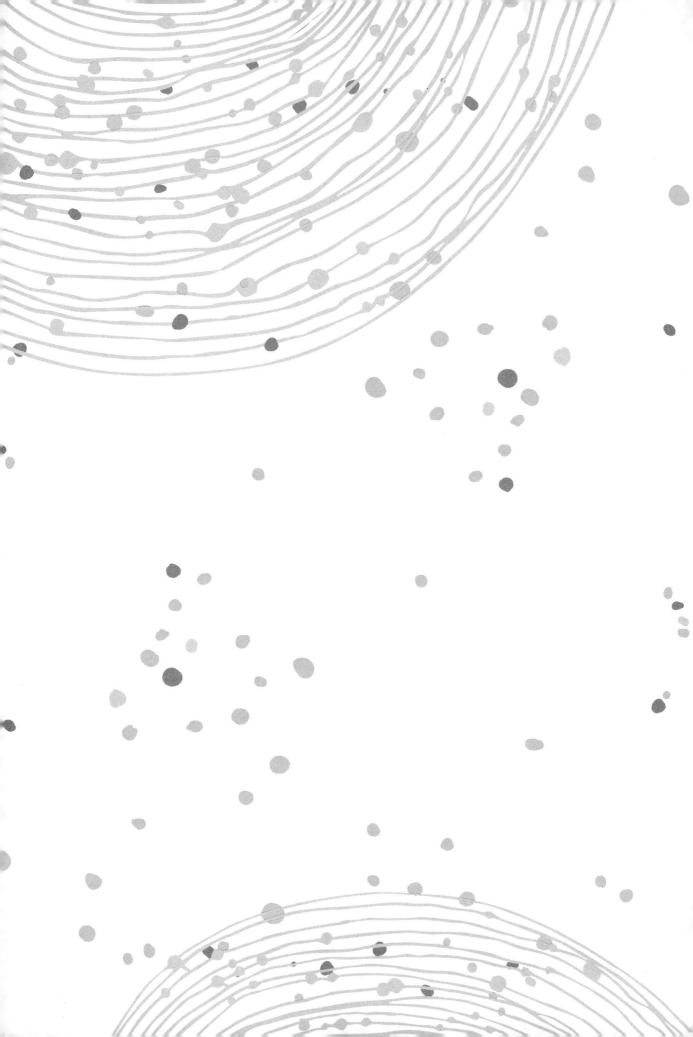

"Forecasting the Weather" Wrap-Up

Create a Comic Strip

Use the information from "Forecasting the Weather" to create a comic strip that explains how to forecast the weather. Include at least two characters in your comic strip. Use signal words for sequence in the dialogue between your characters.

Write a paragraph that explains what happens in each panel of your comic strip. Use signal words for sequence in your explanation.

_____

_____

_____

_____

_____

_____

_____

"Let It Rain"

Write About Clouds

Choose two cloud types from "Let It Rain." For each cloud type, write a main idea and two supporting details that give more information about the main idea. Use complete sentences.

Cloud 1 Main Idea

_____

_____

Cloud 1 Supporting Details

_____

_____

_____

_____

Cloud 2 Main Idea

_____

_____

Cloud 2 Supporting Details

_____

_____

_____

_____

"Let It Rain" Wrap-Up

Teach a Lesson About Clouds

It's time for you to be the teacher! Create a study guide.

• Identify two different cloud types.

• Explain as much as you can about each cloud using the article "Let It Rain" and the Write About Clouds activity page to help you. Use complete sentences.

• Illustrate the clouds.

Can't decide which clouds to write about? Look outside!

Cloud 1 _____

_____

_____

_____

_____

_____

_____

_____

_____

_____

Cloud 2

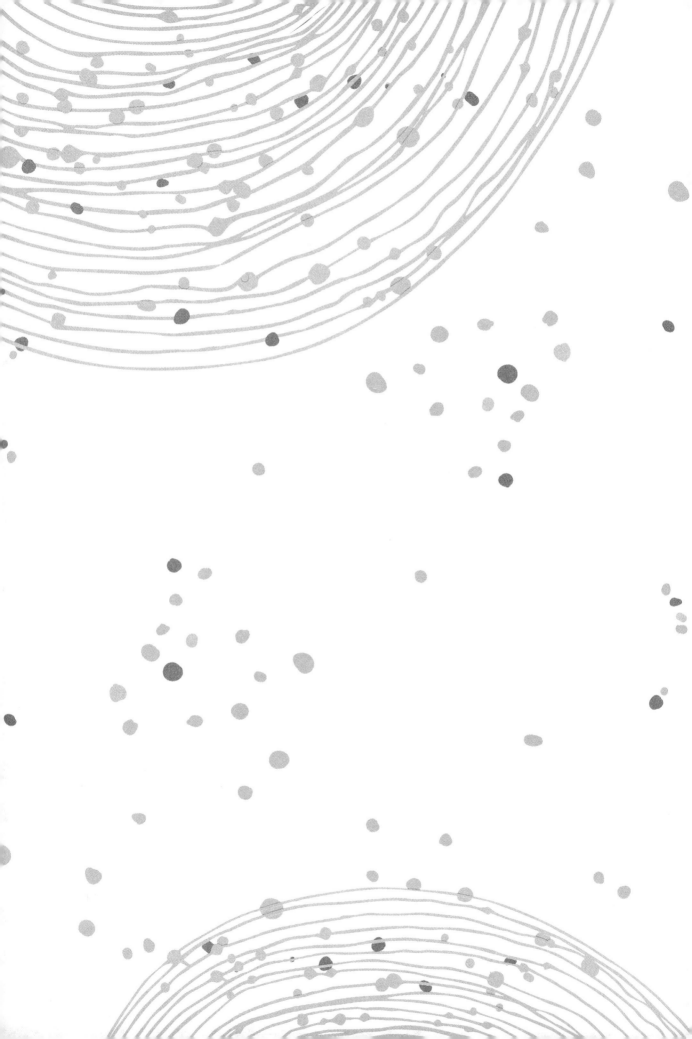

"Winter Storms"

Prepare to Write About Cause and Effect

Think about the weather where you live. What effect does it have on you? Brainstorm a cause and some effects.

Cause: the weather where I live

Effect: what I do or don't do because of the weather

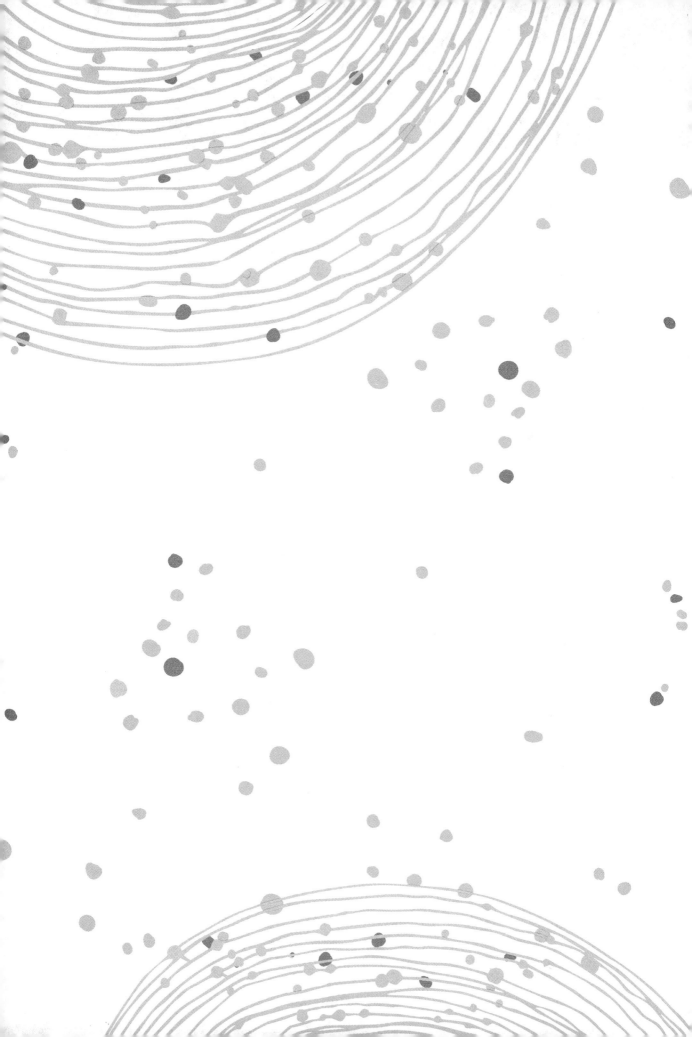

Write About Cause and Effect

Read the writing prompt.

Prompt: **Write a three-paragraph essay about how the weather where you live affects you. Include the following:**

- A title

- Paragraph 1: An introduction to the topic

- Paragraph 2: A body paragraph that explains the effects of the weather

- Paragraph 3: A conclusion

- Signal words that connect your ideas and show cause and effect

Respond to the writing prompt. Use your completed Prepare to Write About Cause and Effect activity page to help you.

Spelling List 20 Pretest

1. **Open the Spelling Pretest activity online. Listen to the first spelling word. Type the word. Check your answer.**

2. **Write the correct spelling of the word in the Word column of the Spelling Pretest table.**

Word	✓	✗
1 blindfold		

3. **Put a check mark in the ✓ column if you spelled the word correctly online.**

Word	✓	✗
1 blindfold	✓	

   Put an X in the ✗ column if you spelled the word incorrectly online.

Word	✓	✗
1 blindfold		✗

4. **Repeat Steps 1–3 for the remaining words in the Spelling Pretest.**

"Wind"

Spelling List 20 Pretest

Write each spelling word in the Word column, making sure to spell it correctly.

	Word	✓	✗
1			
2			
3			
4			
5			
6			
7			
8			
9			

	Word	✓	✗
10			
11			
12			
13			
14			
15			
16			
17			

Compare and Contrast Types of Storms

Complete the T chart to record the ways that hurricanes and tornadoes are alike and different.

One example for each column has been done for you. Write at least two more examples in each column.

Alike	Different
• Both are storms.	• Hurricanes form over warm water. Tornadoes form over land.

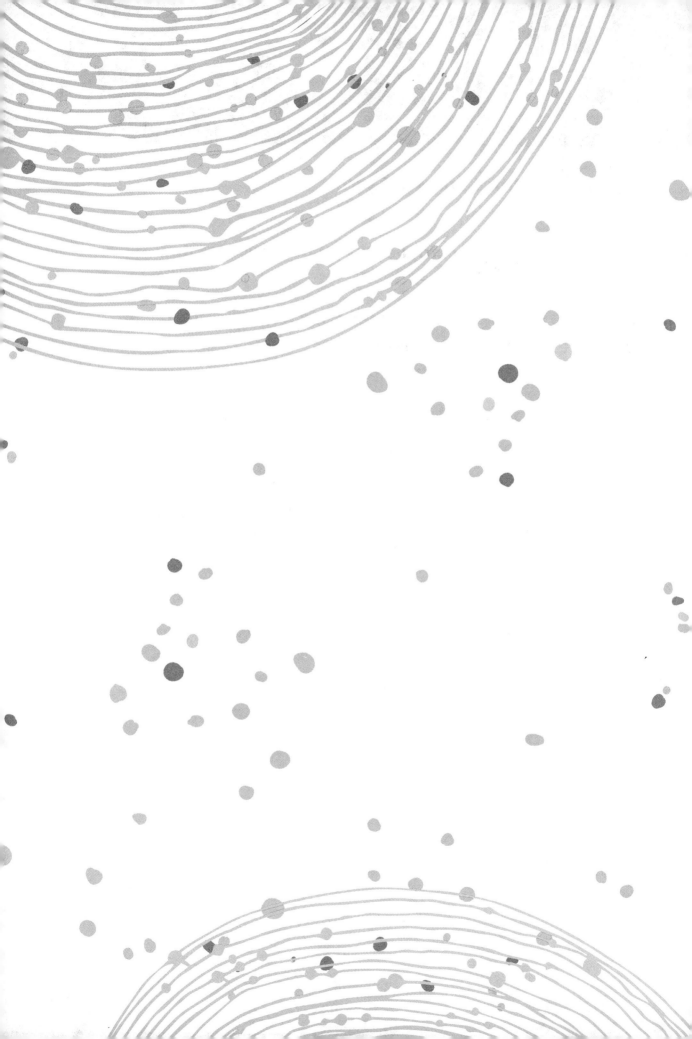

GET READY

"Wind" Wrap-Up

Spelling List 20 Activity Bank

Circle any words in the box that you did not spell correctly on your pretest. Choose one activity to do with your circled words. Do as much of the activity as you can in the time given.

Did you spell all the words on the pretest correctly? Do the one activity with as many spelling words as you can.

bravely	delightful	hopeful	lonely	strangely
careful	fairness	joyful	peaceful	suddenly
dampness	faithful	kindness	quickly	totally
darkness	finally			

Spelling Activity Choices

Create a Crossword

1. Write one of your spelling words going down in the center of the grid.

2. Write another spelling word going across that shares a letter with the first word. See how many words you can connect.

Example:

			p			
		k	i	s	s	e	s
	d		n			
r	o	c	k	s			
	g					
	s					

Word Search Puzzle

1. Draw a box on the grid. The box should be large enough to hold your spelling words.

2. Fill in the grid with your spelling words. Write them across, up and down, and diagonally. You can write them forward and backward.

3. Fill in the rest of the box with random letters.

4. Ask someone to find and circle your words in the puzzle.

Complete the activity that you chose.

My chosen activity: _____

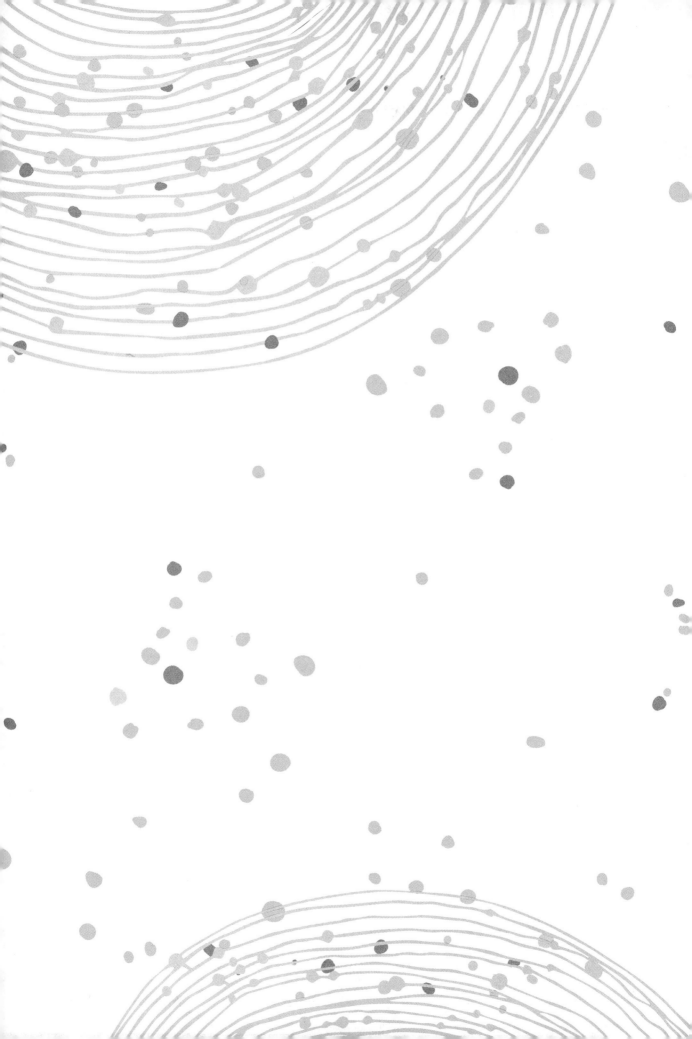

"Wind" Wrap-Up

Write About the Weather

Flip through *K12 World: Weather, Weather Everywhere.*
Choose a topic from the magazine that you'd like to write about.

What topic will you write about?

_____

Read the writing prompt.

Prompt: Write a three-paragraph essay using question-and-answer organization structure.

- Paragraph 1: Ask a question, and explain why you are asking that question.

- Paragraph 2: Answer the question, using details.

- Paragraph 3: Conclude your essay.

Respond to the writing prompt.

_____

_____

_____

_____

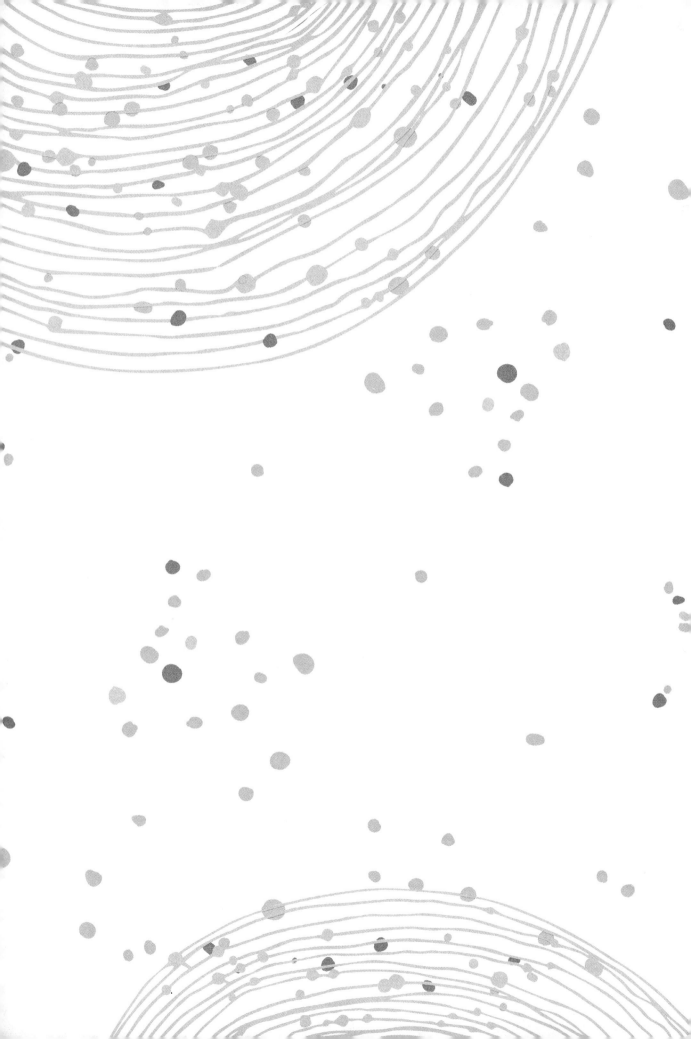

TRY IT

"Storm Chasers"

Brainstorm Steps in a Process

Flip through *K12 World: Weather, Weather Everywhere.*
Choose a process explained in one of the articles. Then,
brainstorm the steps someone would go through to complete
the process you chose. If the steps need to be completed in a
certain order, number the steps.

Process I will write about:

_____

Steps to complete the process:

_____

_____

_____

_____

_____

_____

_____

_____

"Storm Chasers" Wrap-Up

Write About Steps in a Process

Read the writing prompt.

Prompt: **Write a three-paragraph essay that thoroughly explains the process you identified on the Brainstorm Steps in a Process activity page.**

- Paragraph 1: Write a short introduction to the process.

- Paragraph 2: Explain the steps in the process. Use signal words if they help explain the process.

- Paragraph 3: Write why the process is important.

Respond to the writing prompt.

_____

_____

_____

_____

_____

_____

_____

If you would like, illustrate the process you are describing.

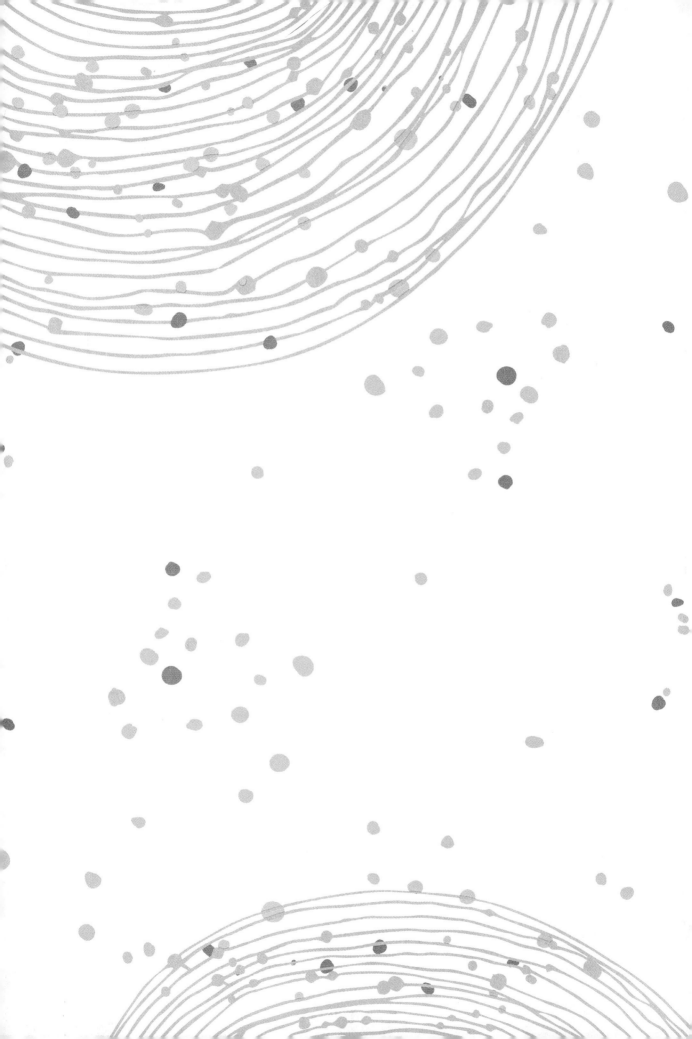

Meteorology Words

Apply: Meteorology Words

Choose the word from the Word Bank that best completes the sentence. Use context clues to help you.

Word Bank

forecast	moisture	humid
frost	gusty	shower

1. Let's watch the weather _____ on the news so we know whether to bring an umbrella today.

2. My dad had to leave extra time to get ready this morning. He had to scrape the _____ off his car.

3. The _____ winds outside make it look like the trees are dancing.

4. The air is so _____; it makes me feel like I need to wipe my face off the minute I step outside.

5. When Anita plays soccer, she likes to wear a shirt that keeps the _____ away from her body.

6. Bella wasn't prepared for the afternoon _____.
She forgot her raincoat at home.

I think the forecast
I read was wrong.

Meteorology Words

Go Write! Reasons to Write

Respond to the prompt. Or, write about a topic of your choice!

Prompt: **What are some reasons for writing to someone? Who have you written to, and what was your reason for writing?**

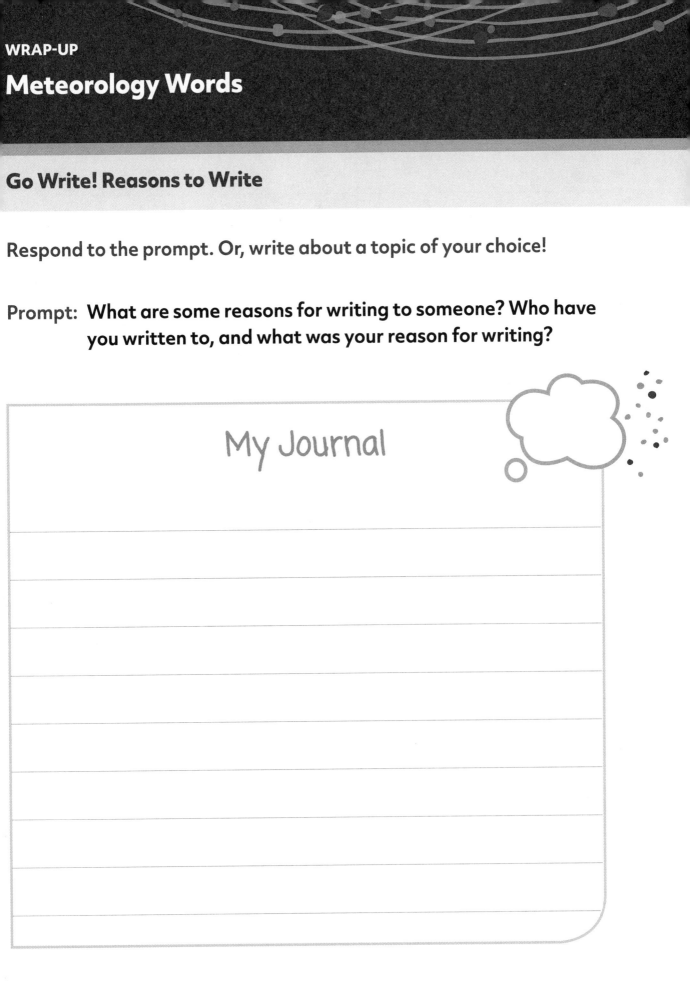

My Journal

Poetry (A)

Spelling List 21 Pretest

1. Open the Spelling Pretest activity online. Listen to the first spelling word. Type the word. Check your answer.

2. Write the correct spelling of the word in the Word column of the Spelling Pretest table.

Word	✓	✗
1 blindfold		

3. Put a check mark in the ✓ column if you spelled the word correctly online.

Word	✓	✗
1 blindfold	✓	

Put an X in the ✗ column if you spelled the word incorrectly online.

Word	✓	✗
1 blindfold		✗

4. Repeat Steps 1–3 for the remaining words in the Spelling Pretest.

Poetry (A)

Spelling List 21 Pretest

Write each spelling word in the Word column, making sure to spell it correctly.

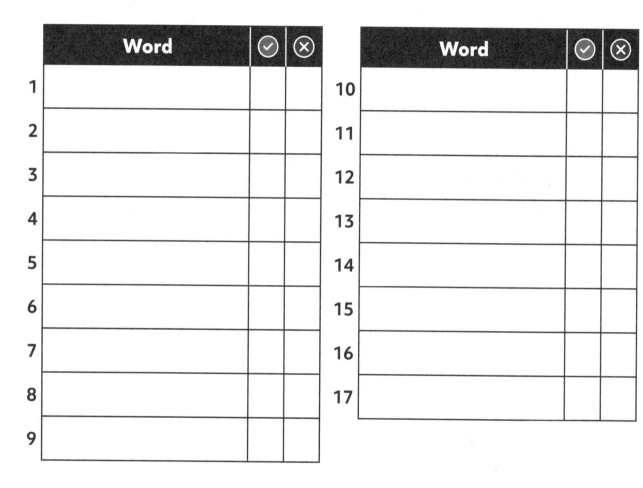

	Word	✓	✗
1			
2			
3			
4			
5			
6			
7			
8			
9			

	Word	✓	✗
10			
11			
12			
13			
14			
15			
16			
17			

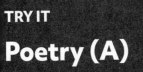

TRY IT

Poetry (A)

Write a Descriptive Poem

Read the writing prompt.

Prompt: Write a descriptive poem about a person, place, object, idea, or feeling.

- Decide who or what you would like to describe.

- Use sensory language.

- Use at least one type of figurative language, such as a simile.

- Use at least one sound pattern in your poem, such as rhyme.

Respond to the writing prompt.

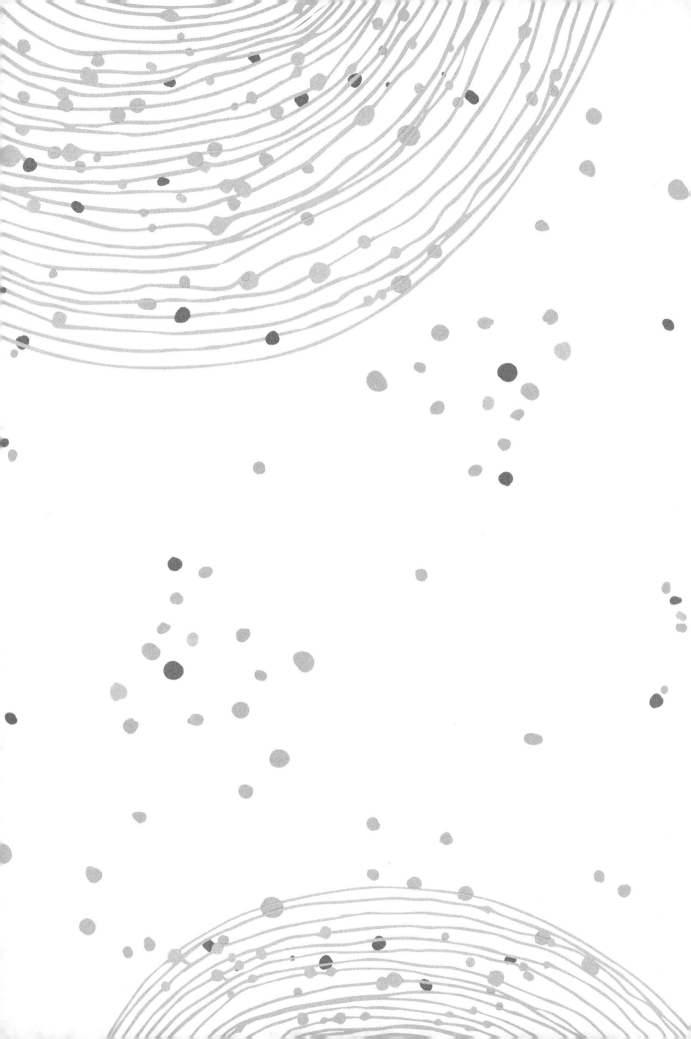

Poetry (B)

Spelling List 21 Activity Bank

Circle any words in the box that you did not spell correctly on your pretest. Choose one activity to do with your circled words. Do as much of the activity as you can in the time given.

Did you spell all the words on the pretest correctly? Do the one activity with as many spelling words as you can.

dishonest	disqualify	reinstall	unbend	unfinished
disobey	disrespect	reissue	underdog	untie
disown	reconsider	rethink	underline	unwrap
displease	reenter			

Spelling Activity Choices

Alphabetizing

1. In the left column, write your spelling words in alphabetical order.

2. Correct any spelling errors.

Vowel-Free Words

1. In the left column, write only the consonants in each of your spelling words. Put a dot where each vowel should be.

2. Spell each word aloud, stating which vowels should be in the places with dots.

3. In the right column, rewrite the entire spelling word.

4. Correct any spelling errors.

Rhymes

1. In the left column, write your spelling words.

2. In the right column, write a word that rhymes with each spelling word.

3. Correct any spelling errors.

Uppercase and Lowercase

1. In the left column, write each of your spelling words in all uppercase letters.

2. In the right column, write each of your spelling words in all lowercase letters.

3. Correct any spelling errors.

Complete the activity that you chose.

My chosen activity: _____

1. _____ _____

2. _____ _____

3. _____ _____

4. _____ _____

5. _____ _____

6. _____ _____

7. _____ _____

8. _____ _____

9. _____ _____

10. _____ _____

11. _____ _____

12. _____ _____

13. _____ _____

14. _____ _____

15. _____ _____

16. _____ _____

17. _____ _____

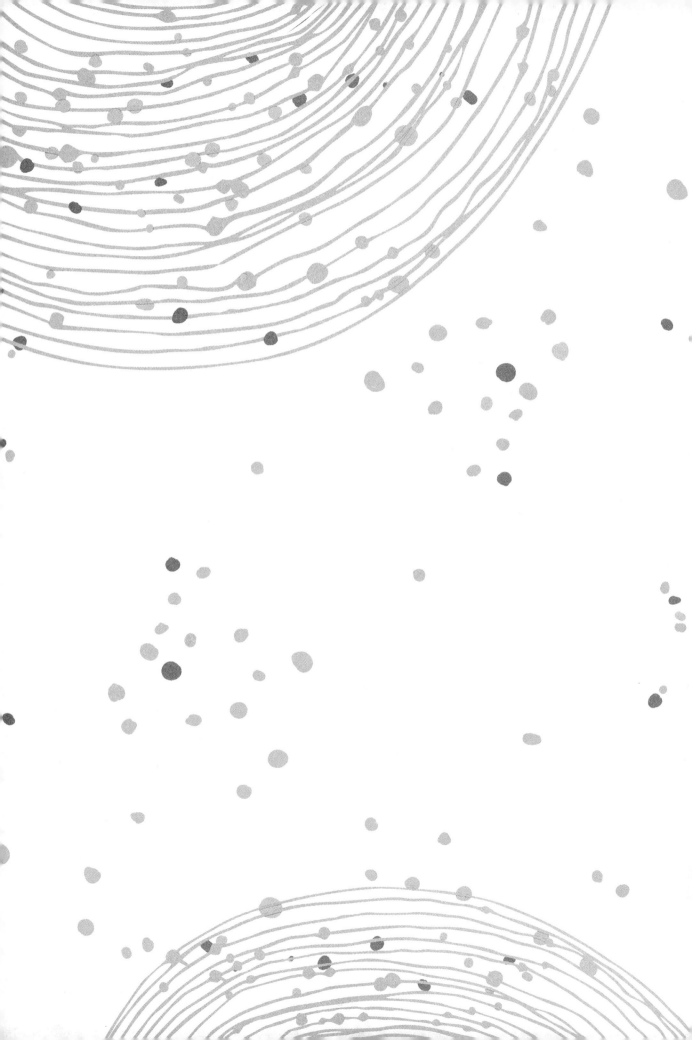

TRY IT

Poetry (B)

Write a Narrative Poem

Read the writing prompt.

Prompt: Write a narrative poem, which is a poem that tells a story.

- Decide on a story you would like to tell.

- Include a beginning, middle, and end.

- Include at least one character.

- Use sensory details and figurative language.

- Use at least one sound pattern in your poem, such as rhyme.

Respond to the writing prompt.

_____

_____

_____

_____

_____

_____

_____

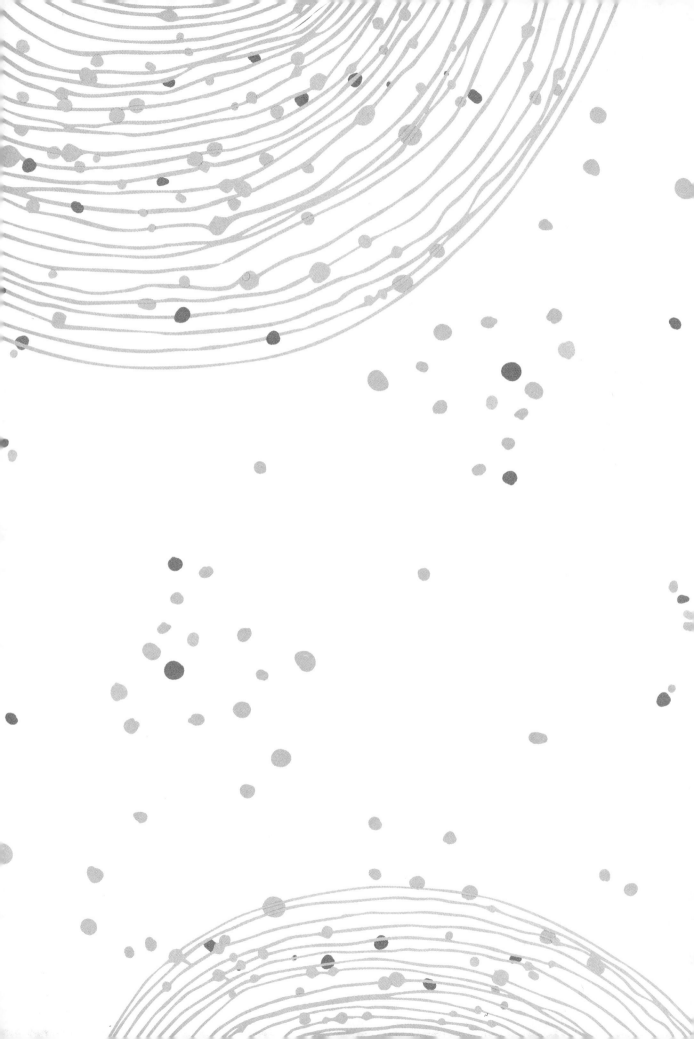

Write or Expand a Poem

Read the writing prompt.

Prompt: **Write another narrative or descriptive poem. Or, expand one of the poems you wrote to make it longer.**

Respond to the writing prompt.

_____

_____

_____

_____

_____

_____

_____

_____

_____

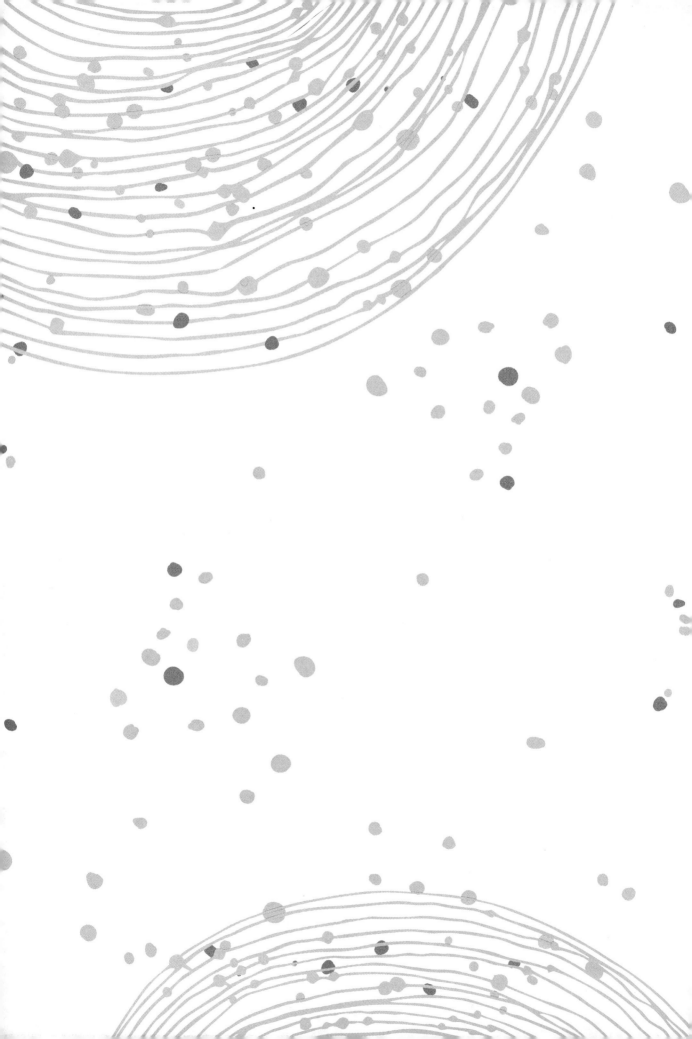

Poetry Wrap-Up

Revise and Publish a Poem

Reread the poems that you wrote. Choose one poem to revise. Use the appropriate checklist to revise your poem. Mark your revisions on your poem.

Checklist for Revising a **Descriptive** Poem

☐ Did I describe a person, place, object, idea, or feeling?

☐ Did I include figurative language to create a picture in readers' minds?

☐ Did I include sensory details?

☐ Did I use any sound elements, such as rhyme?

Checklist for Revising a **Narrative** Poem

☐ Did I include a clear beginning, middle, and end?

☐ Did I include figurative language to create a picture in readers' minds?

☐ Did I include sensory details?

☐ Did I use any sound elements, such as rhyme?

Write or type a clean copy of your poem. Include an illustration if you wish.

Opinion Writing: Revising

Revise Your Persuasive Essay

Read your persuasive essay draft. Then, use the checklist to improve your organization and ideas. Make changes on your draft.

Ideas

- ☐ Does my introduction give background information about my topic?

- ☐ Does my introduction state my opinion clearly?

- ☐ Does each body paragraph begin with a topic sentence?

- ☐ Does each body paragraph give reasons that are facts or reasonable opinions?

- ☐ Do all of my reasons support my opinion? Do any need more details?

- ☐ Are my reasons appropriate for my audience and purpose?

- ☐ Does my conclusion summarize my reasons?

- ☐ Does my conclusion state my opinion differently than I stated it in the introduction?

(continued)

Organization

☐ Does each body paragraph contain related ideas? Do I need to put any ideas in a new paragraph?

☐ Do I use transitions to connect ideas?

Opinion Writing: Proofreading

Proofread Your Persuasive Essay

Read your revised persuasive essay draft and Turn Your Persuasive Essay into a Business Letter activity page. Then, use the checklist to improve your grammar, usage, and mechanics. Make changes on your revised draft and activity page.

Grammar and Usage

- ☐ Are all sentences complete and correct?

- ☐ Is there a variety of sentence types and lengths?

- ☐ Did I form and use verbs correctly?

- ☐ Did I use adjectives and adverbs correctly? Did I choose strong adjectives and adverbs?

- ☐ Is my language appropriate for my audience?

- ☐ Are there any missing or extra words?

(continued)

Mechanics

- ☐ Is every word spelled correctly?

- ☐ Does every sentence begin with a capital letter and end with correct punctuation?

- ☐ Did I put a comma between the city and state in each address?

- ☐ Did I follow the correct format for all parts of a business letter?

Opinion Writing: Publishing

Publish Your Business Letter

Read the assignment.

Prompt: **Write a business letter about a way to improve your city, town, or neighborhood.**

Requirements:

Your business letter should have the following parts:

- Heading

- Inside address

- Salutation

- Body (your revised persuasive essay)

  o An **introduction** that gives information about your topic and clearly states your opinion

  o At least two **body** paragraphs that have well-developed supporting reasons that are facts or reasonable opinions

  o A **conclusion** that restates your opinion in a new way and summarizes your reasons

  o **Transitions** such as *because* and *for example* that connect your opinion and reasons

  o Words and phrases chosen for effect

- A closing

- A signature

- Correct **grammar**, **punctuation**, **capitalization**, and **spelling**

Audience: You will choose an audience based on your topic and opinion.

Purpose: Persuade your audience to agree with your opinion.

Length: 400–500 words long, approximately 2 pages typed and double spaced

Type a clean copy of your business letter. Include your revising and proofreading changes. Follow the format of the Model Business Letter.

I am going to double-check my formatting.

Apply: Suffixes

Write the definition for each suffix.

1. –ly _____   –ish _____

 –ness _____   –er/or _____

 –less _____   –ful _____

Form new words with suffixes, and then use one of the new words in a sentence.

2. Add suffixes from Question 1 to form words that match the definitions.

green _____ : almost the color green

joy _____ : full of joy

sing _____ : someone who sings

3. Choose a word from Question 2. Write 1–2 sentences that show the meaning of the word.

_____

_____

_____

4. Add suffixes from Question 1 to form words that match the definitions.

color _____ : full of colors

teach _____ : someone who teaches

elf _____ : almost like an elf

5. Choose a word from Question 4. Write 1–2 sentences that show the meaning of the word.

_____

_____

_____

Answer the question.

6. Which word correctly completes the sentence? Circle the word.

   careful   reddish   writer

   Marc was _____ not to spill his drink when moving it
   from the counter to the table.

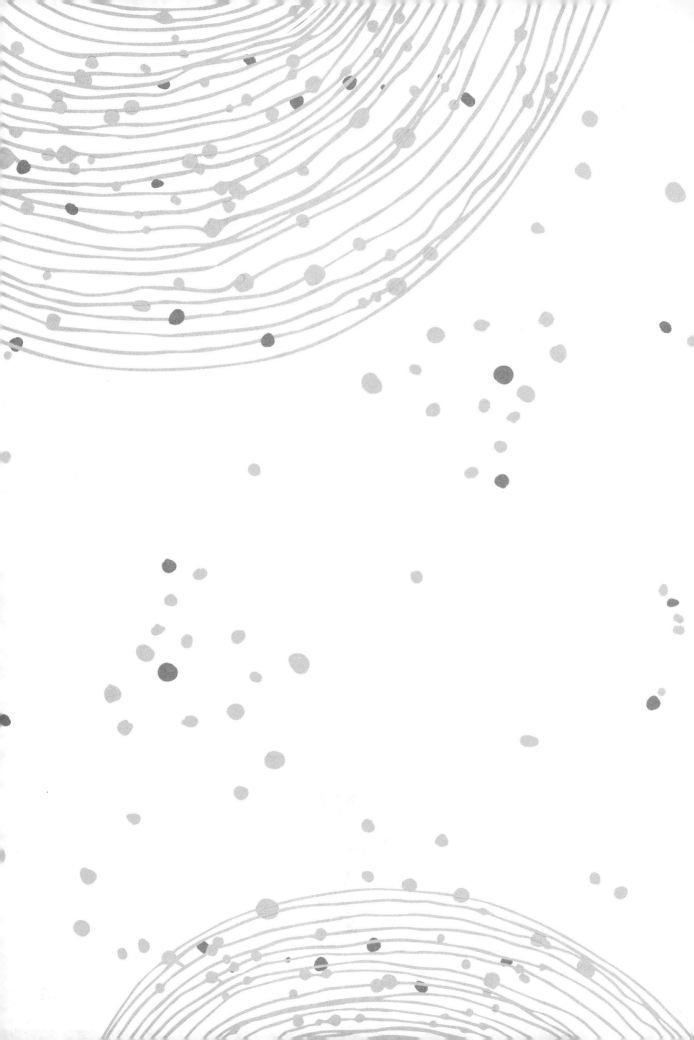

Go Write! Speak to a Group

Respond to the prompt. Or, write about a topic of your choice!

Prompt: **Do you like to speak in front of a group? Explain why or why not.**

My Journal

Presentation Skills (A)

Add the Perfect Picture

Listen to the speech in the online activity. Then, answer the questions.

1. Draw a picture or take a photograph that supports the main idea or an important supporting detail from the speech. (Instead of drawing, you may describe your picture.)

2. Explain how your visual supports the main idea or an important supporting detail from the speech.

_____

_____

_____

_____

_____

_____

_____

_____

Have you ever heard this saying? "A picture is worth 1,000 words."

Read a Poem Aloud

Use the recording tool in the online activity to answer
the questions.

1. Record yourself reading the poem.

My Shoes

I tried to find my shoes today.

I looked both high and low, but

I could not find them anywhere.

I wonder where they go.

I wonder if they take a walk

Without me in the night,

I wonder if they go play ball.

That would be such a sight.

I think they run around the house,

Their eyes all full of dread.

I always seem to find them hiding

Underneath my bed.

2. Listen to what you recorded.

   a. Did you speak too quickly or too slowly during any parts? Identify one way you could improve your pace.

   _____

   _____

   b. Did you read all words clearly? Identify one way you could improve your clarity.

   _____

   _____

3. Record yourself reading the poem again. Use your answers to Question 2 to improve your pace and clarity.

Found you, buddy!

Presentation Skills Wrap-Up

Use Presentation Skills

Use the picture prompt to answer the questions.

1. What is happening in this picture? Identify the main idea and three supporting details.

Main Idea

↓

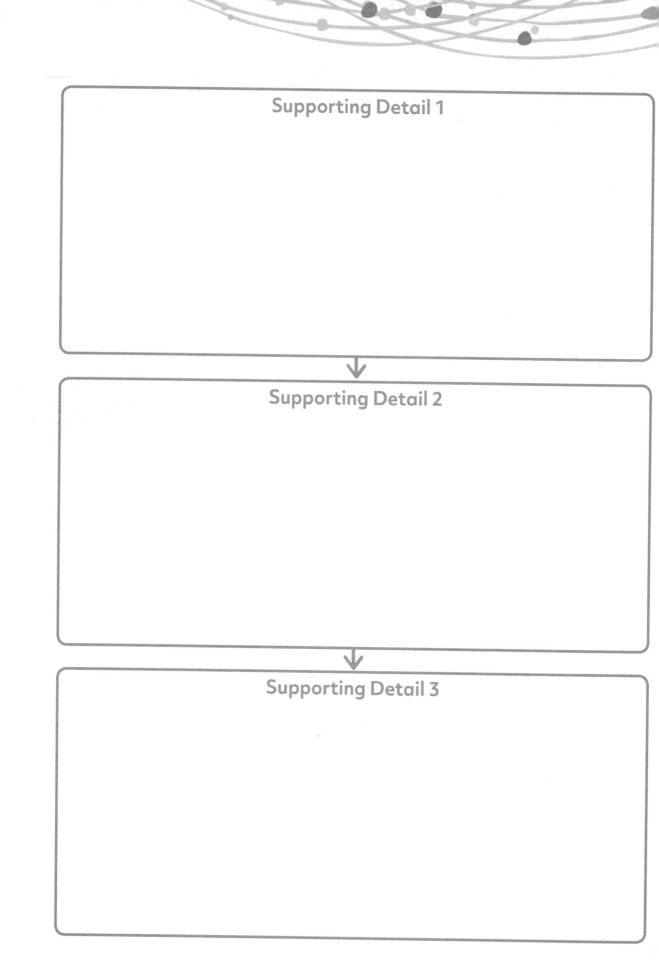

Supporting Detail 1

Supporting Detail 2

Supporting Detail 3

2. Record a speech explaining what is happening in the picture. Begin by explaining the main idea. Then, describe the supporting details. Speak clearly and at a good pace.

3. Listen to your speech.

   a. Describe two strengths of your speech.

_____

_____

_____

_____

   b. Describe two ways you could improve your speech.

_____

_____

_____

_____

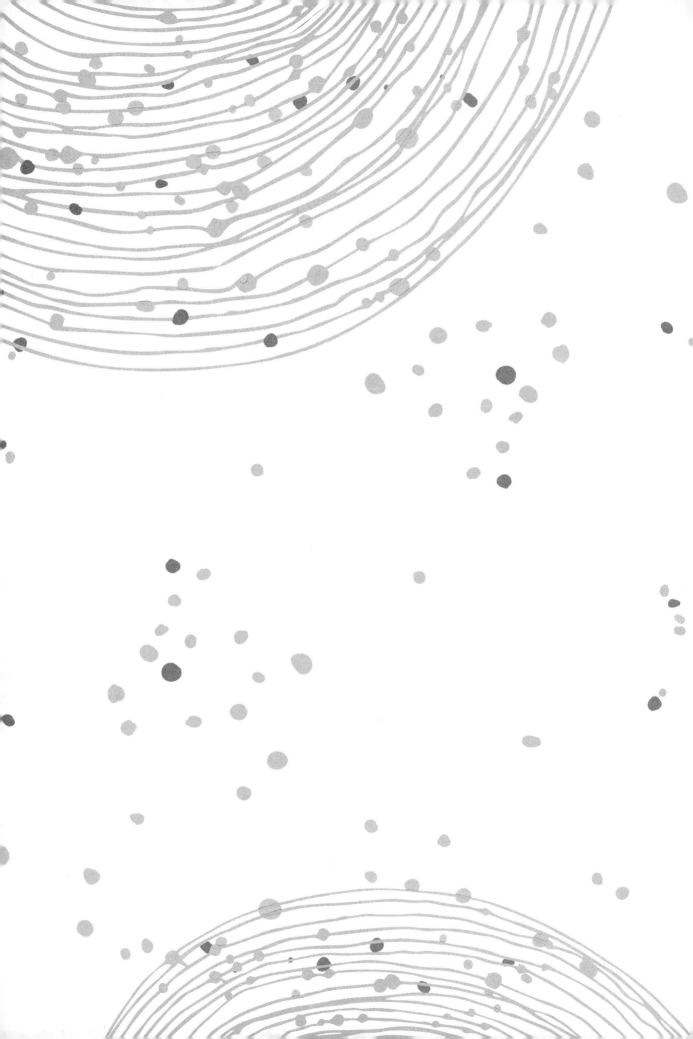

Choice Reading Project (A)

Spelling List 22 Pretest

1. Open the Spelling Pretest activity online. Listen to the first spelling word. Type the word. Check your answer.

2. Write the correct spelling of the word in the Word column of the Spelling Pretest table.

Word	✓	✗
1 blindfold		

3. Put a check mark in the ✓ column if you spelled the word correctly online.

Put an X in the ✗ column if you spelled the word incorrectly online.

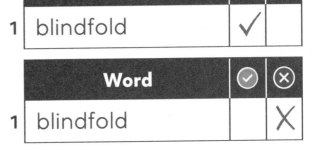

Word	✓	✗
1 blindfold	✓	

Word	✓	✗
1 blindfold		✗

4. Repeat Steps 1–3 for the remaining words in the Spelling Pretest.

Choice Reading Project (A)

Spelling List 22 Pretest

Write each spelling word in the Word column, making sure to spell it correctly.

	Word	✓	✗
1			
2			
3			
4			
5			
6			
7			
8			
9			
10			
11			

	Word	✓	✗
12			
13			
14			
15			
16			
17			
18			
19			
20			
21			

Choice Reading Project (B)

Spelling List 22 Activity Bank

Circle any words in the box that you did not spell correctly on the pretest. Choose one activity to do with your circled words. Do as much of the activity as you can in the time given.

Did you spell all the words on the pretest correctly? Do the one activity with as many spelling words as you can.

badge	general	jellyfish	jungle	ranger
edge	giant	jolly	large	ridge
energy	gorge	judge	ledge	stage
garage	huge	juice	oxygen	strange
gelatin				

Spelling Activity Choices

Silly Sentences

1. Write a silly sentence for each of your spelling words.

2. Underline the spelling word in each sentence.
   Example: The dog was <u>driving</u> a car.

3. Correct any spelling errors.

Spelling Story

1. Write a very short story using each of your spelling words.

2. Underline the spelling words in the story.

3. Correct any spelling errors.

Riddle Me This

1. Write a riddle for each of your spelling words.
   Example: "I have a trunk, but it's not on my car."

2. Write the answer, which is your word, for each riddle.
   Example: Answer: elephant

3. Correct any spelling errors.

RunOnWord

1. Gather some crayons, colored pencils, or markers. Use a different color to write each of your spelling words. Write the words end to end as one long word.
   Example: dogcatbirdfishturtle

2. Rewrite the words correctly and with proper spacing.

3. Correct any spelling errors.

Complete the activity that you chose.

My chosen activity: _____

_____

_____

_____

_____

_____

_____

_____

_____

_____

_____

_____

_____

_____

_____

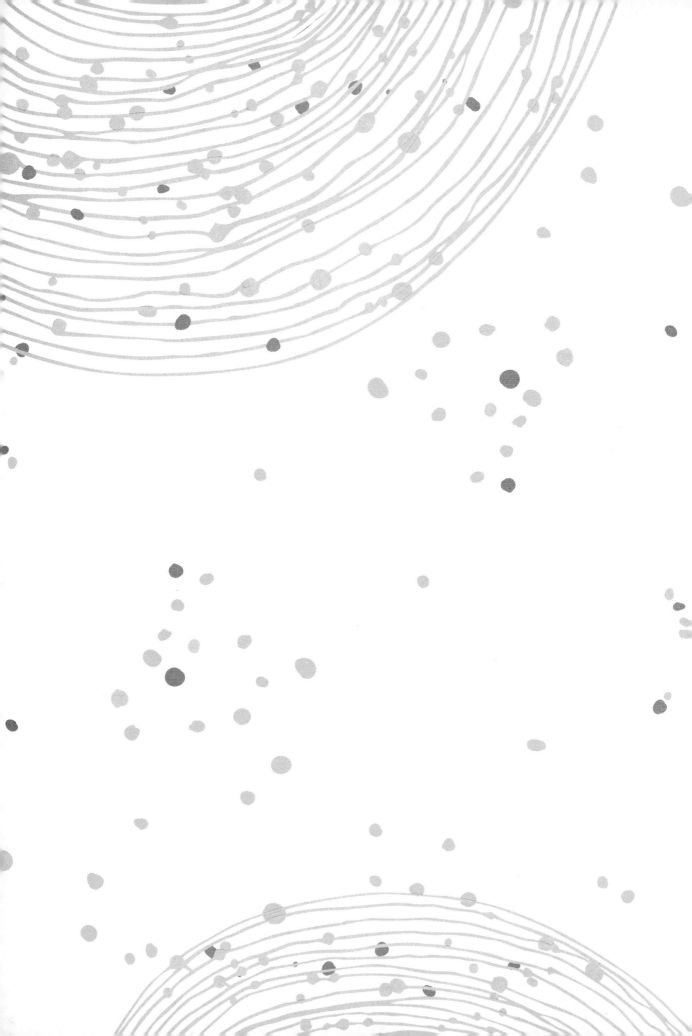

Choice Reading Project (F)

Spelling List 23 Pretest

1. Open the Spelling Pretest activity online. Listen to the first spelling word. Type the word. Check your answer.

2. Write the correct spelling of the word in the Word column of the Spelling Pretest table.

	Word	✓	✗
1	blindfold		

3. Put a check mark in the ✓ column if you spelled the word correctly online.

	Word	✓	✗
1	blindfold	✓	

Put an X in the ✗ column if you spelled the word incorrectly online.

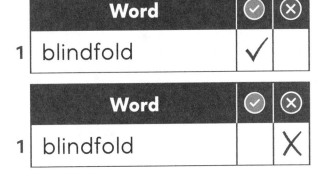

	Word	✓	✗
1	blindfold		✗

4. Repeat Steps 1–3 for the remaining words in the Spelling Pretest.

Choice Reading Project (F)

Spelling List 23 Pretest

Write each spelling word in the Word column, making sure to spell it correctly.

	Word	✓	✗
1			
2			
3			
4			
5			
6			
7			
8			
9			
10			
11			

	Word	✓	✗
12			
13			
14			
15			
16			
17			
18			
19			
20			
21			

Choice Reading Project (G)

Spelling List 23 Activity Bank

Circle any words in the box that you did not spell correctly on your pretest. Choose one activity to do with your circled words. Do as much of the activity as you can in the time given.

Did you spell all the words on the pretest correctly? Do the one activity with as many spelling words as you can.

bagel	marvel	example	possible	shuffle
camel	nickel	jingle	purple	single
damsel	shovel	little	scramble	syllable
funnel	towel	middle	settle	uncle
grovel				

Spelling Activity Choices

Hidden Words

1. Draw a picture. "Hide" as many of your spelling words as you can inside the picture.

2. See if others can find the words you hid in the picture.

Triangle Spelling

Write each of your spelling words in a triangle.

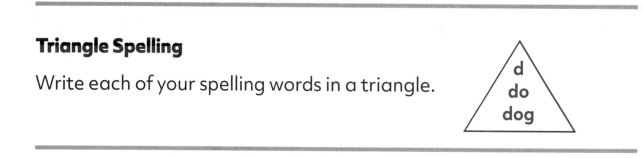

Ghost Words

1. Use a white crayon to write each of your spelling words.

2. Write over the words in white crayon with a colored marker.

Complete the activity that you chose.

My chosen activity: _____

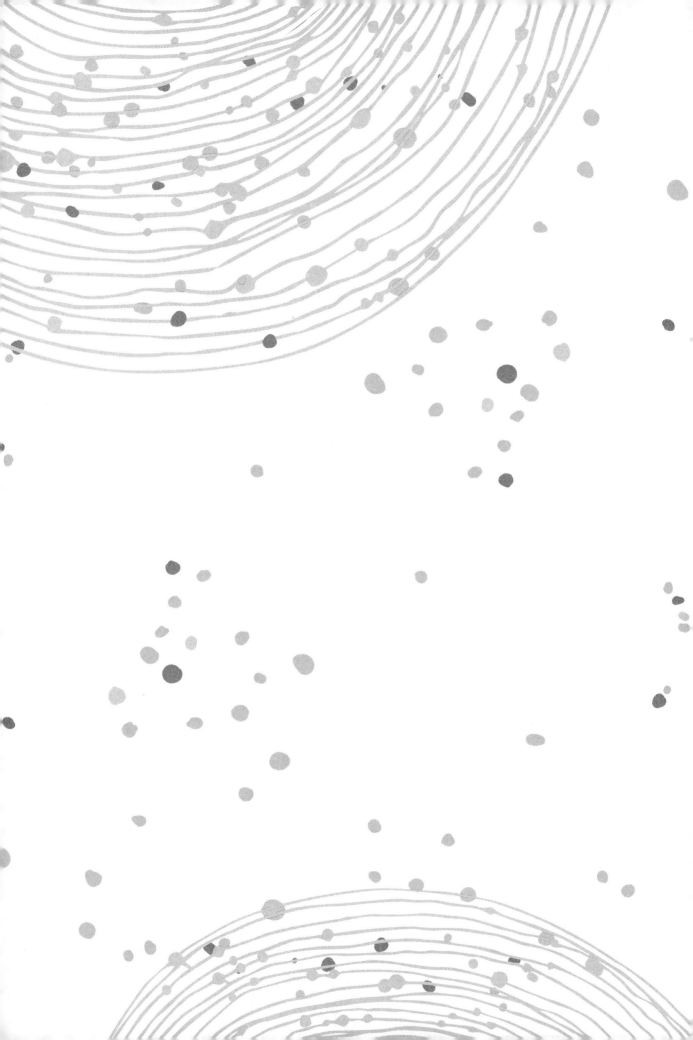

We the People (A)

Spelling List 24 Pretest

1. Open the Spelling Pretest activity online. Listen to the first spelling word. Type the word. Check your answer.

2. Write the correct spelling of the word in the Word column of the Spelling Pretest table.

	Word	✓	✗
1	blindfold		

3. Put a check mark in the ✓ column if you spelled the word correctly online.

	Word	✓	✗
1	blindfold	✓	

Put an X in the ✗ column if you spelled the word incorrectly online.

	Word	✓	✗
1	blindfold		✗

4. Repeat Steps 1–3 for the remaining words in the Spelling Pretest.

We the People (A)

Spelling List 24 Pretest

Write each spelling word in the Word column, making sure to spell it correctly.

	Word	✓	✗
1			
2			
3			
4			
5			
6			
7			
8			
9			
10			
11			
12			
13			

	Word	✓	✗
14			
15			
16			
17			
18			
19			
20			
21			
22			
23			
24			
25			

We the People (A)

Plan a Biography

Read the writing prompt.

Prompt: **Write a three-paragraph biography about a person you know. You do not need to do any research to complete your biography.**

Choose who you will write about. Write notes about this person's life.

Who are you writing about?

_____

First paragraph: Early life/event

_____

_____

_____

_____

Second paragraph: Next part of life/event

_____

_____

_____

_____

Third paragraph: Current life/event

_____

_____

_____

_____

We the People (B)

Spelling List 24 Activity Bank

Circle any words in the box that you did not spell correctly on your pretest. Choose one activity to do with your circled words. Do as much of the activity as you can in the time given.

Did you spell all the words on the pretest correctly? Do the one activity with as many spelling words as you can.

author	bought	fault	sauce	talk
automate	brought	laundry	saucer	taller
awful	chalk	lawsuit	saw	thought
ballpark	draw	mall	small	walk
because	falling	overhaul	stalk	withdraw

Spelling Activity Choices

Create a Crossword

1. Write one of your spelling words going down in the center of the grid.

2. Write another spelling word going across that shares a letter with the first word. See how many words you can connect.

Example:

			p			
	k	i	s	s	e	s
d		n				
r	o	c	k	s		
	g					
	s					

Word Search Puzzle

1. Draw a box on the grid. The box should be large enough to hold your spelling words.

2. Fill in the grid with your spelling words. Write them across, up and down, and diagonally. You can write them forward and backward.

3. Fill in the rest of the box with random letters.

4. Ask someone to find and circle your words in the puzzle.

Complete the activity that you chose.

My chosen activity: _____

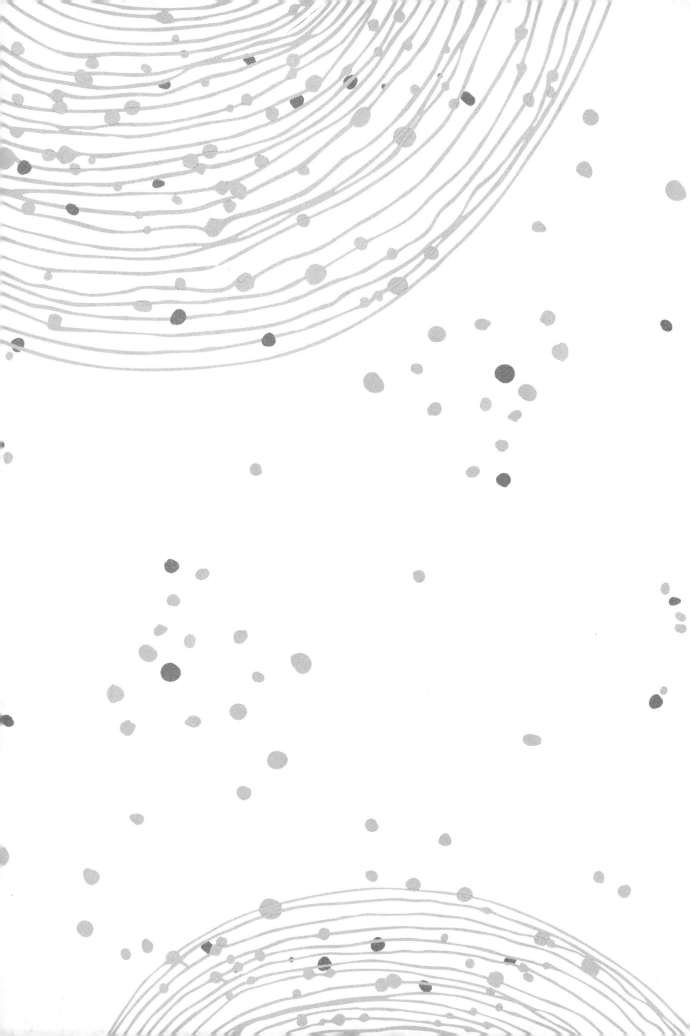

We the People (B)

Draft a Biography

Read the writing prompt.

Prompt: **Write a three-paragraph biography about a person you know.**

- Write the events in chronological order.
- To make your writing more interesting, use an idiom somewhere in your draft.

Respond to the writing prompt. Use your prewriting work to help you.

Revise and Publish a Biography

Read your biography draft. Then, use the checklist to improve your draft. Make changes on your draft.

☐ Did I describe at least three events in the person's life?

☐ Did I include enough details about each event?

☐ Did I organize my biography chronologically?

☐ Did I include an idiom, or example of nonliteral language? Is the idiom clear?

☐ Are all sentences complete?

☐ Do all sentences start with a capital letter and end with a punctuation mark?

Write or type a clean copy of your biography. Include an illustration if you wish.

_____

_____

_____

_____

_____

_____

_____

_____

_____

_____

_____

_____

_____

_____

Write About Biographies

Compare and contrast *Michelle Obama: First Lady, Going Higher* and *I Dissent! Ruth Bader Ginsburg Makes Her Mark*. Find three ways the biographies are alike and three ways they are different. Record your ideas on the T chart.

Alike	Different

Answer the questions in complete sentences.

1. Think about the format of the two biographies you read. Describe the format of each book.

   _____

   _____

   _____

   _____

   _____

   _____

   _____

2. Which format did you like better? Why?

   _____

   _____

   _____

   _____

   _____

   _____

   _____

3. Do you think you're like Mrs. Obama or Justice Ginsburg in any way? If so, how?

_____

_____

_____

_____

_____

_____

I have to choose a favorite? Impossible!

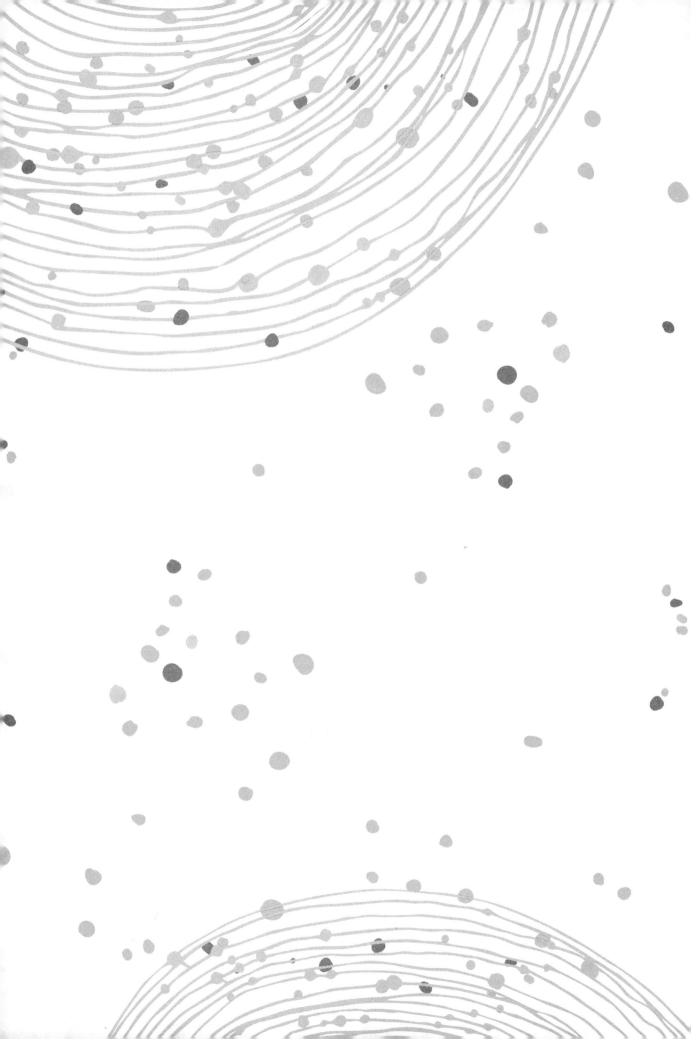

We the People (E)

Complete a Scavenger Hunt

Connect to the Ben's Guide to the U.S. Government website. Select Apprentice Level Learning Adventures. Answer the questions in complete sentences. Use the search bar if you need help finding something.

1. Who gave the Statue of Liberty to the American people?

_____

2. Why was the Pledge of Allegiance written?

_____

_____

3. Which branch of government makes laws?

_____

4. What is a bill?

_____

5. How old do you have to be to vote in an election in the United States?

_____

6. Which city houses the Liberty Bell?

_____

7. What are two powers the federal government has that state governments do **not** have?

_____

_____

8. How many times has the U.S. Constitution been changed?

_____

9. Where would you go if you wanted to see the original Emancipation Proclamation in person?

_____

10. What does GPO currently stand for?

_____

We the People Wrap-Up

Compare and Contrast Information Sources

Answer the questions in complete sentences.

1. You have read biographies in books and looked at information on a website. How are the sources of information alike?

   _____

   _____

   _____

2. How are the sources of information different?

   _____

   _____

   _____

3. Which type of source did you prefer? Why? Use details from the source(s) to explain your answer.

_____

_____

_____

_____

_____

_____

_____

I like websites so much that I just made my own!

Judiciary Words

Apply: Judiciary Words

Circle the word that best completes the passage. Define the word. Explain what context clues led you to choose that word.

1. A woman is accused of going into an unlocked car and stealing a phone. She says she is _____. She shows the judge proof that she was at work when the crime was committed.

   Choices: *innocent* or *guilty*

   Definition:

   _____

   _____

   Context Clues:

   _____

   _____

   _____

2. My father baked a chocolate cake for my birthday. He left it on the counter to cool. When he returned to the kitchen, he found a fistful of cake missing. He knows my younger sister is _____ because he found a huge smear of chocolate icing on the wall in her room.

Choices: *innocent* or *guilty*

Definition:

_____

_____

Context Clues:

_____

_____

_____

Write your own short passage using one of the given words. Leave a blank space where your chosen word belongs. Have someone else read your passage. Ask this person to choose which word best completes the passage. Discuss the answer.

3. Choices: *innocent* or *guilty*

_____

_____

Judiciary Words

Go Write! Who Is Your Hero?

Respond to the prompt. Or, write about a topic of your choice!

Prompt: **Heroes are people we look up to and admire. Who is your hero? Describe someone you admire, and explain why you look up to that person.**

My Journal

Presentation: Brainstorming

Spelling List 25 Pretest

1. Open the Spelling Pretest activity online. Listen to the first spelling word. Type the word. Check your answer.

2. Write the correct spelling of the word in the Word column of the Spelling Pretest table.

Word	✓	✕
1 blindfold		

3. Put a check mark in the ✓ column if you spelled the word correctly online.

Word	✓	✕
1 blindfold	✓	

Put an X in the ✕ column if you spelled the word incorrectly online.

Word	✓	✕
1 blindfold		✕

4. Repeat Steps 1–3 for the remaining words in the Spelling Pretest.

Presentation: Brainstorming

Spelling List 25 Pretest

Write each spelling word in the Word column, making sure to spell it correctly.

	Word	✓	✕
1			
2			
3			
4			
5			
6			
7			
8			
9			
10			
11			

	Word	✓	✕
12			
13			
14			
15			
16			
17			
18			
19			
20			
21			

Presentation: Brainstorming

Brainstorm for Your Oral History Presentation

Read the assignment. You will complete the assignment in steps over multiple lessons.

Prompt: **Interview someone who means a lot to you. Tell an important story that you learned from interviewing that person.**

Requirements:

Your oral history presentation should include the following:

- A **hook** that relates to your main idea and captures your audience's attention

- A story from a person's life that has a clear **beginning**, **middle**, and **end**

- Accurate facts and details gathered from an interview

- Descriptive language

- A piece of media (picture, song, chart) that relates to the story you are telling

Be sure to do the following:

- Speak clearly and at an appropriate pace.

- Use correct grammar.

Audience: Your teacher, peers, and Learning Coach

Purpose: Help others learn about the world by retelling an important experience in someone's life.

Length: $2\frac{1}{2}$–4 minutes

Brainstorm and choose someone to interview for your oral history presentation.

1. Think about people in your life. Create a list or a web of people you may want to interview.

2. Read over the names you brainstormed.

a. Cross off any names of people who may be hard to interview in person or on video.

b. Think about each remaining person you listed.

- Has anyone lived through an interesting event or time period?

- Has anyone experienced something that you have not?

- Might anyone have a story that you want to share?

c. Circle the person whom you think would be the most interesting to interview.

I will interview _____ .

Not all stories make the news. I can't wait to tell an important story.

DAILY NEWS

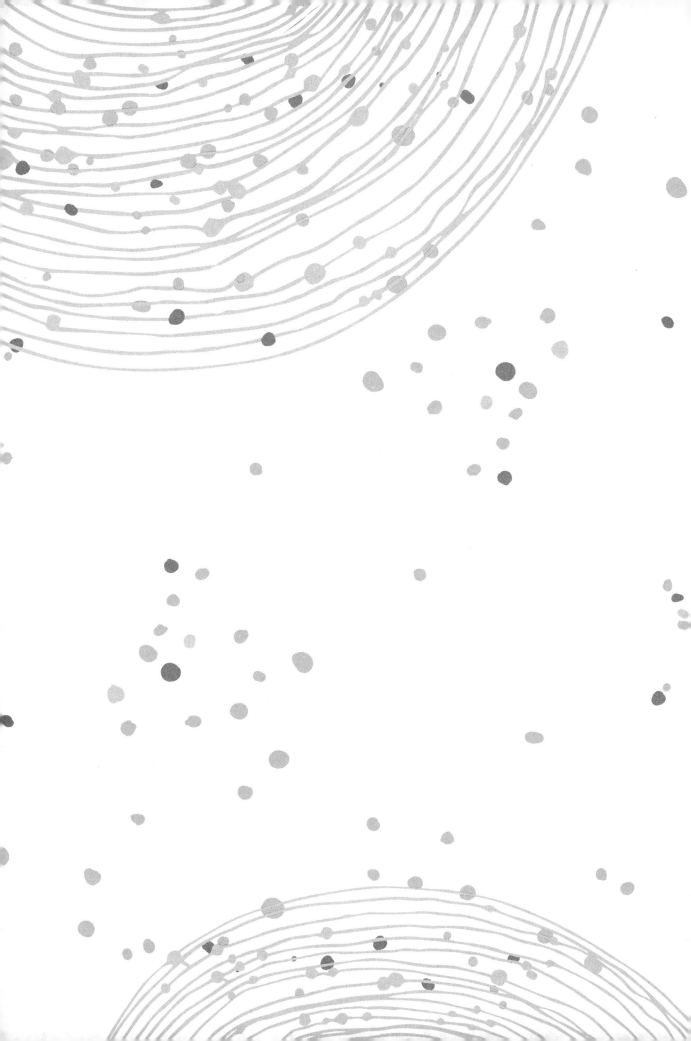

Presentation: Research (A)

Spelling List 25 Activity Bank

Circle any words in the box that you did not spell correctly on your pretest. Choose one activity to do with your circled words. Do as much of the activity as you can in the time given.

Did you spell all the words on the pretest correctly? Do the one activity with as many spelling words as you can.

afternoon	loop	soon	barefoot	stood
bathroom	moonlight	spoon	cookbook	took
food	school	stoop	crooked	undertook
gloomy	scrooge	tool	goodwill	woodwork
groom				

Spelling Activity Choices

Alphabetizing

1. In the left column, write your spelling words in alphabetical order.

2. Correct any spelling errors.

Vowel-Free Words

1. In the left column, write only the consonants in each of your spelling words. Put a dot where each vowel should be.

2. Spell each word aloud, stating which vowels should be in the places with dots.

3. In the right column, rewrite the entire spelling word.

4. Correct any spelling errors.

Rhymes

1. In the left column, write your spelling words.

2. In the right column, write a word that rhymes with each spelling word.

3. Correct any spelling errors.

Uppercase and Lowercase

1. In the left column, write each of your spelling words in all uppercase letters.

2. In the right column, write each of your spelling words in all lowercase letters.

3. Correct any spelling errors.

Complete the activity that you chose.

My chosen activity: _____

1. _____   _____

2. _____   _____

3. _____   _____

4. _____   _____

5. _____   _____

6. _____   _____

7. _____   _____

8. _____   _____

9. _____   _____

10. _____   _____

11. _____   _____

12. _____   _____

13. _____   _____

14. _____   _____

15. _____   _____

16. _____   _____

17. _____   _____

18. _____   _____

19. _____   _____

20. _____   _____

21. _____   _____

TRY IT

Presentation: Research (A)

Make a Research Plan

Fill in the basic information about your interviewee. If you are unsure of anything, fill it out during the interview.

Full name of interviewee:

_____

Age: _____   Year born: _____

Place of birth: _____

Place of current residence:

_____

Write 8–10 interview questions. Use the boxes to record notes during the interview.

1. _____

_____

_____

2. _____

_____

_____

3. _____

_____

_____

_____

4. _____

_____

_____

5. _____

_____

_____

6. _____

_____

_____

7.

8.

9. _____

_____

_____

10. _____

_____

_____

Presentation: Planning (A)

Organize Your Oral History Presentation

You want to tell a story with a beginning, middle, and end. To do that, you need to organize your interview notes. Use your interview notes to complete the graphic organizer. In each box:

- Write 1–2 sentences to summarize that part of the story.

- Write important facts and details from your interview.

Beginning

Summary:

_____

_____

Interview Notes:

_____

_____

_____

_____

Middle

Summary:

_____

_____

Interview Notes:

_____

_____

_____

_____

_____

↓

End

Summary:

_____

_____

Interview Notes:

_____

_____

Presentation: Planning (B)

Create Note Cards for Your Presentation

Follow the instructions to make note cards for your presentation.

1. Gather index cards. Label the first card "Hook" and number it "1."

Hook   ①

2. Write your hook on that card. Use large, neat handwriting. Use more cards for your hook if you need to. Label the cards "2" and so on.

3. Label the next card "Beginning" and number it with the next number in order. Then, begin telling your story! Use your notes from the Beginning box on your Organize Your Oral History Presentation activity page. Add transitions and descriptive language. Use as many cards as you need.

4. Repeat Step 3 for the middle and end of your story.

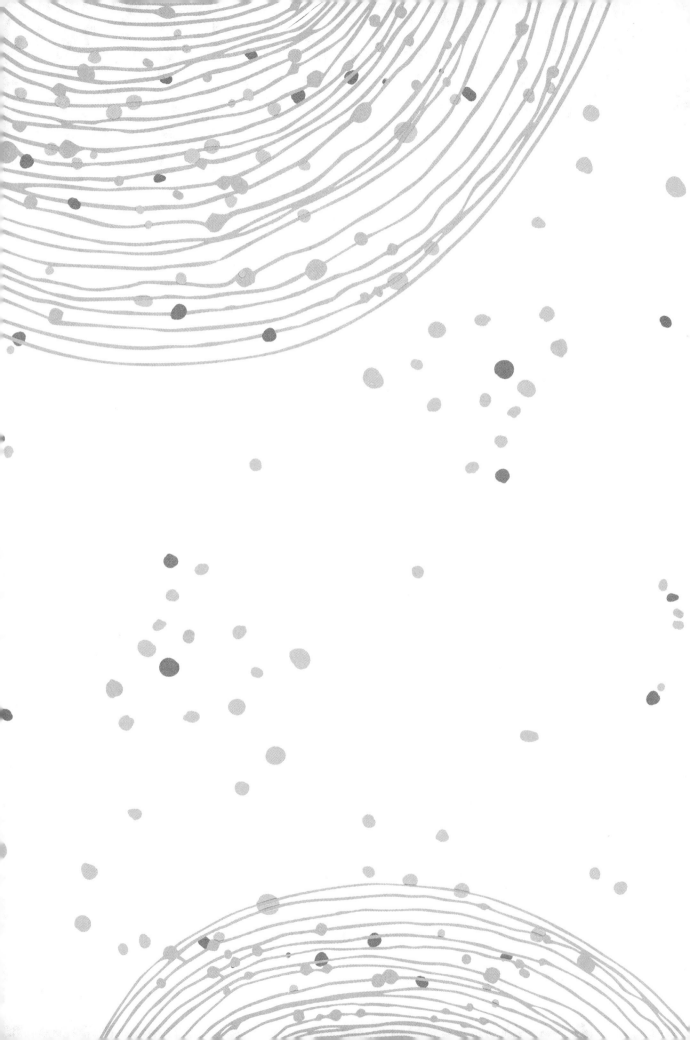

Presentation: Media

Choose Media for Your Oral History Presentation

Answer the questions to choose media for your presentation.

1. What is the main idea of your oral history presentation? Think about what message you want your audience to remember most.

   _____

   _____

   _____

   _____

2. List three details that support your main idea.

   a. _____

   _____

   b. _____

   _____

   c. _____

   _____

3. List three ideas for media that connect with your main idea or supporting details. Examples of media are photographs, drawings, videos, music, objects, and maps. For each idea, explain how it supports your presentation.

Media Idea	How It Supports My Presentation

4. Find or create the media that you will use in your presentation.

5. At what point in your presentation will you show or play the media? Why?

_____

_____

_____

6. Find the note card for your presentation that matches your answer to Question 5. Make a note on that card that will remind you to show or play your media.

_____

_____

_____

_____

Presentation: Practice

Practice Your Oral History Presentation

Use the recording tool in the online activity to record your presentation. Then, use the checklist to improve your ideas, media usage, grammar, and presentation skills. Practice multiple times.

Ideas

☐ Did I begin with a hook?

☐ Did I tell the story from beginning to end?

☐ Did I use descriptive language? Are there words that could be stronger?

Media

☐ Did I present my media at the right time?

☐ Could my audience see or hear my media?

Grammar

☐ Did I use correct grammar? For example, did I use pronouns correctly?

(continued)

Presentation Skills

☐ Was my pace appropriate? Are there times I spoke too quickly or too slowly?

☐ Did I speak too loudly or too quietly?

☐ Did I speak clearly?

☐ Did I look at my audience?

☐ Was I comfortable presenting the information?

It was helpful to record myself!

"Squirrel and Spider"

Spelling List 26 Pretest

1. Open the Spelling Pretest activity online. Listen to the first spelling word. Type the word. Check your answer.

2. Write the correct spelling of the word in the Word column of the Spelling Pretest table.

Word	✓	✗
1 blindfold		

3. Put a check mark in the ✓ column if you spelled the word correctly online.

Word	✓	✗
1 blindfold	✓	

Put an X in the ✗ column if you spelled the word incorrectly online.

Word	✓	✗
1 blindfold		✗

4. Repeat Steps 1–3 for the remaining words in the Spelling Pretest.

"Squirrel and Spider"

Spelling List 26 Pretest

Write each spelling word in the Word column, making sure to spell it correctly.

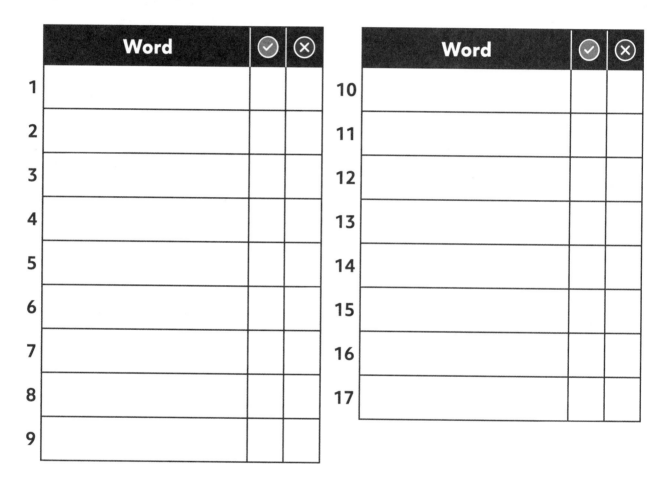

	Word	✓	✕
1			
2			
3			
4			
5			
6			
7			
8			
9			

	Word	✓	✕
10			
11			
12			
13			
14			
15			
16			
17			

"Squirrel and Spider"

Plan a Retelling of a Story

Read the writing prompt.

Prompt: **Retell "Squirrel and Spider" in your own words.**

- Keep the story's sequence of events the same in your retelling.
- State the lesson at the end of your retelling.

Follow the instructions to plan your retelling.

1. List the events of the story in the order in which they happened.

2. What lesson does "Squirrel and Spider" teach readers? Give details from the text to support your answer.

_____

_____

_____

_____

Can't we all just get along?

"Squirrel and Spider" Wrap-Up

Spelling List 26 Activity Bank

Circle any words in the box that you did not spell correctly on the pretest. Choose one activity to do with your circled words. Do as much of the activity as you can in the time given.

Did you spell all the words on the pretest correctly? Do the one activity with as many spelling words as you can.

addressed	clapped	joined	prepared	repeated
behaved	dashed	lifted	printed	scrubbed
believed	dimmed	needed	reached	talented
blinked	discovered			

Spelling Activity Choices

Silly Sentences

1. Write a silly sentence for each of your spelling words.

2. Underline the spelling word in each sentence.

   Example: The dog was <u>driving</u> a car.

3. Correct any spelling errors.

Spelling Story

1. Write a very short story using each of your spelling words.

2. Underline the spelling words in the story.

3. Correct any spelling errors.

Riddle Me This

1. Write a riddle for each of your spelling words.
   Example: "I have a trunk, but it's not on my car."

2. Write the answer, which is your word, for each riddle.
   Example: Answer: elephant

3. Correct any spelling errors.

RunOnWord

1. Gather some crayons, colored pencils, or markers. Use a different color to write each of your spelling words. Write the words end to end as one long word.
   Example: dogcatbirdfishturtle

2. Rewrite the words correctly and with proper spacing.

3. Correct any spelling errors.

Complete the activity that you chose.

My chosen activity: _____

_____

_____

_____

_____

_____

_____

_____

_____

_____

_____

_____

_____

_____

_____

_____

_____

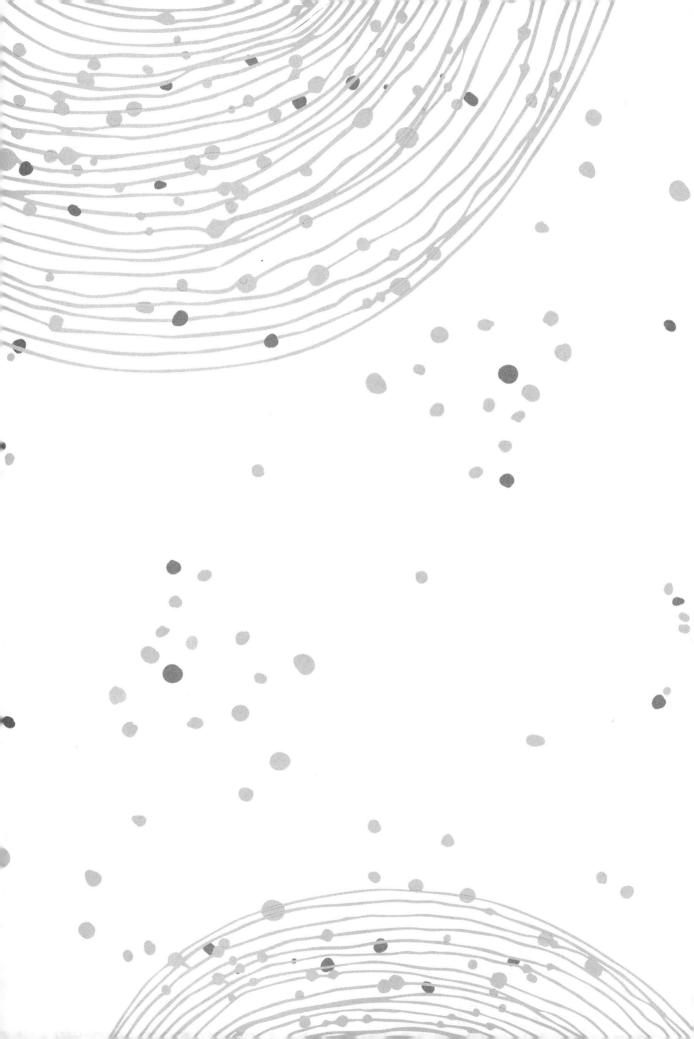

"Squirrel and Spider" Wrap-Up

Retell a Story

Read the writing prompt.

Prompt: Retell "Squirrel and Spider" in your own words.

- Keep the story's sequence of events the same in your retelling.
- State the lesson at the end of your retelling.

Respond to the writing prompt. Use your work on the Plan a Retelling of a Story activity page to help you.

_____

_____

_____

_____

_____

_____

_____

_____

Plan a Story

Read the writing prompt.

Prompt: **Write a short story about a character. Include the following:**

- The name and a description of your main character

- The problem your character faces

- The events of the story

- How your character solves the problem

- How your character feels during the story

- The lesson your character learns in the story

Answer the questions to plan your story.

1. Who is your main character? Give your character a name, and describe him or her.

_____

_____

_____

2. What problem does your main character face in the story?

_____

_____

_____

_____

_____

_____

3. What happens in the story?

_____

_____

_____

_____

_____

_____

4. How does your main character solve the problem?

_____

_____

_____

_____

_____

_____

_____

5. What emotions does your main character feel during the story?

_____

_____

_____

_____

_____

_____

6. What lesson does your main character learn?

_____

_____

_____

My pencil is sharp . . . but my ideas are sharper!

"The Stone-Cutter" Wrap-Up

Write a Story

Read the writing prompt.

Prompt: **Write a short story about a character. Include the following:**

- The name and a description of your main character
- The problem your character faces
- The events of the story
- How your character solves the problem
- How your character feels during the story
- The lesson your character learns in the story

Respond to the writing prompt. Use your work on the Plan a Story activity page to help you.

_____

_____

_____

_____

_____

Apply: Vocabulary in Everyday Life

Circle the word that best completes the passage. Define the word. Explain what context clues led you to choose that word.

1. Rita explained that her _____ grandmother gifted her extended family a vacation. She was excited to visit a new place with all her cousins without worrying how to pay for it.

   Choices: *considerate* or *kindly*

   Definition:

   _____

   _____

   Context Clues:

   _____

   _____

   _____

2. My sister is very _____ . She always gives me hugs when I'm sad. If my early morning swim practice is canceled, she turns off my alarm so I can sleep in.

Choices: _considerate_ or _kindly_

Definition:

_____

_____

Context Clues:

_____

_____

_____

Write your own short passage using one of the given words. Leave a blank space where your chosen word belongs. Have someone else read your passage. Ask this person to choose which word best completes the passage. Discuss the answer.

3. Choices: _considerate_ or _kindly_

_____

_____

_____

Vocabulary in Everyday Life

Go Write! A Finished Project

Respond to the prompt. Or, write about a topic of your choice!

Prompt: What is one project you have completed?
What did you like about doing it?

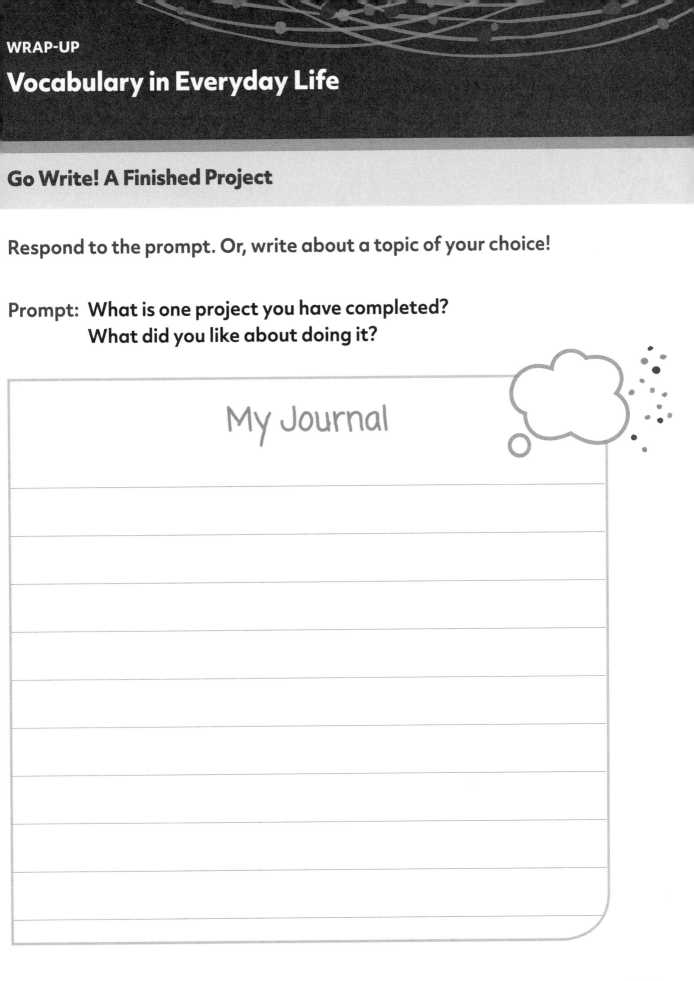

My Journal

"The Bundle of Sticks"

Spelling List 27 Pretest

1. Open the Spelling Pretest activity online. Listen to the first spelling word. Type the word. Check your answer.

2. Write the correct spelling of the word in the Word column of the Spelling Pretest table.

Word	✓	✗
1 blindfold		

3. Put a check mark in the ✓ column if you spelled the word correctly online.

Word	✓	✗
1 blindfold	✓	

Put an X in the ✗ column if you spelled the word incorrectly online.

Word	✓	✗
1 blindfold		✗

4. Repeat Steps 1–3 for the remaining words in the Spelling Pretest.

"The Bundle of Sticks"

Spelling List 27 Pretest

Write each spelling word in the Word column, making sure to spell it correctly.

	Word	✓	✗
1			
2			
3			
4			
5			
6			
7			
8			
9			

	Word	✓	✗
10			
11			
12			
13			
14			
15			
16			
17			

TRY IT
"The Bundle of Sticks"

Plan an Essay with a Metaphor

Read the writing prompt.

Prompt: When in your life have you learned the lesson, "We are stonger together"? Write an essay about that time.

- Use details to explain how you learned the lesson.
- Include a metaphor in your essay.

Answer the questions to plan your essay.

1. How did you learn the lesson, "We are stronger together"?

_____

_____

_____

_____

_____

_____

_____

_____

_____

_____

_____

_____

_____

_____

_____

_____

2. Write a metaphor that you can include in your essay. Think of something that only becomes strong when there is a lot of it. For example, sticks aren't very strong unless many of them are bundled together.

_____

_____

_____

_____

"The Bundle of Sticks" Wrap-Up

Spelling List 27 Activity Bank

Circle any words in the box that you did not spell correctly on your pretest. Choose one activity to do with your circled words. Do as much of the activity as you can in the time given.

Did you spell all the words on the pretest correctly? Do the one activity with as many spelling words as you can.

autumn	doubt	knife	lamb	wrap
bright	flight	knit	subtle	wrist
column	highlight	know	thumb	wrong
crumb	knee			

Spelling Activity Choices

Hidden Words

1. Draw a picture. "Hide" as many of your spelling words as you can inside the picture.

2. See if others can find the words you hid in the picture.

Triangle Spelling

Write each of your spelling words in a triangle.

```
    d
   do
  dog
```

Ghost Words

1. Use a white crayon to write each of your spelling words.

2. Write over the words in white crayon with a colored marker.

Complete the activity that you chose.

My chosen activity: _____

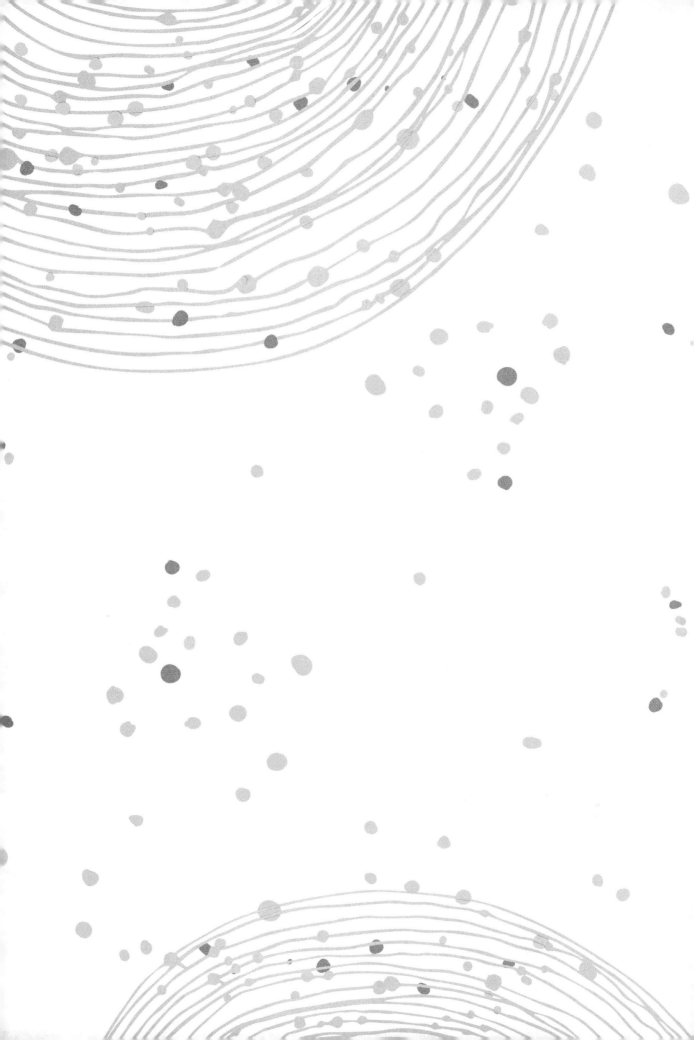

"The Bundle of Sticks" Wrap-Up

Write an Essay with a Metaphor

Read the writing prompt.

Prompt: **When in your life have you learned the lesson, "We are stronger together"? Write an essay about that time.**

- Use details to explain how you learned the lesson.

- Include a metaphor in your essay.

Respond to the writing prompt. Use your work on the Plan an Essay with a Metaphor activity page to help you.

_____

_____

_____

_____

_____

_____

_____

TRY IT

"The Necklace of Truth"

Plan a Play

Read the writing prompt.

Prompt: **Write stage directions and dialogue for a scene from a play.**

Answer the questions to plan your play. (You will plan the full play, but you will only write a scene.)

1. What is the name of your play?

   _____

2. What is the setting of your play?

   _____

   _____

3. What lesson will your play teach?

   _____

   _____

4. Who are the characters in your play? Write a sentence to describe each one.

_____

_____

_____

5. What problem are the characters in your play trying to solve?

_____

_____

_____

6. What happens in each scene?

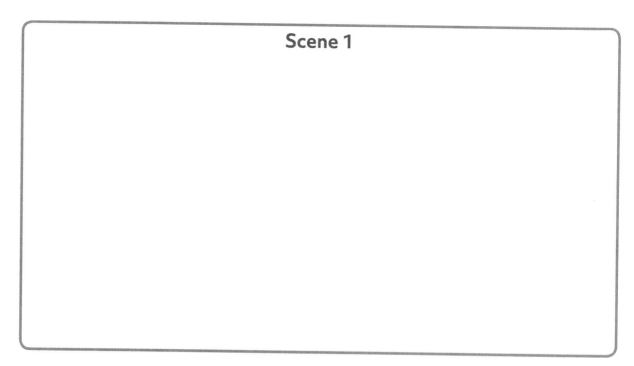

Scene 1

Scene 2

Scene 3

7. How do the characters solve the problem?

_____

_____

_____

_____

8. How do the characters feel while they are trying to solve the problem?

_____

_____

_____

I'm looking for actors for my play. Want to try out?

Director

"The Necklace of Truth" Wrap-Up

Write a Scene

Read the writing prompt.

Prompt: Write stage directions and dialogue for a scene of a play.

Respond to the prompt. Use your work on the Plan a Play activity page to help you. Follow the format of this model scene.

The Magic Cookie Jar

Scene 2

SAM and MAX are sitting at the kitchen table with the magic cookie jar between them.

SAM: Where did Sophie go?

MAX: She said she had to help a friend with some math homework. (*MAX eyes the cookie jar*) I want some more cookies.

SAM: Me too! Do you remember the magic words that Sophie said to get cookies?

MAX: I think so. Wasn't it something like "Chocolate, sugar, oatmeal and spice, three little cookies would be so nice?"

SAM: It worked! I wonder what would happen if we asked for 10 cookies?

MAX: Let's try it. Chocolate, sugar, oatmeal and spice, 10 little cookies would be so nice. *(Ten cookies appear in the jar. MAX and SAM eat them. Then, 10 more appear.)*

SAM: I'm getting full. I don't know how many more cookies I can eat.

MAX: Ugh. My stomach is starting to hurt. How do we stop the cookies from coming?

SAM: I don't know! Do you remember?

MAX: No. I was trying to wrestle you off the couch. I didn't hear what Aunt Peg said!

SAM: Oh no! What are we going to do with all these cookies?

Glossary

abstract noun – a word that names an idea

adjective – a word that describes a noun or pronoun

adverb – a word that describes a verb, an adjective, or another adverb

affix – a word part attached to a root or base word to create a new word

alphabetical order – a way to put things in order according to the alphabet Example: in alphabetical order, *at* comes before *bat*, which comes before *cat*

antecedent – the noun or pronoun that a pronoun points back to

antonym – a word that means the opposite of another word

author's purpose – the reason the author wrote a text: to entertain, to inform, to express an opinion, or to persuade

autobiography – the story of a person's life written by that person

biography – the story of a person's life written by another person

body – the main text of a piece of writing

body (of a business letter) – the main text of a business letter

brainstorming – before writing, a way for the writer to come up with ideas

business letter – a letter written to an organization or a person at a business

caption – text that tells more about an illustration, photograph, or other graphic

cause – the reason something happens

cause and effect – when one thing—the cause—makes another thing—the effect—happen

chapter – a main part of a written work, such as a book, usually numbered or titled

character – a person or animal in a story

character trait – a quality of a person or character; part of a personality

chronological order – a way to organize that puts details in time order

clarity – the quality of being easy to understand

closing (of a business letter) – the part of a business letter that follows the body text, containing a phrase such as "Sincerely" or "Yours truly"

common noun – a noun that names any person, place, thing, or idea Examples: *girl, mountain, book,* and *joy*

comparative form – the form of an adjective or adverb used to compare two things

compare – to explain how two or more things are alike

compare-and-contrast organization – a structure for text that shows how two or more things are similar and different

complex sentence – a sentence that has one independent part and at least one dependent part

compound predicate – two or more predicates that have the same subject

compound sentence – a sentence that has at least two independent parts

compound subject – two or more subjects that have the same predicate

conclusion (a decision) – a decision made made, or opinion formed, about something not stated, using information provided and what is already known

conclusion (a final paragraph) – the final paragraph of a written work

conflict – a problem or issue that a character faces in a story

content-specific word – a word that has to do with a certain job or activity

context clue – a word or phrase in a text that helps you figure out the meaning of an unknown word

contrast – to explain how two or more things are different

coordinating conjunction – one of seven words—*and, but, for, nor, or, so, yet*—that connects words, phrases, or independent clauses

description – writing that uses words that show how something looks, sounds, feels, tastes, or smells
Example: The sky is a soft, powdery blue, and the golden sun feels warm on my face.

detail – a fact or description that tells more about a topic

dialogue – the words that characters say in a written work

drafting – of writing, the stage or step in which the writer first writes the piece

drama – another word for *play*

effect – the result of a cause

fact – something that can be proven true

fiction – make-believe stories

figurative language – words that describe something by comparing it to something completely different; figure of speech
Example: Rain fell in buckets and the streets looked like rivers.

first-person point of view – the telling of a story by a character in that story, using pronouns such as *I, me*, and *we*

folktale – a story, which usually teaches a lesson important to a culture, that is passed down through many generations

free verse – poetry whose rhythm follows natural speech patterns and does not rely on regular rhyme or meter

future tense – a form of a verb that names an action that will happen later

glossary – a list of important terms and their meanings that is usually found in the back of a book

graphic – a picture, photograph, map, diagram, or other image

graphic organizer – a visual tool used to show how ideas connect with each other; types of graphic organizers include webs, diagrams, and charts

heading – a title within the body of a text that tells the reader something important about a section of the text

heading (of a business letter) – the first part of a letter that has the writer's address and the date

historical fiction – a story set in a historical time period that includes facts about real people, places, and events, but also contains fictional elements that make the story exciting or interesting

hyperlink – a word or words in an online text that you can select; a hyperlink is usually blue and underlined

idiom – a group of words that does not actually mean what it says
Examples: raining cats and dogs; a month of Sundays

illustration – a drawing

infer – to use clues and what you already know to make a guess

inference – a guess that readers make using the clues that an author gives them in a piece of writing

informative essay – a kind of writing that informs or explains

inside address – the part of a business or formal letter that comes after the heading and before the greeting, made up of the name and address of the person to whom the letter is written

interview – to ask someone questions to gather information

introduction – the first paragraph of an essay, identifying the topic and stating the main idea

legend – a story that is passed down for many years to teach the values of a culture; a legend may or may not contain some true events or people

literal – exact or strict meaning

literal language – language that uses words according to their exact, or factual, meanings

main character – an important person, animal, or other being who is central to the plot

main idea – the most important point the author makes; it may be stated or unstated

media – ways to express ideas, such as pictures, photographs, videos, and songs

metaphor – a figure of speech that compares two unlike things, without using the word *like* or *as*
Example: The cat's eyes were emeralds shining in the night.

mood – the feeling that an author shows with words and pictures

moral – the lesson of a story, particularly a fable

myth – a story that explains how something came to be and that usually contains magical figures as characters

narrative – a kind of writing that tells a story

narrative poem – a poem that tells a story

narrator – the teller of a story

nonfiction – writing that presents facts and information in order to explain, describe, or persuade
Example: newspaper articles and biographies are nonfiction

nonliteral language – figures of speech or words and phrases that change their usual meaning based on how they are used in a sentence

noun – a word that names a person, place, thing, or idea

nuance – a very small difference in meaning

opinion – something that a person thinks or believes, but which cannot be proven to be true

outline – an organized list of topics in an essay

pace – the speed, and the change of speeds, of a speaker's delivery

paragraph – a group of sentences about one topic or subject

paraphrase – to restate information in one's own words

past tense – the form of the verb that tells what has already happened

personification – giving human qualities to something that is not human Example: The thunder shouted from the clouds.

perspective – the way someone sees the world

plot – what happens in a story; the sequence of events

plural noun – a word that names more than one person, place, thing, or idea

poem – a piece of poetry

poetry – writing that is made up of lines that often rhyme and follow a specific rhythm

point of view – who is telling the story

possessive noun – the form of a noun that shows ownership

predicate – tells what the subject of a sentence is or does

prefix – a word part with its own meaning that can be added to the beginning of a base word or root to make a new word

present tense – the verb form that tells what is happening now

presentation – an oral report, usually with visuals

prewriting – the stage or step of writing in which a writer chooses a topic, gathers ideas, and plans what to write

primary source – a record made by a person who saw or took part in an event or who lived at the time

problem – an issue a character must solve in a story

problem-solution structure – organizational pattern in which a problem is described, followed by descriptions of its solution or possible solutions

pronoun – a word that takes the place of one or more nouns

proofreading – the step of the writing process for checking and fixing errors in grammar, punctuation, capitalization, and spelling

proper noun – noun that names a particular person, place, thing, or idea

publishing – the step of the writing process for making a clean copy of the piece and sharing it

quotation marks – punctuation that encloses a quotation, or the exact words of a speaker or writer

reason – a statement that explains why something is or why it should be

research (n.) – a careful search for information about a subject

research (v.) – to find information through study rather than through personal experience

research report – a type of essay based mainly on the author's research

resolution – the outcome of a story

revising – the step of the writing process for reviewing and fixing ideas and organization

rhyme – the use of words that end with the same sounds
Example: *cat* and *hat* rhyme

rhythm – a regular pattern of sound and beats within a poem

root – a word part with a special meaning to which prefixes and suffixes can be added
Example: *spec* is a root that means "see"

salutation – the greeting of a business letter, which usually says, "Dear (name of recipient)"; it is followed by a colon

scene – a part of an act of a play that happens at a fixed time and place

sensory detail – descriptive detail that appeals to any of the senses—sight, hearing, touch, smell, or taste

sensory language – language that appeals to the five senses

sentence – a group of words that tells a complete thought

sequence – the order in which things happen

sequence of events – the order in which things happen in a story

setting – when and where a story takes place

sidebar – a short text within a larger text that tells about something related to the main text

signature – the part of a business letter following the closing, consisting of the writer's signature above the writer's typed name

simile – a comparison between two things using the word *like* or *as*
Example: I didn't hear him come in because he was as quiet as a mouse.

solution – how a character solves a problem in a story

source – a provider of information; a book, a historical document, online materials, and an interviewee are all sources

speaker – the imaginary person who speaks the words of a poem, not the poet

speaker tag – the part of a dialogue that identifies who is speaking

stage directions – instructions in a play that tell the actors what to do

stanza – a group of lines in a poem

subject – a word or words that tell whom or what the sentence is about

subject-verb agreement – the way a subject and verb match when both are singular or both are plural

subordinating conjunction – a word that is used to introduce a dependent clause

suffix – a word part added to the end of a base word or root that changes the meaning or part of speech of a word

summarize – to tell in order the most important ideas or events of a text

summary – a short retelling that includes only the most important ideas or events of a text

superlative form – the form of an adjective or adverb that compares more than two things

supporting detail – a detail that gives more information about a main idea

synonym – a word that means the same, or almost the same, as another word

tense – the time that verbs show, such as present, future, or past

text feature – part of a text that helps a reader locate information and determine what is most important
Examples: title, table of contents, headings, pictures, glossary

text-based evidence – proof in a text that supports an idea or answers a question

theme – the author's message or big idea

third-person point of view – the telling of a story by someone outside of the action, using the third-person pronouns *he*, *she*, and *they*

time order – the arrangement of ideas according to when they happened

topic – the subject of a text

topic sentence – the sentence that expresses the main idea of a paragraph

transition – a word, phrase, or clause that connects ideas

URL – the Internet address of a website; stands for uniform resource locator

verb – a word that shows action or a state of being

website – a place on the Internet devoted to a specific organization, group, or individual